Actual Proof of My Existence signed: God of the Bible

By Don Christie

PRESS

Xulon Press
10640 Main Street
Suite 204
Fairfax, VA 22030
(703) 934-4411
XulonPress.com

To order additional copies, call 1-866-909-BOOK (2665).

This book is lovingly dedicated to my:

Wife: Ruth
Daughters: Rachel and Sharon
Son: Donald
Grandson: Scotty Gabler

And to those who seek the truth.

The truth is simple; it is sin that causes complexity.

Don Christie

Contents

⟨══════⟩

CHAPTER 1

The Psalm verses that landed on the **correct years: 1900-2050**

Introduction

This book is designed to be the simple, and yet convincing truth that the Bible is the infallible "Word of God." Most of the book will look on the surface of the Bible; we will not have to go very deep to see the actual proof of God's existence. The evidence to be presented is simple and easy to see. The book will match many of the Bible's verse numbers to science, showing that the scientific number matches the meaning of the content of the *same numbered* verse. The book will also show that many **historical events** are found in verses that match the number of the **year of the event**, especially in the **Psalms**. The book will show that many of the Bible's number patterns, written thousands of years ago, will match what science has discovered within the last two hundred years. There are no mathematical formulas required to understand this book. In fact, by using the Psalms we are merely going to match one number with another. This is like simply saying; I recognize that science says '**creation fire**' was 10^{29} power degrees, and Psalm **29** also says "The LORD divideth the **flames of fire**"; that's all there is to it! You don't have to understand the science, because all we will be doing is matching simple numbers using 'key words' like this: Psalm 19 = 19 electricity, Psalm 27 = 27 light, Psalm 38 = 38 gravity, and so on. We are going to see in a few moments, that many scientific **power numbers** such as 10^19 power for electricity and 10^-27 for light, have a '**key word**' describing that **constant** in the Psalm of the same **number**; it's a really amazing pattern. There are over **23** of these science constants found in the **Psalms**, and they are **all** contained in the **first few verses** of the **Psalms**! Many of these 'key words' also actually appear in the Bible the exact number of times that matches the power number of the constant. An example is Psalm **38** where 10^-38 power is gravity, and "**heavy**" is the *key phrase*. The word '**heavy**' actually appears in **38** verses of the Bible. There are **many others** like this. We will also see that all of the major events from the years **1900** through **2050** (yes even **future** events), are contained in the **150** Psalms, and are described on the Psalm number that is the **same year** of the **event**! For instance Psalm **46** says "He maketh **wars** to cease"; and the year **1946** is the year after **World War II**; or **1998** and Psalm **98:7** "Let the **sea** roar, and the fulness thereof; the world, and they that dwell therein", because (1998)was the year of **El Niño**. In **1987 Saddam Hussein** restored the old **Babylonian** empire and hosted a **party** for a **month** with **bands** and **musicians** from all over the world; it was predicted in Psalm **87:4** "I will make mention of Rahab and (*Babylon*) to them that know me: behold *Philistia*, and Tyre, with Ethiopia; this man was born there." Psalm **87:7** "As well the **singers as the players on instruments** shall be there: all my springs are in thee."

This book is guaranteed to reveal mind-boggling things about the Bible that you haven't seen before. The books' goal is to deliver the most *evidence* of the 'God of the Bible' in the **simplest** way possible. I am not going to have to offer my opinion on whether the Bible is the "Word of God"; I will let the Bible do that for you. You understand how a lotto works; for instance to get 6 numbers correct out of 53 to win takes 23,000,000 to 1 odds; that is 1 chance out of 23 million to win. This is only 23 x 10^6 power or 6 zeroes. The book will be showing odds on the level of 10^22 power to 1 and higher that these Bible patterns would occur by random accident or chance. Ten to the twentieth power or 10^20 is roughly equivalent to the number of grains of sand on Coney Island Beach. This book is also going to look into the **Tabernacle of Moses**, the **Ark of the Covenant**, New Testament verse numbers and science, and in nature using the **Fibonacci** numbers (8, 13, 21, 34, 55 etc. which are preva-lent in all of nature, flowers, plants, and nautilus shells) to see how these relate to the **Bible**. The book will show an incredible relation-ship between the 'Ark of the Covenant' in the **Torah**, and the **Tora, Tora, Tora**, of the attack on **Pearl Harbor**. There are also some interesting surprises using the **English language** as a **code**, such as A=1, B=2, C=3, and the summing of sentences related to **historical events** and Bible words. You will see that the actual 'proof for God' in this book is **way beyond** question and **chance**. Just reading the Psalms alone and seeing the simple **pattern** and **number matching** should be enough to convince anyone, that the information in the Psalms, written 3,000 years ago, describes everything we have just recently learned. The book isn't designed to be complex but simple, showing how the complexity of the universe funnels into the simplicity of the scriptures. The hand and inspiration of God had to be with David and others, as the Psalms and other parts of the Bible prophetically show many things that were impossible to know in their day. If you are a Christian you will find the material very inter-esting and an excellent witnessing tool and discussion piece, to be taken into schools, colleges, universities, or clubs. The book is also a great way to study the Bible, making you aware of the spiritual and natural laws of the universe, and how these relate to each other. There is a study chapter at the end of the book that lists **400** scrip-tures. These scriptures are organized in numerical **groups** of **related** (science and Bible number) **data**, where the verse numbers equal the content of the verse. There are between **500** and **600** scriptures listed throughout the entire book that relate the meaning of the verse to the verse number. The book is also a great way to memorize scripture; this is done by associating the **meaning** of scriptures with their (biblical and scientific) **numerical values**. If you are not a Christian, but are willing to look at the **evidence**, then I present to you: the "Bible's evidence" using simple numbers, science, nature, and simple logic, that there is a God who wrote the Bible through His mighty prophets, and that He has a Son named Jesus Christ.

The **Historically** correct Psalms **1900-2050**

The Psalms were written for the most part by King David about

1000 years before the birth of Jesus Christ. The Psalms are some of the most beautiful verses in the Bible. They show the character of Jesus Christ and prophesy about Jesus, as in Psalm 22. The Psalms are designed to lead the way to God.

If you are having a battle with sin and temptation, and who doesn't, the Psalms are a great comfort.

Now consider that the Psalms are the **19**th book of the Bible and consider these next Psalms as if Psalm 1 is the year **1901**; Psalm 12 is year 1912 and so on. Get ready to go on a time-travel trip through the Psalms as both past and future years will be explored!

Psalm 12: Year **1912**

Psalm 12 is the year **1912** and the sinking of the Titanic if you remember: "Not even God can sink this ship!" This era in 1912 was called the *'Gilded age'* where many rich people flourished and had forgotten about God. We've all seen the movie and know the facts.

Psalm 12:3	"The LORD shall cut off all flattering lips, and the tongue that speaketh proud things:"
Psalm 12:4	"Who have said, With our tongue will we prevail; our lips are our own: who is lord over us?"
Psalm **12:3**	at the end says "…the tongue that speaketh proud things."
Psalm **12:4**	"...who is the lord over us?"

This is Psalm **12:4** in relation to 1912 and the Titanic sank in the **4**th month (April). The Titanic was written up in many papers and magazines as unsinkable because of her **16** watertight compartments and our Psalm numbers 12:4 (12 + 4) =**16**. Our other Psalm numbers 12:3 (12 + 3) = **15** the morning she sank April **15**th 1912 at 2:20 am!

There was an expedition of the French and the Americans in 1985 to find the Titanic, headed by Robert Ballard. In 1985 on

September 1ˢᵗ the wreckage of the Titanic was found about 350 miles from the coast of Nova Scotia. It was 2 miles below the surface of the ocean. It wasn't until **July 14**, 1986, that everything was ready to explore the wreckage of the Titanic. This exploration was **74** years after the Titanic sank. The exploration began on **714** (July is the **seventh** month on the **fourteenth** day) July 14ᵗʰ and look at 2ⁿᵈ Chronicles **7:14** "If my people, which are called by my name, shall **humble themselves**, and pray, and seek my face, and turn from their **wicked ways**; then will I hear from heaven, and will forgive their sin, and will heal their land." Here we have traveled **74** years from the sinking of the Titanic in 1912 of Psalm 12:3 saying "…the tongue that speaketh **proud things**" to "shall **humble** themselves and pray." This was **74** years after the sinking; just put a '1' in the middle of **74** and you have the **7:14** of 2ⁿᵈ Chronicles again. This whole country, which was started based on religious freedom, was declared independent on a **74** day: **July 4ᵗʰ**, 1776. Add all of the numbers for the birthday of our nation: $(7 + 4 + 1 + 7 + 7 + 6) =$ **32**; 32 is the Bible number of covenant; One nation under God…"

Psalm 18: Year **1918**

The ending of the first World War, WWI in 1918.

Psalm 18:29	"For by thee I have run through a **troop**; and by my God have I **leaped over a wall**."
Psalm 18:34	"He teacheth my hands to **war**, so that a **bow of steel** is broken by mine arms."
Psalm 18:37	"I have pursued **mine enemies**, and overtaken them: neither did I turn again till they were consumed."
Psalm 18:39	"For thou hast girded me with strength **unto the battle**: thou hast subdued under me those that rose up against me."
Psalm 18:40	"Thou hast also given me the necks of **mine enemies**; that I might destroy them that hate me."

Veteran's Day was once called Armistice Day. The day WWI ended, peace was declared on the 11ᵗʰ hour, of the 11ᵗʰ day, of the

11th month, November 11th, 1918.

Psalm 33: Year **1933**

This is the end of the great depression in 1933 when many were without jobs and hungry.

Psalm 33:19   "To deliver their soul from **death**, and to keep them alive in **famine**." This one even lands on verse 19 as in **1933**.

Psalm 41: Year **1941**

The attack on Pearl Harbor was December 7th, **1941**. Remember how the Japanese ambassadors were falsely negotiating peace right up to the time of the attack; Psalm **41**:9 "…familiar friend, in whom I trusted, which did eat of my bread, hath *lifted up his heel against me*." Notice verse 41:11 "…because mine **enemy** doth not *triumph* over me." Take the end of the 11th month of November in **1941** as in verse numbers 41:11 and add our verse numbers (4 + 1 + 1 + 1) and you get 7, the day of the attack in the next month, December!

Psalm 41:9   "Yea, mine own familiar friend, in whom I trusted, which did eat of my bread, hath **lifted up his heel** against me."

Psalm 41:10   "But thou, O LORD, be merciful unto me, and raise me up, **that I may requite them**."

Psalm 41:11   "By this I know that thou favourest me, because mine **enemy doth not triumph over me**."

Psalm 41:12   "And as for me, thou **upholdest me in mine integrity**, and settest me before thy face for ever."

War was declared on Japan on December 8, 1941 and our verse numbers for Psalm 41:12 are year 1941 and month twelve (12). Verse 12 is the 12th month December; and all verse numbers (4 + 1 + 1 + 2) = **8**, the day we declared war; and Psalm 41:12 says that God will '*upholdest me in mine integrity*' referring to the United

States of America and her allies.

Psalm 43: Year **1943**

Psalm 43:1 "Judge me, O God, and plead my cause against an **ungodly nation**: O deliver me from the *deceitful and unjust man*." Psalm 43:2 "For thou art the God of my strength: why dost thou cast me off? why go I mourning because of the *oppression of the enemy*?" Jesus is talking to the Jews about missing their day of visitation: Luke **19:43** "For the days shall come upon thee, that thine **enemies** shall cast a **trench** about thee, and **compass thee round**, and keep thee in on every side."

The year is **1943** and Psalm 43:1 says "...plead my case against an ungodly nation"; and 43:2 says "...oppression of the enemy." This of course relates to the Nazi's and the oppression of the Jews during World War II in **1943**.

Psalm 44: Year **1944**

Psalm 44:5	"Through thee will we **push down** our **enemies**: through thy name will we tread them under that rise up against us." . Notice this has a future tense to it with "will we push down our enemies" and "will we tread them under." We were getting ready for D-day in May the (5th month), **1944**.
Psalm 44:6	"For I will not *trust in my bow*, neither shall my sword save me." In June (the sixth month) the 6th day 1944 you really needed to trust in God, and not just in your **bow or sword** on this beachhead.
Psalm 44:7	"But thou hast *saved us from our enemies*, and hast put them to shame that *hated us*." We landed our troops and pushed the enemy back in July (7th month), **1944**.

Psalm 45: Year 1945

Psalm 45:5 "Thine *arrows are sharp* in the heart of the *king's enemies*; whereby the people fall under thee." The Germans attacked the '**King and Queen'** (*king's enemies*) of England. This is the falling of our **enemies** in Germany because of the sharp arrows of our **armed forces and allies**! This is verse **45:5** and the **5**th month is May and **May** 8th is when Germany surrendered in **1945**.

Psalm 46: Year 1946

Psalm 46:8 "Come, behold the works of the LORD, what **desolations** he hath made in the **earth**."

Psalm 46:9 "He maketh **wars to cease** unto the end of the earth; he **breaketh the bow**, and cutteth the spear in sunder; he **burneth** the **chariot in the fire**." The year is **1946** and Psalm 46 says "He maketh **wars** to cease", the first full year after 1945 and **WWII**.

Psalm 48: Year 1948

Psalm **48**:2 says "Beautiful for situation, the joy of the whole earth, is **mount Zion**, on the sides of the north, the city of the great King." The city of the great king (*mount Zion*) is of course **Jerusalem** and in **1948** Israel became a nation. Psalm **48**:12 "Walk about **Zion**, and go round about her: tell the towers thereof."

Psalm 87: Year 1987

Psalm 87:4 "I will make mention of Rahab and (*Babylon*) to them that know me: behold *Philistia*, and Tyre, with Ethiopia; this man was born there." This was the restoration of the ancient Babylonian (**Babylon**) empire in **1987** by Saddam Hussein. There was actually a big feast (party) that lasted thirty days from October to November. This was one of the largest celebrations in history with famous **singers and bands** invited from all over the world and Psalm 87:7 declares "As well the **singers as the players on instruments** shall be there: all my springs are in thee." In **1987** Saddam

Hussein rebuilt the palaces and temples, and announced to the world that the old **Babylonian** empire with the spirit of *Nebuchadnezzar* had been restored within him (**Saddam Hussein**).

Psalm 89: Year **1989**

Psalm 89:40 "Thou hast broken down all his **hedges**; thou hast brought his **strong holds to ruin**." Thou hast broken down all his '**hedges**' referring to the Berlin wall falling; which came down on November 9, **1989**. The word '**hedges**' is only in the whole Bible 6 times and this one happens to land here.

We know that the Berlin wall led to the breakup of the Soviet Union which fell in 1991.

Psalm 89:10 "Thou hast broken (***Rahab***) in pieces, as one that is slain; thou hast *scattered thine enemies* with thy strong arm." The beginning of the coming down of the Soviet empire and the "*scattering of thine enemies*"; the breaking up of the USSR into other countries which occurred in 1991.

Psalm 91: Year **1991**

Psalm 91:5 "Thou shalt not be afraid for the terror by night; nor for the **arrow that flieth** by day." This is the terror (***terror by night***) from Saddam Hussein and the scud missiles (arrow that flieth by day) during the Gulf War in **1991**. Israel has now built its own new anti-missile defense system to combat scud missiles in 2002 and it's called the '**Arrow**' system.

Psalm 93: Year **1993**

Psalm 93:3 "The **floods** have lifted up, O LORD, the floods have lifted up their voice; the **floods** lift up their **waves**." Psalm 93:4 "The LORD on high is mightier than the noise of many **waters**, yea, than the **mighty waves of the sea**." In **1993** the Midwest floods happened by over 70 events that spread over a several month period of rainfall. This was because of a tremendous rainfall and flooding, which occurred over areas up to 200 miles wide and up to 600 miles long. Flash flooding and the flooding of rivers threatened life and property. The **1993 floods** and winter super-storm was among the worst in U.S. history.

Psalm 98: Year **1998**

Psalm 98:7 "Let the **sea roar**, and the fulness thereof; the world, and they that dwell therein." This was the year of El Niño, and of course the **seas** really did roar and affected parts of the whole earth with flooding. In late January and the early parts of February 1998, the California Coast was slammed with a series of very powerful El Niño winter storms. There were 27 counties in California that were declared **National Disaster Areas**, and hundreds of millions of dollars in property was lost. There were large **waves**, that went along with high tides and elevated seas, which produced a lot of beach erosion. The term El Niño (Spanish for "the Christ Child") was originally used by fishermen along the coasts of Ecuador and Peru to refer to a warm ocean current that typically appears around Christmas time and lasts for several months. Fish are less abundant during these warm intervals, so fishermen often take a break to repair their equipment and spend time with their families.

Psalm 99: Year **1999**

Psalm 99:**8** "Thou answeredst them, O LORD our God: thou wast a God that forgavest them, though thou tookest **vengeance of their inventions**." God took vengeance on our inventions, the **computers** and the **Y2K** problem and all of the expense and time involved to fix them. This is verse **8** and we know that all computers are based on the number **8**, especially seen in memory chips: 64k 128k, 256k, 1024k etc..; numbers all evenly divisible by eight (8). The **Y2K** problem itself was because the computers could not know the century year "**00**" in the date such as (12/31/**00**) which is 6 digits. In order to fix the problem we needed to go from 6 to **8** digits in the date like this (12/31/**2000**); and 8 is the verse number here.

Psalm 100: Year **2000**

Psalm 100:1 "Make a **joyful noise** unto the LORD, all ye lands." The **millennium celebration** in the Year **2000**. This is on the first verse and the first month is **January**, like January 1st 2000.

Psalm 101: Year **2001**

Psalm 101:8 "I will early destroy all **the wicked** of the land; that I may cut off all **wicked doers** from the (**city**) of the LORD." Looks like something is about to happen (WTC attack of September 11, 2001) in New York (**city**) and God is going to judge the **wicked terrorists**. Notice also this is the last verse of Psalm 101 verse 8 (August is the 8th month), if there was a next verse (9 for September) it would have been 101:9 or **9:101** backwards!

Psalm 102: Year **2002**

Psalm 102:3 "For my days are **consumed like smoke**, and my **bones are burned** as an hearth." Psalm 102:9 "For I have eaten **ashes** like bread, and mingled my drink with **weeping**." The mood and grieving of the people after the smoke and **ashes** of the World Trade Center attack. Psalm **102:8** "Mine *enemies reproach me all the day*; and they that are mad against me are sworn against me." The constant threats of the **terrorists** in America and in Israel. Here is some hope: Psalm **102:13** "Thou shalt arise, and have mercy upon **Zion**: for the time to **favour her**, yea, the set time, is come." Psalm **102:14-21** "For thy servants take pleasure in her **stones**, and **favour the dust thereof**. So the **heathen** shall fear the name of the LORD, and all the kings of the earth thy glory. When the LORD shall build up **Zion**, he shall appear in his glory. He will regard the **prayer of the destitute**, and not despise their prayer. This shall be written for the **generation to come**: and the people which shall be created shall praise the **LORD**. For he hath looked down from the **height of his sanctuary**; from heaven did the LORD behold the earth; To hear the **groaning** of the prisoner; to loose those that are appointed to **death**; To declare the name of the LORD in **Zion**, and his praise in **Jerusalem**."

Psalm 103: Year **2003**

Psalm 103:5 "Who satisfieth thy mouth with good things; so that thy youth is renewed like the **eagle's**." Is this good things and spiritual renewal for America in **2003** (renewed like the American **eagle**)? Don't ever lose sight of this: Psalm 103:11 "For as the heaven is high above the earth, so great is his mercy toward them that fear him." Psalm 103:6 "The LORD executeth righteousness and judgment for all that are oppressed."

You might want to watch out for this one in 2006 and our 'inventions'.

Psalm 106: Year **2006**

Psalm 106:29 "Thus they provoked him to anger with their **inventions**: and the **plague brake** in upon them." Psalm 106:39 "Thus were they defiled with their **own works**, and went a whoring with their own **inventions**."

Psalm 110: Year **2010**

Psalm 110:6 "He shall **judge among the heathen**, he shall fill the places with the **dead bodies**; he shall wound the **heads over many countries**."

Keep in mind that there are **150** Psalms so if you want to get a hint of what else is coming ahead, just read the rest of them. If there are only 150 Psalms starting from the year 1900, then what? A hint will be given later in regard to this.

These **18** Psalms have significant key words, describing major events for the same year as the Psalm numbers starting at the year 1901. The years are 1912, 1918, 1933, 1941, 1943, 1944, 1945, 1946, 1948, 1987, 1989, 1991, 1993, 1998, 1999, 2000, 2001, and 2002. Many of these also have verses that land on the correct number of the month. This would be like getting **(18)** matching Psalm numbers correct, landing on significant related data out of a total of **150** Psalms on the first try. The odds are about 8 x $10\verb|^|22^{nd}$ power to **1** that this would happen by random accident or chance; $10\verb|^|22^{nd}$ power is about the number of stars in the universe.

CHAPTER 2

The **Scientific** and **Mathematical** correct Psalms

U nder the leading of the Holy Spirit I have made some amazing discoveries about the Psalms and their Psalm numbers in
the area of scientific power numbers. This has to do with the meaning of a scientific power number showing up in the Psalm of that
same number. All of the numbers that I will show are international
constants that would be easily recognized by any scientist, or
student of science, or that you can look up for yourself. These
numbers are all powers of the number 10; such as 10 to the 8th
power would be: $(10x10x10x10x10x10x10x10)$ or $100,000,000$,
which is ten multiplied by itself eight times $(1 + 8$ zeroes$)$. It's not
as important to understand all of the following scientific explana-
tions as much as it is to notice that the actual number of a particular
Psalm seems to contain the meaning of the same scientific power
number! These are what I call *obvious numbers*, based on already
known scientific data existing on the surface of the text, along with
the 'key words' pertaining to that scientific power number.

There are four basic forces known to the universe, the strong
force, the weak force, electromagnetism and gravity. Electromagnetism (*electricity*) and *gravity* are somewhat familiar to us.
The strong force and the weak force are not so familiar. The strong
force is the strongest force known and holds the proton and neutron
together in the center of the atom, but has a very short range of

influence. The weak force has to do with the beta decay of subatomic particles and also has a very short range. The weak nuclear force is also responsible for reactions that fuel the sun. Gravity has a long range, but is a very weak force compared to the other forces. Electromagnetism is much stronger than gravity and has a long range also, but is balanced out by the existence of positive and negative forces that cancel and balance each other out. In these Psalms we are looking for the beauty and symmetry of how the Word of God agrees with science and nature.

The strong force of the universe is the force holding the nucleus of the atom together and is the strongest physical force known. If we set the strong force to a value of (1), which is what scientists do, then we can gauge the other forces relative strengths. In this case, the electromagnetic force would be a power of (2), actually 1.37×10^2 power or 137 times weaker than the strong force. The weak force would be (13) or 10^{13} power times weaker than the strong force; and gravity would be (38) or 10^{38} power times weaker than the strong force. If we added all of these forces $(1 + 2 + 13 + 38)$ they equal 54, which is interesting as the weight of the entire universe is somewhere around 10^{53} power expressed in kilograms. A kilogram is 2.2 pounds. Throughout the Psalms we will use a measurement called the Planck length named after Max Planck who discovered this around the year 1900. The Planck length is the smallest measurement known in the universe at about 1.6×10^{-33} centimeters. Anything smaller than this measurement has no meaning in our world, it would either be a black hole or what is known as quantum foam. This is the size of where the 6 or 7 extra dimensions of the universe would exist in our eleven-dimensional universe. The concept of the eleven-dimensional universe will be discussed later in the book. In other words, the known universe has a finite limit in smallness of size at 10^{-33} centimeters. It also has a known radius of about 10^{61} powers magnitude in centimeters greater than the Planck length, which equates to about 15 billion light years. These measurements put the size of the earth at 10^{42} power magnitudes greater than the Planck length.

Psalm 8:3   "When I consider thy heavens, the work of thy fingers, the moon and the stars, which thou hast ordained."

Key words: **heavens**, moon, stars.

Eight (**8**) is Jesus' number in the Bible and (**150 x 10^8th power**) is the radius size of the universe in billions of light years (15,000,000,000). The numerical value of the word "Jesus" in the Greek language is "**888**". There are **150** Psalms total and this is **Psalm 8** talking about the one who created the heavens by the work of His fingers. The equation for the temperature of black holes and the equation for the warping of space by a massive body both contain (**8** times pi (3.14159)). There are **8** messenger particles that mediate the 'strong force' holding all atoms together in the universe called **gluons**. Each neutron and proton in the (center of the atom) is composed of **3** quarks held together by using these **8** gluons of the strong force; now consider again our verse numbers **8:3** and what this Psalm is talking about. The name for this in science is called "**The Eightfold Way**" of particle physics; we will talk more on this later.

Psalm 13:1   "… O LORD my God: **lighten mine eyes**, lest I sleep the **sleep of death**."

Key words: lighten, sleep of death.

10^-13th power is the relative power of the weak force (*compared to the strong force set to 1*) and beta decay, the *death* of particles. The weak nuclear force is also responsible for reactions that fuel the sun. This **Psalm 13** deals with the weak force which is 10 to the -13 power. Scientists set the strong force, the strongest force known, to a value of one (1) and then compare all of the other forces based on this force. The strong force holds the atom's nucleus together. If the strong force is set to the number one (1) then the weak force is 10 to the -13 power times weaker than the strong force. Written out, the weak force is 10,000,000,000,000 times weaker than the strong force. This weak force is also known as 'beta decay' or death of the particle. In this process the particle such as a neutron decays (***dies***) and is transformed into another particle. Particles of (***light***) like **photons** with mass called vector bosons are also involved in this process. The weak force is carried by three particles called bosons, the W+, W-, and Z bosons. These particles of the weak force are extremely short lived and can only travel a very short distance on the subatomic scale, and then they disappear. In this Psalm 13 it says *"lighten mine eyes"* and *"the sleep of death"*, just like the power number **10 to the -13 power** *weak force* implies by the ***death*** of a particle involved with a particle of *light* called a boson. What happens in nature to particles is a natural picture of what can happen to us in life spiritually. In the *weak force* all of the particles in nature take turns turning into the other particles. Another power of 13 weakness scripture: 2nd Corinthians 13:4 "For though he was crucified through **weakness**, yet he liveth by the power of God. For we also are **weak** in him, but we shall live with him by the power of God toward you." Another reason that the weak force is 13 is that its range of influence is about $10^\wedge$-13 power centimeters, the size of the atom. The weak force can be expressed another way as $10^\wedge$**-6** power on a different measuring scale other than this relative scale of comparing it to the strong force set at (1). With that in mind look at Psalm **6**:2 says "Have mercy upon me, O LORD; for (**I am weak**): O LORD, heal me; for my bones are vexed." Now put together these two Psalm numbers of the weak force and paste them together as (6 and 13) = **613**. There were actually exactly **613** laws for the Jews in the Old Testament! Romans 8:3 "For what the law could not do, in that it was **weak** through the flesh, God sending his own Son in the likeness of sinful flesh, and for sin, condemned sin in the flesh." Now mirror 613 and you have John 3:16 "For God so loved the world...." a (613 | 316) reflection of the Old and New Testament. Galatians **6:13** "For neither they themselves who are circumcised keep the **law**, but desire to have you circumcised, that they may glory in your flesh." Romans 6:14 "For sin shall not have dominion over you: for ye are not under the **law**, but under grace." Here we add one to the law (613 + 1) = 614 because we are no longer under the law but grace. And who brought the grace, the number 14 of the 6(14) of course is Jesus as the generational number in the very next Psalm, number 14!

Psalm 14:5   "There were they in great fear: for God is in the **generation** of the righteous."

Key word: generation.

$10\wedge14^{th}$ power is the number of cells in your body and **Psalm 14** talks about "God is in the **generation** of the righteous"; having to do with our **genes** (*cells*). This is 100,000,000,000,000 cells. Also in the book of Matthew 1:17 "So all the generations from Abraham to David are **fourteen** generations; and from David until the carrying away into Babylon are fourteen generations; and from the carrying away into Babylon unto Christ are fourteen generations." These are three (3) **generations** of (14) and 3 x 14 = 42. 10 to the 42nd power is the size of the earth above the Planck length. Ecclesiastes 1:4 "One **generation** passeth away, and another generation cometh: but the **earth** abideth for ever." Numbers 14:18 "The LORD is longsuffering, and of great mercy, forgiving iniquity and transgression, and by no means clearing the guilty, visiting the iniquity of the fathers upon the children unto the third and fourth **generation**." The word 'generations' is found in the Bible **114 times**; John **1:14** "And the Word was made flesh..." See also Psalm 114.

Psalm 19:1   "The heavens declare the glory of God; and the firmament sheweth his handywork. Day unto day uttereth speech, and night unto night sheweth knowledge. There is no speech nor language, where their voice is not heard. Their line is gone out through all the earth, and their words to the end of the world. In them hath he set a **tabernacle for the sun**, Which is as a bridegroom coming out of his chamber, and rejoiceth as a strong man to run a race. His going forth is from the end of the heaven, and his **circuit** unto the ends of it: and there is nothing hid from the **heat** thereof."

Key words: tabernacle for the **sun**, end of the heaven, **circuit**, **heat**.

The number for electrical energy (*heat*) is 10 to the **-19th power** and this is also referred to as the Planck mass. This number 10 to the -19th power joules is associated with one electron volt. A joule is a unit of energy required to lift something weighing one pound about nine inches. Another use is 10 to the **+19th power** (GeV) this is the Planck energy. The word (GeV) refers to Giga electron Volts, Giga means billion. This is 10 to the 19th power (10,000,000,000,000,000,000) billion electron volts. This **Psalm 19** talks about a tabernacle for the **sun**, **heat** and a **circuit**, all about electrical energy and power! The meaning of the Psalm matches the scientific power number **19**. Also note that the Psalms are the **19th book** of the Bible and is filled with the '**power**' of God. Luke 10:**19** says "Behold, I give unto you (**power**) to tread on serpents and scorpions, and over all the power of the enemy: and nothing shall by any means hurt you." The number 19 also speaks of faith in the Bible. In the book of Hebrews in the 11th chapter (the faith chapter), there are 19 instances of 'faith' or 'by faith' listed. Psalm 119 is the longest Psalm with 176 chapters. God's victory number is 17 and (7 x 17) = 119. The words '**sun**' and '**light**' appear together in **19** scriptures of the Bible. 10^-**19th** power is also the charge of the **electron**.

Psalm 23:4　　　　"Yea, though I walk through the valley of the shadow of death, I will fear no evil: for thou art with me; thy rod and thy staff they comfort me."

Key words: 23:4 "valley of the shadow of death", 23:3 "He restoreth my soul".

We know that if we carbon-based *oxygen breathing* beings don't breathe air for a few minutes, we die and Psalm 23 talks about the "*valley of the shadow of death*" and "*He restoreth my soul.*" Remember that man was created by God '*breathing*' into him and then man became a *living soul*: Genesis 2:7 "And the LORD God formed man of the dust of the ground, and (**breathed**) into his nostrils the (**breath**) of life; and man became a living (**soul**). Ten to the **23rd power** (6.022 x **10^23**) is the Avogadro constant that matches our **Psalm 23** number; this constant is all about the air (**gases**) we breathe. This science constant is special because it is the number of carbon atoms that makes exactly 12 grams of carbon, i.e. if you had 6.022 x 10^23 power carbon atoms on a scale, it would read exactly 12 grams. Although the Avogadro constant is officially defined in terms of carbon, it is probably easier to think of it in terms of the simplest atom, hydrogen. Equal volumes of different gases at the same temperature and pressure contain the same number of molecules. The entire system of measuring pure substances (elements and compounds) is based on this fact. The number of particles in 22.4 liters of any gas at STP (*Standard Temperature and Pressure*) is a standard unit called a mole. This (mole) unit is important because it forms the basis of writing chemical formulas and equations. This volume of gas is known as the molar volume of a gas. Each mole contains 6.022 x 10^{23} particles; Avogadro's number. Therefore, 22.4 Liter of any gas contains 6.022 x 10^{23} representative particles of that gas; this is true of any gas, such as the air or '**oxygen**' that we breathe to keep alive. Please note that the verse numbers for our **Psalm 23:4 (23 x 4) = 92** the number of natural elements of the earth, and this 10^23 power number is all about gases and molecules and their measurement, simply awesome. Also in Christian circles we have that song saying "He is the air that I breathe"; He being Jesus of course, who is the number eight (**8**) in the Bible, and oxygen is number (**8**) in the chemical table of elements. Another major constant having to do with the number (**23**) related to gases is the Boltzmann constant; it's 1.3806 x **10^-23 power** and is defined as: the ratio of the 'universal gas constant' to the Avogadro number.

Psalm 24:1   "The **earth** is the LORD's, and the fulness thereof; the world, and they that dwell therein."

Key words: Earth, world.

6 * 10^24^th^ power is the mass (*weight*) of the **Earth** as measured in kilograms (1 kilogram = 2.2 pounds); and this is Psalm **24** talking about the **Earth** in the first verse! Also the Earth is 10^42 power times larger than the Planck length; so we have a (**24 | 42**) mirror of weight and size. The earth's weight can also be expressed as 6 x 10^{21st} power metric tons: Psalm **21:10** "Their fruit shalt thou destroy from the **earth**, and their seed from among the children of men." A metric ton is 2204.6 pounds. The word 'earth' is found 906 times in the Bible. Take 905.6 (almost 906) and divide by the earth's weight number **24**; (905.6 / 24) = **37.73**. The Genesis creation verse of the Bible: **Genesis 1:1** "In the beginning God created the heaven and the **earth**" in the Hebrew language, has a numerical value of 2701 or mirror multiples (**37 x 73**) = 2701 when all of its letters are added. Speaking of 2701, Psalm 27:01 or rather stated Psalm 27:1 is next.

Psalm 27:1   "The LORD is my **light** and my salvation; whom shall I fear?"

Key word: **light**.

10^{-27th} power is the number for the minimum energy of a photon of *light* in erg seconds. This is also called Planck's constant and is one of the most important constants in physics. The words '**lightning**' and '**lightnings**' together are found **27 times in the Bible**. The words '**God and light**' appear together in **27** different scriptures of the Bible. Matthew **10:27** "What I tell you in darkness, that speak ye in (**light**): and what ye hear in the ear, that preach ye upon the housetops." See also Psalm **34**.

Psalm 29:7   "The voice of the LORD divideth the **flames of fire**."

Key words: **divideth**, flames of fire.

10^{29th} **power** is the temperature of the heat of the creation event when the universe was 10^{-37th} power of a second old. This is 100,000,000,000,000,000,000,000,000,000 degrees on the Kelvin scale. This would be real hot on any scale! This Psalm 29 shows the Lord **dividing** the *flames of fire* in creation, and matches the number of **10^{29} power**. This is what science says also; that there was just one super-force in the beginning, and that it broke off and *divided* into the four different basic forces we experience today.

Combining Psalm 29 with Psalm 92 (coming ahead about the 92 natural elements) we have a **(29 | 92)** mirror of energy (29) and the number of natural elements of earth (92); energy and matter. Also Deuteronomy **29:29** says "The secret things belong unto the LORD our God: but those things which are revealed belong unto us and to our children for ever, that we may do all the words of this law." Hebrews 12:**29** says "For our God is a consuming **fire**." The number **29** in the Bible means: ***departure***; here something departed and took off in a real hurry, the universe!

Psalm 31:2	"Bow down thine ear to me; deliver me **speedily**: be thou my strong rock, for an house of defence to save me."
Psalm 31:4	"Pull me out of the **net** that they have laid privily for me: for thou art my strength."

Key words: Psalm 31:2 speedily, Psalm 31:4 out of the net.

 10^{-31} power is the mass of the electron; actually 9.10938 x 10^{-31} power expressed as kilograms. The key to the electron is its incredible ***speed*** as it orbits the atom and Psalm 31:2 says "...deliver me **speedily**." The tiny electron orbits the atom at 2.2 million meters per second! Electron spin is a quality that gives rise to its ***angular momentum*** about an axis within the electron. We also know that without electrons there would be no computers. What are most of the world's computers hooked up to? The **net** (internet) of course; and Psalm 31:4 says "Pull me out of the **net**...." The **number 31** as the mass of the electron is a mirror to the weak force of Psalm 13, a **(13 | 31)** mirror and these two forces actually work together in physics. Now look at something really strange as the two verse numbers where the key words *'speedily'* and *'net'* are found is 31:2 (31 x 2) = 62 and 31:4 (31 x 4) = 124. Just add the results as (62 + 124) = **186**. Why is light found ***speed*** here for the electron? Because electrons are constantly absorbing and sending out photons of **light**! The first chapter of the Book of Genesis, being the creation chapter has **31** verses in it. (**186** x 1000 God's glory number) is **186,000** miles per second, light speed. Regarding 1000 being God's glory number of light: Exodus 40:25

"And he **lighted** the lamps before the LORD; as the LORD commanded Moses." These Exodus verse numbers (40 x 25) = 1000. The words *lighted* and *lamps* from our Exodus 40:25 scripture are found together in only 2 scriptures in the whole Bible. The word *'lamps'* appears **31** times in the Bible, the word *lamp* appears **13** times in the Bible, another (**13 | 31**) mirror. To go with our word lamps, the word *'flame'* occurs in **31** different scriptures of the Bible. In reference to Psalm 31:2 "Bow down thine ear to me; deliver me *speedily*..." The word *'speedily'* is found **19** times in the Bible, the word *'speed'* is found **11** times, and *'speedy'* is found **1** time. Of all words with 'speed' as the root word in the Bible there are (**19 + 11 + 1**) = **31**; and *'speedily'* was our key word in Psalm **31**. In regards to 'speed' being found (**19 + 11 + 1**) = **31** times; in **1911** Ernest Rutherford discovered that the atom has a nucleus and electrons surrounding it! A term related to the electron is its spin; the word spin is found in the Bible only 3 times, but the word 'spindle' is only found once in the whole Bible and it's in a **31** numbered scripture: **Proverbs 31:19** "She layeth her hands to the (**spindle**), and her hands hold the (**distaff**)." The word 'distaff' here in the Hebrew means: (pelek, a 'circle', the instrument used for twisting threads by a whirl)." One can picture many electrons *whirling* around the atom in a *circle*. What is really interesting also is that $10^{\wedge}-19^{th}$ power is the charge of the electron making our Proverbs verse of **31**(*electron mass*) + **19** (*electron charge*) even more significant. The word 'spin' is found (**3**) times and 'spindle' is found (**1**) time; 3 pasted to 1 equals **31**.

Later on in the book we will see this fact repeat, that when a key word is found just once in the Bible, the verse numbers scientifically equal what the scriptures verse meaning implies.

Psalm 33:1-2   "Rejoice in the LORD, O ye righteous: for praise is comely for the upright. Praise the LORD with harp: sing unto him with the psaltery and an instrument of **ten strings**."

Key words: instrument of **ten strings**, harp, psaltery.

The number of the Planck length, the smallest length measurement in the universe is 10 to the -33rd power expressed as centimeters of length. If you were the size of an atom you would still have to shrink 10 to the 20th power times smaller to get to the Planck length. This is the place where time and space merge into quantum foam. Length and time no longer have any meaning as in the classical world of size where we live. This **10 to the -33 power** is the basic length (or a multiple of this length) of the length of vibrating loops of energy called strings. In string theory the strings are the dimensions that are curled up into a six or seven dimensional ball. The theory of the universe where these strings vibrate in the *ten dimensions* of space is called super-string theory. This Psalm 33 is about vibrating **ten strings** in the universe.

The **Psalm 33** says *"an instrument of ten strings"* in the second verse. The latest theory of the universe says that the universe has eleven dimensions; ten dimensions are space dimensions, and one of time. These vibrating loops of strings at the Planck length, **10 to the -33rd power** centimeters, are said to be vibrating like strings of music in the 10 *dimensions* of space. This theory looks very promising and says that the universe must contain exactly 11 dimensions. Four dimensions are the everyday dimensions, including time, and six or seven of these dimensions are real tiny, and rolled up at the Planck length, out of our everyday experience. Psalm **33** matches the important measurement of the Planck length of quantum physics; 10^{-33} centimeters by talking about **10** strings. A string's length (10^{-33}) is the measurement size or is a multiple of the size of the Planck length. Consider Ecclesiastes **3:11** "He hath made every thing beautiful in his time: also he hath set the **world in their heart**, so that no man can find out the work that God maketh from the beginning to the end." Even though God has *"set the world in their heart"* no man can find out the work! It's a mystery, why? Because this is Ecclesiastes **3:11** and $(3 \times 11) = $ **33**, the smallest measurement possible called the Planck length, made of tiny vibrating loops of matter called **super-strings**! Colossians **3:3** "For ye are dead, and your life is **hid** with Christ in God." Jesus lived **33** years on the earth. String theory also has objects called **membranes** (referred to as '**branes**') in the theory. A string is a 'one-brane' object because it exists in just one dimension. There are however, higher dimensional branes possible. For example, a 'three-brane' is an object existing in 3 spatial dimensions. These strings are called membranes if they have more space dimensions than one. These **strings** can have extra space dimensions up to **nine** spatial dimensions, **nine** is the limit. The word '**string**' shows up exactly **nine (9)** times in the Bible in all of its forms. Here is the list of all **nine;** they all seem to land on very significant numbered verses.

Psalms 11:2 "For, lo, the wicked **bend their bow**, they make ready their **arrow** upon the (**string**), that they may privily **shoot at the upright in heart**." The escape velocity to get off of the earth is **11.2** kilometers per second (overcoming **gravity**). (11 x 2) = **22,** the number of letters in the **Hebrew alphabet** and Bible number of **light**!

Psalms 21:12 "Therefore shalt thou make them turn their back, when thou shalt make ready thine **arrows** upon thy (**strings**) against the face of them." (21 + 12) = **33,** this Psalm's number and the Planck length.

Psalms **33:2** "Praise the **LORD** with **harp**: sing unto him with the psaltery and an instrument of **ten** (**strings**)." This is Psalm **33** and the **ten-dimensional** (strings) of the universe! (33 x 2) = **66** the number of books of the Bible and (33 + 2) = **35;** man is about 1.8 x **10^35** powers in size (centimeters) greater than the Planck length!

Psalms **92:**3 "Upon an instrument of (**ten strings**), and upon the psaltery; upon the harp with a solemn sound." **92** is the number of natural elements on the earth.

Psalms 144:**9** "I will sing a new song unto thee, O God: upon a psaltery and an instrument of (**ten strings**) will I sing praises unto thee." **144** is the size of the man/angel from Revelation 21:17. The number **1.44** in science deals with (**half life**) and radioactive decay.

Psalms 150:**4** "Praise him with the timbrel and dance: praise him with (**stringed**) instruments and organs." The **15** billion light year radius of the universe with **4** seen dimensions; see Psalm **8**. (**150 x 4**) = **600**. Genesis 7:6 "And Noah was **six hundred years old** when the **flood of waters** was upon the earth." Genesis 7:24 "And the **waters** prevailed upon the earth an **hundred and fifty days**."

Isaiah 38:**20** "The **LORD** was ready to save me: therefore we will sing my songs to the (**stringed**) **instruments** all the days of our life in the house of the LORD." **38** (Psalm 38) is **gravity** and a string is $10^{\wedge}\text{-}20^{th}$ power (centimeters) times smaller than the **atom**. The atoms' size is $10^{\wedge}\text{-}13^{th}$ power centimeters (13 + 20) = **33**.

Habakkuk 3:19 "The LORD God is my strength, and he will make my feet like hinds' feet, and he will make me to walk upon **mine high places**. To the chief singer on my (**stringed**) instruments." (3 + 19) = **22** again like Psalm **11:2**. (3 x 19) = **57**, the base number of carbon **14** (**half-life**) about (**5700**) years.

Mark 7:35 "And straightway his ears were opened, and the (**string**) of his **tongue** was loosed, and he spake plain." 10 to the 35th power (**10^35**) is the size of **man** above the Planck length, and (7 + 35) = **42**, the size of the **earth** above the Planck length: 10^42.

All of the subjects in these **nine** verses will be talked about more later on in the book. The number 33 in the Bible means: *promise*.

Psalm 34:5 "They looked unto **him**, and were **lightened**: and their faces were not ashamed."

Key word: **Lightened**

$10^{\wedge}\text{-}34^{th}$ power is the number for the minimum energy of a photon of **light** in joule seconds. Actually it is 6.626 x $10^{\wedge}\text{-}34$ power. This is also called Planck's constant and is one of the most important constants in physics. This is the same value as Psalm 27 which used erg seconds. We are just using a different scale of measurement called joule seconds for our **10^-34 power** number. It's amazing that both of the Psalms (**27** and **34**) mention *light* and *lighten* in the first 5 verses. This Planck's constant relates the *quantum* of energy of a ***photon of light*** to its frequency and is used in many equations in quantum theory. The words 'Lord' and 'light' appear together in **34 verses** in the Bible!

Psalm 38:3   "There is no soundness in my flesh because of thine anger; neither is there any rest in my bones because of my sin. For mine iniquities are gone over mine head: as an **heavy** burden they are too **heavy** for me."

Key words: **heavy burden**, too **heavy** for me.

Gravity is **10^-38th power** compared to the *strong force*, and Psalm 38 talks of "***an heavy burden***" and something "***too heavy***" called sin. The word '*heavy*' is found in exactly **38 different verses** of the Bible! The word *heavy* is in this verse twice, and this is the only verse that it's in twice in the whole Bible, for a total of 39 times. The number 38 in the Bible means slavery. Jesus is talking about a *heavy* thing to carry: **Matthew 10:38** "And he that taketh not his **cross**, and followeth after me, is not worthy of me." If 10^-38 power is gravity, then what power is anti-gravity, 10^+83 power? Look at Psalm 83:18, "That men may know that thou, whose name alone is **JEHOVAH**, art the **most high** over all the earth." We have a (**-38 | +83**) Psalm mirror of these two opposite forces with the "*too heavy for me*" of Psalm 38, and the "JEHOVAH, art the most high" of Psalm 83. The power of sin (-38) drags you down, and the power of JEHOVAH (+83) lifts you up into *the "most high"*; gravity and anti-gravity. Now consider again what Psalm **8:3** says "When I consider thy heavens, the work of thy fingers, the moon and the stars, which thou hast ordained", and relate it to Psalm **83**:18. To go along with our Psalm 83:18 meaning of anti-gravity, the 83rd element is called Bismuth. This element has an atomic number of **83**. This Bismuth element (no. 83) has the highest electrical resistance when placed in a magnetic field (*qualities of anti-gravity*), than any other element. Also this element Bismuth (83) has an atomic weight of **208.98**. In relation to Bismuth at a weight in the 208-209 range look at **Psalm 20:8** "They are brought **down and fallen**: but we are **risen**, and stand upright." Again gravity *"brought down and fallen"* and anti-gravity *"we are risen"*. It's amazing that these words just happen to fall on these numbers of Psalm 20:8. Look at our verse number 38:3 as gravity at the power of (38 x 3) = 114; see Psalm 114 for the power of the 114 number.

Psalm 39:1   "I said, I will take heed to my ways, that I sin not with my **tongue**: I will keep my **mouth** with a bridle, while the wicked is before me."

Key words: tongue, mouth, bridle.

This is a prophecy of Jesus Christ who said nothing to Pilate just before He was crucified and was also beaten with **39 stripes**. Imagine the strength of His **tongue** and what it took for Him to say nothing to free His self, knowing He was facing the cross. There are **39** different categories of diseases and Jesus was beaten with a stripe for each one of them for us. The Old Testament has **39** books in it and (3 x 9) = 27, the number of books of the New Testament; also 27 (2 x 7) = 14, the generational number of Psalm 14. It just so happens that 10^{+39th} **power** (*a number with 39 zeroes in it*) tons is the tension exerted by one of these tiny vibrating loops of matter called *strings*. A related scripture having to do with the *tongue and strings* is Mark 7:35 "And straightway his ears were opened, and the **string** of his **tongue** was loosed, and he spake plain." Using Planck units as a standard of measurement, a six foot man is about 1.82×10^{35th} power times larger than the Planck length *in centimeters* and this is Mark 7:35. Science says we live in an eleven dimensional universe; so take the 4 seen dimensions of (length, height, width, and time) and minus them from eleven (11 – 4) = 7. That leaves only 7 tiny curled up dimensions like *string theory* says, and again this is Mark 7:35! Ten to the 35th power (relating to Mark: 7:35) or stated as 10^{35} powers of the Planck length, is the size of a man! This 10^{+39th} **power** number seems to have to do with the power of **speech** and **words** through 'string vibrations'. In fact in computer language a '*string*' is a group of letters that form a word. Proverbs 18:21says "Death and life are in the power of the **tongue**: and they that love it shall eat the fruit thereof." This is chapter 18 and verse 21 in Proverbs and (18 + 21) = **39**. Isaiah 28:11 "For with **stammering lips** and **another tongue** will he speak to this people"; (28 + 11) = **39**. Psalm **39**:3 "My heart was hot within me, while I was musing the fire burned: then spake I with my **tongue**." This is 10 to the 39th power and words: Luke **10:39** "And she had a sister called Mary, which also sat at Jesus' feet, and heard his (*word*)." Mark 9:**39** "But Jesus said, Forbid him not: for there is no man which shall do a miracle in my name, that can lightly (*speak*) evil of me." Look even at Psalms **139**:4 "For there is not a **word** in my **tongue**, but, lo, O LORD, thou knowest it altogether!" **Strings** have to do with **music** vibrations also: 1st Samuel **16:23** "And it came to pass, when the **evil spirit from God** was upon Saul, that David took an **harp**, and played with his hand: so Saul was refreshed, and was well, and the **evil spirit departed** from him"; verse numbers (16 + 23) = **39**. The weak force is a power of 13 *see Psalm 13,* and (3 x 13) = 39. If you add the weak force (13) to the number of characters in the English or Greek language (26), you get (26 + 13) = **39**!

Psalm 42:7   "Deep calleth unto deep at the noise of thy waterspouts: all thy **waves** and thy **billows** are gone over me."

Key words: waves, billows

This **Psalm 42** talks about '*waves*' which relates to the Planck frequency. This frequency is a kilogram (2.2 pounds) of mass whose energy equals the energy of a group of photons (*of light*) whose frequencies sum to 10^{42} power. This Planck frequency means *cycles per second* or frequency of **waves at 10^42** power matching Psalm 42 talking about **waves**. This is a number with **42** zeroes in it and that is a whole lot of (*light wave*) cycles per second! The 'm' here is meters and m/s = meters per second; with a wavelength fixed at the Planck limit of 10^{-34} m, and for a velocity of c (light speed), the frequency becomes $3.10^{8}[m/s]/10^{-34}m = \mathbf{3.10^{42}}$ cycles per second. We see here from this formula, dealing with wavelengths and light, that **10^42 power** is the result dealing with **waves**. Also the earth is 10 to the 42nd power times larger than the Planck length. These waves going over you are God's thoughts. Psalms 139:17 "How precious also are thy thoughts unto me, O God! how great is the sum of them!" The word '*waves*' shows up in 26 verses and the word '*wave*' appears in 16 different verses of the Bible for a total of (26 + 16) = **42 verses**.

Psalm 44:1   "We have heard with our ears, O God, our fathers have told us, what work thou didst in their days, in the **times** of old."

Key words: **times of old**, in their days.

This next number is similar to the Planck length and is called the *Planck time*. It's 10 to the **-44th power** of a second. This is the smallest *time* that can be measured! This is the time that it takes light to cross the Planck length. If you divide a second into 100,000,000,000,000,000,000,000,000,000,000,000,000,000,000 pieces, this is how small of a time that this is. This Psalm 44 has to do with the major physics constant of the smallest measurement of time, 10^-44 power of a second. Notice that this Psalm 44 talks of "in the **times of old**" in the very first verse of the Psalm, matching our **10^-44 power** scientific number with **Psalm 44**. Also consider this important New Testament scripture: Galatians **4:4** "But when the fulness of the (**time**) was come, God sent forth his Son, made of a woman, made under the law, To redeem them that were under the law, that we might receive the adoption of sons." Only 4 verses in the whole Bible have the words 'times' and 'fathers' in the same verse including this Psalm, and Nehemiah **10:34** says "And we cast the lots among the priests, the Levites, and the people, for the wood offering, to bring it into the house of our God, after the houses of our (**fathers**), at (**times**) appointed year by year, to burn upon the altar of the LORD our God, as it is written in the law"; and (**10 + 34**) = **44**. Isaiah **44:8** "Fear ye not, neither be afraid: have not I told thee from that (**time**), and have declared it? ye are even my witnesses. Is there a God beside me? yea, there is no God; I know not any." The Planck length of Psalm 33 at 10^-33 centimeters and

Planck time 10^44 seconds were not known until the year 1900; these Psalms were written **2,900** years before this information was known.

Psalm 60:1   "O God, thou hast cast us off, thou hast scattered us, thou hast been displeased; O turn thyself to us again. Thou hast made the **earth to tremble**; thou hast **broken it**: heal the breaches thereof; for it shaketh."

Key words: **broken it**, earth to tremble.

The key phrase to Psalm **60** is "**thou hast broken it**" and this is exactly what science says; that the universe exists as a **broken symmetry**. You can say that the whole universe spans a range of about (**60-61**) magnitudes of the power of 10 using the Planck length. This is from 10 to the -33rd power, the smallest size in centimeters; to the largest (radius size of the whole universe) which is about 10 to the 27th power expressed in length as centimeters. Adding the two powers we get ($33 + 27 = 60$). The universe that we live in is said by scientists to have a *broken symmetry* and not a perfect symmetry. At much higher energies or heat, all of the four forces of nature, the strong force, the weak force, the electromagnetic force, and gravity all become equal or symmetric. At lower energies where we live, these forces exist in a broken symmetry and the forces behave in a different way. Scientists are trying to come up with a Theory Of Everything (**TOE**) to explain all of these **broken** and higher energy forces and thus describe the entire universe. This **Psalm 60** is about the whole universe, with a size of sixty (**60**) magnitudes of the powers of ten existing in a broken symmetry and how it affects the earth.

Psalm 61:2   "From the **end of the earth** will I **cry unto thee**, when my heart is overwhelmed: lead me to the **rock** that is higher than I."

Key words: end of the **earth**, **rock** that is higher than, will I **cry** unto thee.

This is the Psalm of the stretched universe at **10^61** magnitudes above the Planck length. Later on we will talk more of string theory and the **10^61** power radius size of the universe. This Psalm mentions the earth, which we know is **10^42** powers above the Planck length, it also mentions 'cry unto thee'. If we cry unto God with the 'power' of faith (which is **19** from **Psalm 19**), from the end of the earth **(42)** we have (19 + 42) = **61**, the radius size of the stretched universe and this Psalms number! This makes Jesus **(61)** the rock that is higher than I.

Psalm **72:5**   "They shall fear thee as long as the sun and **moon** endure, throughout all generations."

Key words: sun and **moon** endure, generations.

This is **Psalm 72:5** talking about the sun and **moon** and of course the moon orbits the earth and the earth orbits the sun and the verse numbers of 72:5 multiplied (72 x 5) = **360**, as in a 360 degree orbit. This Psalm says "throughout all **generations**" at the end of the verse, and (7 + 2 + 5) the verse numbers added together equal fourteen **(14)** the generational number (see Psalm 14:5). Verse numbers (7 x 2) = (14) and (72 / 5) = **14.4**! We landed on the **moon** on **(7/20/1969)** and this is **Psalm 72** talking about the moon. We landed on the **moon** at 4:18 pm EDT and (4 x 18) = **72**, this Psalm's number again! All particles of matter in the universe called fermions (named after Enrico Fermi) have what is called spin ½; this means that they have to spin **720** degrees (2 full 360 degree orbits) before returning to their normal state. What does the moon do at night? It reflects light from the sun, and Psalm **27** says "The LORD is my **light** and my salvation..." a (**72 | 27**) mirror of the moon and its light. Using the moon's mirror numbers we have (72 | 27) so let's multiply them (7 x 2) = 14 and (2 x 7) = 14; adding the two fourteens we get (14 + 14) = **28**, the average number of days of the moon's rotation period. The moons' shortest period of rotation is about **27.3** days. I am writing this book in December of 2002. The last time that a man was on the moon so far, was Apollo 17 in **1972**. The Apollo 17 mission left the earth on December **7th** and December is the **12th** month; it left on **127** a (**127 | 721**) mirror of the **moon** and its light again. Psalm **72:7** "In his days shall the righteous flourish; and abundance of peace so long as the **moon** endureth."

Proverbs **7:20** "He hath taken a bag of money with him, and will come home at the (day appointed)." The 'day appointed' at the end of this scripture in Proverbs in the Hebrew means the '**full moon**'.

Only 2 scriptures in the whole Bible have the words '**moon**' and '**appointed**' in the same verse.

Psalm 81:3   "Blow up the trumpet in the new **moon**, in the time **appointed**, on our solemn feast day."

Psalms 104:19   "He **appointed** the **moon** for seasons: the sun knoweth his going down."

Please read this about the "*Moon Trees*." Apollo **14** launched in the late afternoon of January 31, 1971 on what was to be our third trip to the lunar surface. Five days later Alan Shepard and Edgar Mitchell walked on the Moon while Stuart Roosa, a former U.S. Forest Service smoke jumper, orbited above in the command module. Packed in small containers in Roosa's personal kit were hundreds of tree seeds, part of a joint NASA/USFS project. Upon return to Earth, the seeds were germinated by the Forest Service. Known as the "*Moon Trees*", the resulting seedlings were planted throughout the United States (often as part of the nation's bicentennial in **1976**) and the world. They stand as a tribute to astronaut Roosa and the Apollo program.

In regards to Psalm **104:19** mentioning 'appointed the moon for seasons' the verse numbers (**104 x 19**) = **1976**, the year of our nation's bicentennial and when most of the **moon** trees were planted!

Psalm 80:1   "Give ear, O Shepherd of Israel, thou that leadest Joseph like a flock; **thou that dwellest between the cherubims, shine forth**."

Keywords: **between the cherubims, shine** forth.

There are **10^80** power particles in the universe and this Psalm 80 is talking about "thou that **dwellest** between the **cherubims, shine forth.**" This is the place where God's Spirit and matter met in the **Ark of the Covenant.** Keep in mind that the *'Ark of the Covenant'* and the *'Tabernacle of Moses'* are actual models of the universe as we shall see later on in the book. The *"thou that dwellest between the cherubims"* is referring here to the Lord God who dwelt between the cherubims (angels) that are on top of the Ark of the Covenant. Here is the reference to these in Exodus 25:18 "And thou shalt make two cherubims of gold, of beaten work shalt thou make them, in the two ends of the mercy seat." Exodus 25:19 "And make one cherub on the one end, and the other cherub on the other end: even of the mercy seat shall ye make the cherubims on the two ends thereof." Exodus 25:20 "And the cherubims shall stretch forth their wings on high, covering the mercy seat with their wings, and their faces shall look one to another; toward the mercy seat shall the faces of the cherubims be."

The Greek symbol for pi (π) has a numerical value of **80** (all Greek letters have a numerical value). Let's multiply our eighty **(80)** number by pi (3.14159) and see what happens; as we see it yields **(80 x 3.14159) = 251. 3**. The **Psalm 80** verse number: **(80** times pi) refers to the same area of Exodus 25:10-13 or **(25:13)** and both are talking about the **Ark of the Covenant!** Look at where the Lord first talks to Moses about building the Ark in (25:10); Exodus 25:10-13 "And they shall make an ark of shittim wood: two cubits and a half shall be the length thereof, and a cubit and a half the breadth thereof, and a cubit and a half the height thereof. And thou shalt overlay it with pure gold, within and without shalt thou overlay it, and shalt make upon it a crown of gold round about. And thou shalt cast four rings of gold for it, and put them in the four corners thereof; and two rings shall be in the one side of it, and two rings in the other side of it. And thou shalt make staves of shittim wood, and overlay them with gold." The last verse here is verse number **25:13** and we get **251.3** when we multiplied **(80 x pi)**, incredible! Consider that 251 is the 54th prime number and (54 is all of the 4 forces of the universe combined).

Take **251** and divide by **61** (61 is the radius of the universe in Planck lengths) (251 / 61) = 4.**114**. How about this meaning the 4 seen dimensions of the universe and the Word made flesh of John **1:14** (4.**114**) holding it all together. The Psalm 80 verse number (80 times pi) refers to the same area of Exodus 25:10-13 and both are talking about the Ark of the Covenant! We saw in Psalm 38 that Bismuth (the antigravity element no. 83) has an atomic weight of **208**. Rev 21:17 "And he measured the wall thereof, an hundred and forty and four cubits, according to the measure of a man, that is, of the angel." Notice also that the verse numbers in Revelation added (21 + 17) equal 38 (gravity). The measure of the angel is **144** cubits. **1st Samuel 4:4** "So the people sent to Shiloh, that they might bring from thence the **ark of the covenant** of the LORD of hosts, which (**dwelleth** between the **cherubims**)…" Putting all the numbers of this verse together 1st and 4 and 4 = **144**, the size of the angel and it also talks about (dwelleth between the cherubims). We have two cherubim here or two angels on the mercy seat of the ark. Multiply the size of two angels (**144 x 2**) and you have **288**. Now we are talking about Psalm **80** (and there are **10^80 power** particles in the universe), so just add (**80 to the 208** atomic weight of Bismuth) and you have **288** (the size of the 2 angels), utterly amazing! Why is this so amazing? Because the 'Ark of the Covenant' actually was an anti-gravity device! Studies that were done show that the mercy seat (which is pure gold); weighed **2.8** tons. Exodus 25:17 "And thou shalt make a mercy seat of **pure gold**: two cubits and a half shall be the length thereof, and a cubit and a half the breadth thereof." The whole ark weighed in at 4 tons! There was no way that a few men could carry 8,000 pounds on their shoulders by themselves; it had to be an ark with anti-gravity (element no. **83**) qualities.

Here is the opposite of anti-gravity (gravity or burden as stated in Psalm **38**) in 2nd Chronicles **35:3** "And said unto the Levites that taught all Israel, which were holy unto the LORD, Put the holy (**ark**) in the house which Solomon the son of David king of Israel did build; it shall not be a (**burden**) upon your shoulders: serve now the LORD your God, and his people Israel." There are only 36 chapters in 2nd Chronicles and verse numbers $(35 + 3) = 38$, the burden or weight and mirror to 83 a $(38 \mid 83)$ mirror of the weight of the Ark. Joshua **3:8** "And thou shalt command the priests that (**bear**) the ark of the covenant, saying, When ye are come to the brink of the water of Jordan, ye shall stand still in Jordan." How about some anti-gravity (**83**) relief with Joshua **8:33** "And all Israel, and their elders, and officers, and their judges, stood on this side the (**ark**) and on that side before the priests the Levites, which **bare** the (ark of the covenant) of the LORD, as well the stranger, as he that was born among them; half of them over against mount Gerizim, and half of them over against mount Ebal; as Moses the servant of the LORD had commanded before, that they should bless the people of Israel."

Also remember that the universe has $10\wedge80$ power (*a number with 80 zeroes*) particles in it, and if we add eight (8) as in Jesus we get $(80 + 8) = 88$. There are $10\wedge88$ power photons of light in the universe and we know that *Jesus is the light of the world*; and in Psalm **88** coming we shall see "all thy waves", referring to waves of light. In quantum physics entities are either waves or particles depending on how we decide to measure them. This Psalm 80 also says *"...shine forth"* in the first verse.

Now take our **288** number (size of 2 angels 144 x 2) from the Ark of the Covenant and add these things that were actually inside the Ark to see that we get the number 300. Hebrews **9:4** "... and the ark of the covenant overlaid round about with gold, wherein was the golden pot that had manna, and Aaron's rod that budded, and the tables of the covenant." The word angel or angels shows up **286** times in the Bible, and the word seraphim(s) shows up only **twice** in Isaiah Chapter 6; (286 angels + 2 seraphims) = **288**!

288	Size of 2 angels (144 x 2)
10	Commandments
1	Rod that budded of Aaron
+ 1	Golden pot of manna
———	
300	

Now look at the measurements of Noah's Ark.

Genesis 6:15 "And this is the fashion which thou shalt make it of: The length of the ark shall be **three hundred cubits**, the breadth of it fifty cubits, and the height of it thirty cubits."

Noah's Ark had for its first measurement **300** also, because the Ark was **300** x 50 x 30 cubits. The number 300 is always associated with great victory in battle and complete deliverance in the Bible. Judges 7:7 "And the LORD said unto Gideon, By the **three hundred men** that lapped will I save you, and deliver the Midianites into thine hand: and let all the other people go every man unto his place."

Psalm 83:18   "That men may know that thou, whose name alone is JEHOVAH, art the most high over all the earth."

Key words: **most high** over all the earth, **JEHOVAH**

This is the anti-gravity Psalm with the expression: "**JEHOVAH**, art the **most high** over all the earth" and mirror to Psalm 38 (gravity); a **(-38 | +83)** mirror. If you want to escape the gravity and weight of sin in Psalm **38** then you must **rise** and experience the anti-gravity of JEHOVAH the "*most high*" in **Psalm 83**. To go along with the Psalm 83:18 meaning of anti-gravity, the **83rd** element is called Bismuth. This element has an atomic number of 83. This Bismuth element has the *highest electrical resistance* when placed in a magnetic field (*qualities of anti-gravity*), than any other element. Also this element Bismuth (83) has an atomic weight of 208.98. In relation to Bismuth at a weight of **208** look at Psalm **20:8** "They are brought down and fallen: but we are *risen*, and *stand upright*." Again gravity (*brought down and fallen*) and anti-gravity (*we are risen*); amazing that these words just happen to fall on these numbers of Psalm **20:8**. **John 20:8-9** "Then went in also that other disciple, which came first to the sepulchre, and he saw, and believed. For as yet they knew not the scripture, that he must *rise* again from the dead." Acts **20:8** "And there were many lights in the ***upper*** chamber, where they were gathered together." 2nd Kings **20:8** "And Hezekiah said unto Isaiah, What shall be the sign that the LORD will heal me, and that I shall go ***up into the house*** of the LORD the (third day)?" Revelation **20:9** "And they **went up on the breadth of the earth**, and compassed the camp of the saints about, and the beloved city: and **fire came down from God** out of heaven, and devoured them." In regards to the number **208** and the name 'JHVH', (which is the real Hebrew way to spell JEHOVAH) has the Hebrew numerical value of 26 (J=10, H=5, V=6, H=5) = **26**. The number of Jesus is **(8)** and **(26 x 8) = 208**, the atomic weight of our anti-gravity like element Bismuth. This is the only Psalm out of all of the Psalms where the key word is not in the first seven verses. These key words "JEHOVAH, art the **most high** over all the earth" are in the last and highest numbered verse appearing in verse **(18)**; what would one expect of anti-gravity anyway but to **rise** above! The word **HIGHEST** appears **18** times in the Bible.

The measurements of the Ark of the Covenant are 2½ by 1½ by 1½ cubits. If you add the two widths (1½) measurements (1.5 + 1.5) you get **3**. Now divide **2.5** (the first measurement) by **3** and you get **.83** our anti-gravity number! Super-symmetry is the idea that for every particle of matter in the universe that there is a corresponding particle of light and vise-versa. This theory has not been verified yet but we may be closer when a more powerful particle accelerator is built. Also science is looking for a particle called the graviton. The graviton has a spin number of 2 (meaning it makes ½ spin or 180 degrees) before it returns to its original state. The electron has spin ½ which means that it makes 2 full revolutions (720 degrees) before it returns to its' original state. The gravitons possible super-symmetry partner would have to have a spin of **3/2** which is the same as 1.5, one of the measurements of the Ark of the Covenant. We just added these 2 spins of the possible super-partner to the graviton (3/2) + (3/2) and got 3 as (1.5 + 1.5) = 3. We then used the first measure of 2.5 or 5/2 to divide as in (2.5 / 3) = **.83** to get (anti-gravity).

Also there really are (5) types of (regular matter) fermion particles with ½ spin (5/2) called the Electron, Muon, Tau, Neutrino, and Quark. Five times one half or (5 x ½) = 5/2 the first measurement of the Ark of the Covenant. There are also five (5) types of regular force carrying particles of light called bosons (with whole integer number 1, 2, 3 etc. spin) called the Photon, Gluon, W particles, Z particle, and the Higgs particle. These are thought to have super-symmetry partner particles all with spin ½ and again 5 x ½ = (5/2). It appears that the two length sides of the '**Ark of the Covenant**' with their (**5/2** measurement of particles at ½ spin and 5/2 super-symmetry particles at ½ spin); and the two (3/2 width sides meaning: (the spin 2 (sides) of the graviton and the **3/2** spin of its possible super-partner); equals the basic structure of all the (particles and force carriers in the universe), and their possible super-symmetry partners. These sides of (5/2 x 5/2 x 3/2 x 3/2) equal the measurement of the whole basic structure of particles and were made 3,400 years ago! We will talk more about this later in the chapter about the Ark of the Covenant.

Psalm 88:7   "Thy wrath lieth hard upon me, and thou hast afflicted me with all thy **waves**. Selah."

Keywords: all thy **waves**, afflicted me

This one goes along with **Psalm 42** that says "…**all thy waves** and thy billows are gone over me." 10^{42} is a power number that measures the frequency of photons of (light wave) cycles per second in one kilogram of mass. We are talking about (waves of photons) in **Psalm 88** and 10 to the **88th power** is the number of photons in the universe with "all thy **waves**". Also remember that God says that He is light!

Psalm 90:4 "For a **thousand years** in thy sight are but as yesterday when it is past, and as a watch in the night."

Key words: **thousand years**, yesterday, watch in the night.

Here we have Einstein's relativity in a **circular** universe where even time is curved and has its own shape. Psalm number 90 times verse number 4 (**90 x 4) = 360**, the number of degrees in a circle. 2nd Peter 3:8 says, "But, beloved, be not ignorant of this one thing, that one day is with the Lord as a **thousand years,** and a thousand years as one day." This is verse **3:8** in 2nd Peter and gravity is **10^-38** power; knowing also that the curvature (360 degrees) of the universe is gravity. The word 'heavy' (from our gravity Psalm 38) is in the Bible in 38 different verses. The word compass (*as in circular 360 degrees*) is also found in the Bible in 38 different verses. These are the **only two** verses (Psalm **90:4** and 2nd Peter **3:8**) where these relativity scriptures (*thousand years* as a **day**) can be found, and they both contain numbers defining the *curvature* and *gravity* of the universe, utterly amazing! **Peter** was the one who walked **on the water** with Jesus and thus defied gravity. Jesus started His ministry when He was thirty (30) and **30** in the Bible is Jesus' number of blood and divine service. Adding **208** (anti-gravity) to Jesus **(30)** gives us **238,** and this scripture is 2nd Peter 3:8. Matthew **14:25** "And in the fourth watch of the night **Jesus** went unto them, **walking on the sea.**" Now Jesus is a little higher than *gravity* because He is walking on the water and verse numbers (14 + 25) = **39**.

Albert Einstein was born on March 14, 1879. March is the 3rd month of the year and he was born on the 14th day; this is (3.14) if the date is expressed as a decimal. Einstein was born on 3.14 (pi), the number we all know to determine the circumference of a circle by its radius. If you multiply pi by itself you get (3 x 14) = 42; the earth is a size of 42 magnitudes greater than the Planck length. Now an interesting one, our verse numbers (90 / 4) = 22.5; 22 being the Bible number of light and number of characters in the Hebrew alphabet. The Hebrew alphabet also has 5 final letters as in (22.5) that give the word a prophetic sense. The Jews say that the universe is constructed out of the Hebrew alphabet! We will talk more about the number 22 later. Oh there is just one more small thing (*I sound like Columbo here)*; take our verse numbers and add them as in (90 + 4) = 94. Now let's figure the approximate circumference of whole universe: take a 15 billion light year radius and use the formula 2 x pi = (6.28) x RADIUS (15) = **94.2** billion light years and our verse numbers are (**90 + 4**) = **94**. The Word **Jesus** appears **942** times in the King James version of the Bible, all in the New Testament (942 / 10) = **94.2**. Psalm **94:2** "Lift up thyself, thou judge of the earth: render a reward to the proud." Even (**94 x 2**) = 188 or (94 x .2) =

1.88, and we know that this is the number of photons of light in the universe at 10^88 power from Psalm 88. He is the light and size of the universe and *'judge of the earth'* in Psalm **94:2**!

Psalm 92:3   "Upon an instrument of **ten strings**, and upon the psaltery; upon the harp with a solemn sound."

Key word: **ten strings**

There are **92** natural elements that are known to exist on earth and the **vibration frequency** of a string is what gives the **92 natural elements** their masses and force charges. This Psalm 92 represents strings defining atoms at atomic size. Only Psalms 33, **92**, and 144 say *"an instrument of ten strings"*, and this shows a natural three level progression of size from the tiniest strings at size (10^-33 centimeters), to atomic size with 92 (natural elements), and size 144 (size of the man or angel) in Psalm 144 coming up. Combining Psalm 29 with Psalm 92 we have a (**29 | 92**) mirror of creation energy (29) and the number of elements (92); energy and matter.

Psalm 104:2   "Who coverest thyself with **light** as with a garment: who **stretchest out the heavens** like a curtain:"

Key words: **stretchest** out the **heavens** like a **curtain**, coverest thyself with **light**.

The name Jehovah which is **JHVH** in the Hebrew language has a numerical value of (J=10, H=5, V=6, H=5), which when added are (10 + 5 + 6 + 5) = **26**. Also the latest theory of the Universe called super-string theory says that the universe has **26** dimensions in their original calculations, ending up with 10 space dimensions after doing 16 mathematical cancellations (**26 – 16**) = 10. Another fact of the number 26 is that the limit of the observable universe (*cosmic horizon*) is 10 to the 26th power meters. There are four (**4**) seen dimensions to the universe: length, width, height, and time and (**4 x 26 = 104**). It is **Jehovah (26)** who "stretchest out the heavens

(4) like a curtain" in **Psalm 104**! Also notice our Psalm 104:2 verse number if we put them together as **1042** because the size of the earth is $10\wedge42^{nd}$ powers of magnitude above the Planck length! Also a large *galaxy* has a mass of $10\wedge42$ power *kilograms*! Also using our verse numbers and multiplying them (**104 x 2**) we get **208**, the number of the atomic weight of Bismuth, the anti-gravity like element talked about in Psalms 38, 83 and 80. Is this *mind-boggling* or what?

Psalm **104:19**   "He appointed the **moon for seasons**: the sun knoweth his going down."

In regards to Psalm **104:19** mentioning 'appointed the moon for seasons' the verse numbers (**104 x 19**) = **1976**, the year of our nation's bicentennial and when most of the **moon trees** were planted! See also Psalm **72:5** for the full story.

Psalm 114:4-7   "The mountains **skipped like rams**, and the little hills like lambs. What ailed thee, O thou sea, that thou fleddest? thou Jordan, that thou wast driven back? Ye mountains, that ye skipped like rams; and ye little hills, like lambs? **Tremble, thou earth**, at the presence of the Lord, at the **presence of the God of Jacob**."

Keys words: mountains skipped like rams, tremble thou earth, presence of the God of Jacob.

$10\wedge114$ power is the energy of the quantum vacuum. This 114 power number is actually the measurement of the energy of a cubic meter of empty space using the joules measurement system, a power number with 114 zeros in it. The power of the God of Jacob in **Psalm 114** can certainly make the whole earth to **shake and tremble**, remembering that the **fear of the Lord** is the beginning of wisdom. 1st Samuel 4:5 "And when the ark of the covenant of the LORD came into the camp, all Israel shouted with a great shout, so that the **earth rang again**." We will see later that the number **114** also refers to the measurements of the '*Ark of the Covenant*'.

Science is also looking for a particle or field called the **Higgs boson**. This Higgs field is what is supposed to give all of the matter in the universe its mass. Finding the Higgs is a really big deal, as it would complete the standard model of particle physics and maybe lead the way to find super-symmetry particles predicted by string theory. Super symmetry means: (for every particle of matter there is a corresponding particle of light and vise-versa). Most information I have seen says that the HIGGS is expected to be found at about **114 GeV** (Giga electron Volts), Giga means billions. When you square all of the numbers of the total number of characters in the Torah (first 5 books of the Bible) which is (304,805) characters: (9 + 0 + 16 + 64 + 0 + 25) they equal **114**.

The main reason that the 114 number is so powerful: the gospel of **John 1:14** says "And the **Word** was made flesh, and dwelt among us, (and we beheld his glory, the glory as of the only **begotten** of the Father,) full of grace and truth." Science says that the universe is made of information. This **114** power number is a mirror to the number that we call information **411**; a (**114 | 411**) mirror. Also consider that gravity at power number 38 for Psalm 38 times 3 space dimensions: (38 x 3) = 114, and electromagnetism for Psalm 19 times 6 (19 x 6) = 114 also; 6 is the number of man. We know that Psalm 14 is the generational number in Psalm 14:5 "There were they in great fear: for God is in the **generation** of the righteous", and that (100 + 14) = 114; the word '**generations**' shows up **114** times in the whole Bible and John **1:14** talks about the generation of Jesus: "And the **Word** was made flesh..."

Psalm **144**:9   "I will sing a new song unto thee, O God: upon a psaltery and an instrument of **ten strings** will I sing praises unto thee."

Key words: instrument of **ten strings**, new **song, praises** unto thee.

The (half life – radioactive decay) of carbon **14** is a little bit over 5700 years. A small number of particles stay around quite a bit longer than the half life (called the mean life); and the decay process obeys strict rules. The mean life of these particles that stick around are equal to **1.44** times the half life, and we know that 144 or (1.44 x 100) = **144**.

Only Psalms 33, 92, and **144** say "an instrument of ten strings", and this shows a natural three level progression of size from the tiniest strings at size (10^-33 centimeters), to atomic size with 92 (natural elements), and size 144 (size of the man or angel) defined in: Revelation 21:17 "And he measured the wall thereof, an hundred and forty and four cubits, according to the measure of a man, that is, of the angel."

Revelation 14:3   "And they sung as it were a new song before the throne, and before the four beasts, and the elders: and no man could learn that song but the **hundred and forty and four thousand**, which were redeemed from the earth."

Notice that both of these verses (Psalm **144:9** and Rev. **14**:3 speak of "a new song" being sung, and this is the last Psalm (144) that mentions ten strings (like the 10 space dimensions of the universe made of strings). The universe would be made of strings as God is a God who desires our worship and praise played on stringed instruments. In fact we are the ten-stringed instruments that He desires to play!

Revelation **14:4**   "These are they which were not defiled with women; for they are virgins. These are they which follow the Lamb whithersoever he goeth. These were redeemed from among men, being the firstfruits unto God and to the Lamb."

Here we have Revelation **14:4** to match our Psalm number **144**. This is the reason that they are singing with '**ten strings**' as these are the redeemed from among men and **14.4** (referring to the **Rev. 14:4** verse) times 10 *strings* = 144, this Psalm's number. Here is Jesus as the number (**8**) writing His Ten **10** (*stringed dimensions*) as Commandments (*laws*) into our hearts and mind in a 8:10 scripture: Hebrews **8:10** "For this is the **covenant** that I will make with the house of Israel after those days, saith the Lord; I will put my **laws** into their **mind**, and write them in their **hearts**: and I will be to them a God, and they shall be to me a people." (8 x 10) = **80** as in Psalm 80 talking about the former *'Ark of the Covenant'*. How about another **10** numbered scripture dealing with God's laws: Hebrews **10:16** "This is the *covenant* that I will make with them after those days, saith the Lord, I will put my **laws** into their **hearts**, and in their **minds** will I write them." (10 x 16) = 160 a multiple of **80** (80 x 2) = **160**.

Revelation 21:17   "And he measured the wall thereof, an hundred and forty and four cubits, according to the measure of a man, that is, of the angel."

This Revelation scripture has to do with the new city of Jerusalem coming out of heaven, and the walls (or measure of a man) of this city are 144 cubits wide. A cubit is 18 inches (1.5 feet) which equals (144 times 1.5 feet) = 216 feet. Take 216 feet and divide it by a 6 foot man: (216 / 6) = 36. This wall (or man size) of the New Jerusalem is 36 times larger than a 6 foot man. If the Talmudist cubit is used (and many scholars feel that this is what was used by the Israelites), then the measure of the cubit would be about 21 inches. In this case our wall would be 252 feet wide!

Summary of the Scientific Psalms

It would be one thing if just a few of these Psalms *numbers and meanings* were to match the scientific power number, but here we have twenty three Psalms that have significant 'key words' matching the actual meaning of the scientific power number or mathematical constant of the Psalms number. Also consider that all of these 'key words' for the scientific constants (except Psalm 83) are in the first seven verses of each Psalm which shows an incredible pattern. Nineteen (**19**) of the **23** Psalms have the keyword(s) in the first 5 verses! Many of the actual key words such as *'heavy'* appear that many times in the Bible like Psalm 38 as gravity at 10^-38 power. We are not going to count the *'number of times'* appearing for the 'key expressions' or the fact that they are all in the first seven verses, but you can imagine how much greater the odds would be!

Here are some mathematical odds to consider; we are using the way odds are figured by using the lotto. For instance, in the state of Florida the odds of winning the lotto are 23,000,000 to one, where you have to get 6 correct numbers out of a possible 53 numbers. Imagine having to guess by random chance 20 or more correct numbers out of a possible 150 numbers on the first try! This is just what the scientific Psalms did and they were written 2,900 years before these constants were known. The Lord is subtle, but the pattern matching is easily seen when all of these Psalms "*key words*" are looked at as a whole, noticing that all of the correct meanings land on the Psalm's number that is the power of 10 for the particular force. The odds of this happening by accident or random chance out of **150** Psalms are quite high as we shall see.

If only 1 power number meaning landed on the correct Psalm number: the odds are 150 to 1.

If only 2 power number meanings landed on the correct Psalm number: the odds are 11,175 to 1.

If only 3 power number meanings landed on the correct Psalm number: the odds are 551,300 to 1.

If only 5 power number meanings landed on the correct Psalm number: the odds are 591,600,030 to 1.

If 10 power number meanings landed on the correct Psalm number: the odds are 1,169,554,298,222,310 to 1 or about 10^{15th} power.

If 20 power number meanings landed on the correct Psalm number: the odds are about (3.6×10^{24th}) power or about 3,600,000,000,000,000,000,000,000 to 1 that this would happen by random accident or chance.

The number of grains of sand on Coney Island beach is about

4 x 10^{20th} power. So this means that our 10^{24th} power number of the odds of 20 matching scientific Psalms is the equivalent of the number of grains of sand on 10,000 Coney Island beaches! Obviously God has left His fingerprint throughout the Psalms written 3,000 years ago, and many other parts of the Bible as we shall see.

Both Psalm sets of 'historical' and 'scientific data' would be like getting **38** (20 + 18) matching Psalm numbers correct, landing on significant related data out of a total of **150** Psalms on the first try. The odds would be about $\mathbf{10^{38th}}$ power or: **100,000,000,000,000,000,000,000,000,000,000,000,000** to **1** that all of these science constants and historical events would all appear by random accident or chance and land on these Psalm numbers. If this book ended right here after all of these matching Psalms, we would have plenty of evidence of the *fingerprint* and *proof* of the **God** of the **Bible**. There is however, much more *evidence* to be seen. A more condensed list of all the matching Psalms and major facts of the book is provided at the end of the book.

CHAPTER 3

The Torah, the Ark of the Covenant, and the number 114

I f you square all the numbers of the Torah and then add them you have (9 + 0 + 16 + 64 + 0 + 25) = 114. 114 is the number of the energy of the quantum vacuum using the joules measurement system; this is (one cubic meter of empty space) at $10\wedge114^{th}$ power, *a number with 114 zeroes*! Look at the power of Psalm 114 "…Tremble, thou earth, at the presence of the Lord, at the presence of the God of Jacob." It should also be noted that if we add Jesus number of 30, *which means blood and dedication* to 114 we get (114 + 30) = 144, the size of the man. Finally we have the powerful John 1:14 "And the Word was made flesh, and dwelt among us, (and we beheld his glory, the glory as of the only begotten of the Father,) full of grace and truth." Science is looking for a particle or field that gives mass to everything in the universe called the Higgs boson; they expect it to come in at about 114 GeV (Giga electron volts), but they need a more powerful particle accelerator to generate more energy in order to find it, which they expect to have in about 3 or 4 years with the CERN accelerator. The Ark of the Covenant has the following measurements: (2 ½ cubits by 1 ½ cubits by 1 ½ cubits), or if fractions (5/2 by 3/2 by 3/2). Exodus 25:10 "And they shall make an ark of shittim wood: **two cubits and a half** shall be the length thereof, and a **cubit and a half** the breadth thereof, and a **cubit and a half** the height thereof." Notice that the verse numbers of Exodus (**25 / 10**) = **2.5** or 5/2 or (52 inches as we shall see), the first length measurement of the Ark!

Go back two verses to Exodus **25:8** "And let them make me a sanctuary; that I may dwell among them", as these verse numbers divided (**25 / 8**) = **3.12** or (3 / 2) or (31.2 inches as we shall see), are the width of the Ark. The cubit's size used at the time of the Jews and the Ark was believed to be 21 inches. Let's use a form of our anti-gravity number of (**20.8**) as it's so close to **21** inches, to convert the Ark's measurements from cubits to inches! **Bismuth** which is element no. 83 (see Psalm 83) has an atomic weight of 208 also see Psalm 20:8. If you multiply 20.8 inches x 2.5 (the Arks length) you get exactly **52** inches, which amazingly looks like the **5/2** fraction (52) or (2.5 cubits). If you multiply (20.8) x 1.5 you get **31.2** inches and there are two of these 1.5 cubit sides; 31.2 inches (**312**) looks amazingly like the **3/2** fraction (1.5 cubits)! Our **31.2** number matches Psalm **31:2** "Bow down thine ear to me; deliver me **speedily**..."; referring to the speed of he **ELECTRON**. All dimensions added together (52 + 31.2 + 31.2) = **114.4 inches**. As you see we have our **114** number again embedded in the measurement of the Ark of the Covenant. Not only that but the **144** (size of the man) is also embedded in this number (1(**14.4**)). These measurements agree with data I have seen from those who have actually explored resting places of the Ark; with sides of 4 feet 4 inches (**52 in.**) and (**2** sides) of 2 feet 7inches (**31** in.). I don't think that they realize that this multiple number of (**20.8**) is based on the anti-gravity element **Bismuth 83**. Using the cubit measures of the Arks' sides (**2. 5 /** (1.5 + 1.5) = 3) = **.83**, the chemical element number of Bismuth. We will see why the inches measurement here is important as a conversion factor when we get to the **Torah numbers**. Psalm 80 contains the expression "...dwellest between the cherubims" referring to the Ark; and there are **2** cherubims on the Ark. The word *'cherubims'* appears in the Bible **57** times and (57 x 2 cherubims) = **114** our measurement of the Ark. **2ⁿᵈ** Chronicles 5:7 "And the priests brought in the **ark of the covenant** of the LORD unto his place, to the oracle of the house, into the most holy place, even under the wings of the **cherubims**"; and again (**2ⁿᵈ** x 57) = **114**. One more very interesting thing is that the measurements of 52, 31.2, and 31.2

inches for the Ark contain the actual super-symmetry numbers of **spin** that science is looking for. These are talked about in Psalm 83 in relation to the length of the Ark with **5/2** (5 regular matter particles times ½ spin) or (**5** super-symmetry particles times ½ spin) and two widths of **3/2** (2 Gravitons (or spin 2) with a super-symmetry partner (Gravitino) with a spin of **3/2**).

Here is a list of the known particles that transmit forces, and their possible super-partners according to their spin. If a particle has a spin of 1 it makes one full revolution (360 degrees) before returning to its original state of being. If it has a spin of 2 like the graviton, it looks the same after only (180 degrees) of spin. If it has a spin of ½ then it looks the same after 2 full (720 degrees) of revolution.

Name	Spin	Super-partner	Spin
Graviton	**2**	Gravitino	**3/2**
Photon	1	Photino	½
Gluon	1	Gluino	½
W +, W-	1	Wino+, -	½
Z	1	Zino	½
Higgs	0	Higgsino	½

As you can see there are 5 force carrying particles, each of which has a possible super-partner with a spin of ½, just like the Ark's dimension of 5/2 or (5 x ½) = 5/2 cubits. If these super-partners exist then super-symmetry would be proven to be true. Super-symmetry is the fact that for each particle of matter in the universe, there is a corresponding particle of light and vice-versa. The other two sides of the Ark at a length of 3/2 cubits match the fact that the graviton with spin 2 (sides) has a super-partner particle with a spin of 3/2.

Here is a list of the known particles that make up matter and their possible super-partners.

Name	Spin	Super-partner	Spin
Electron	½	Selectron	0
Muon	½	Smuon	0
Tau	½	Stau	0
Neutrino	½	Sneutrino	0
Quark	½	Squark	0

From these 5 regular matter particles we see also that there are 5 basic kinds of particles with a spin of ½ and that (5 x ½) = 5/2, which again is the measurement of the Ark of the Covenant in cubits. If we take all of the numbers of the Ark multiplied 3/2, 5/2, and 3/2 as in: (3 x 5 x 3 x 2 x 2 x 2) they equal 360, like one full spin of a circle!

Just think, these measurements of the Ark of the Covenant equal the basic structure of particles and spin, and even some of the things that science is looking for, and were given by God to Moses about 3,400 years ago. The Higgs Boson and the super-symmetry of string theory are the most sought after things in physics today! Scientists also have discovered traces of a new element called Ununquadium, and its Atomic number is **114**; knowing also that our inches measurement of the Ark of the Covenant is 114. This new element is said to be an island of stability surrounded by a group of more unstable elements. The atomic weight of this element is 289 and (2 x 8 x 9) = **144**, the size of the man or angel from Revelation 21:17 and (21 + 17) = 38 gravity! If you take our **114** number of inches measurement from the Ark of the Covenant and convert it to centimeters as in (114 x **2.54**) it equals **289.65** the atomic weight of Ununquadium the **114**th **element**. God's perfect victory number is **17** and (**17 x 17**) also equals **289**, the atomic weight of the 114th element! We also know that (**114 + 30** *Jesus number of blood and divine service*) = 144 the size of the man. Look at Jesus as the 114 of (the Word made flesh in John 1:14) as Melchizedek visiting Abraham in Genesis 14:18 "And Melchizedek king of Salem brought forth **bread and wine**: and he was the priest of the most high God." They are having communion and verse numbers (14 + 18) = **32**, the Bible number of **Covenant**! Hebrews

7:1 "For this **Melchisedec**, king of Salem, priest of the most high God, who met Abraham returning from the slaughter of the kings, and blessed him." Verse number **7:1** is the mirror to **17**. Psalm **110:4** "The LORD hath sworn, and will not repent, Thou art a priest for ever after the order of **Melchizedek**" and (110 + 4) our verse numbers = **114**. Verse numbers multiplied (**110 x 4**) = **440** or (10 x 44) or how about Psalm 44 and 10^-44 power the Planck time, with the phrase: "a priest for ever." One time dimension (44) times ten (10) space dimensions = **440**.

Pearl Harbor and the power of the 'Ark of the Covenant'

Let's now look at the measurements of the Ark this way, knowing that they measure 2 ½ by 1 ½ by 1 ½ cubits or as fractions: 5/2, 3/2 and 3/2.

$$\frac{3}{2} \quad \frac{5}{2} \quad \frac{3}{2}$$

In the Bible God renames Abram to Abraham by adding an '**H**' to his name; God does the same for Sarai by renaming her Sarah. God added a letter ('**H**') from His own name JeHoVaH to these two people. When God adds a letter of His very own name to you it's the most powerful covenant promise for your life. The name JEHOVAH is just JHVH with no vowels in the original Hebrew. The letter '**H**' in the Hebrew has a numerical value of 5, and 5 is the number of '*grace*' in the Bible.

The codeword for the Japanese during the attack on Pearl Harbor December 7, 1941 was Tora, Tora, Tora! Lets see what happens when we add an '**H**' to Tora, we get Torah, Torah, Torah; knowing that the Ark of the Covenant is the place where God actually dwelt in the Tabernacle of Moses, written about in the Torah. What was God's answer to Tora, Tora, Tora and the United States of America being attacked at Pearl Harbor? Keep in mind these figures are within 1 or 2 aircraft, 1 or 2 minutes, and 1 or 2 miles, as I have seen slightly different figures on these.

The Ark's measurements of **3/2**, **5/2**, and **3/2** are displayed.

3	5	3
—	—	—
2	2	2

3 5 3   There were **353** planes in the attack on Pearl Harbor.

2 2 2   There were **6** Japanese aircraft carriers $2 + 2 + 2 = $ **6**.
The attack was launched from about **222** miles away.

God's answer:

$3 \times 5 \times 3 =$ **45** (as in **1945**)

$2 \times 2 \times 2 =$ **8** (the 8th month, **August**)

$2 + 2 + 2 =$ **6** (the 6th day of the month of **August**)

If you look at the Arks measurements they read **235** from the bottom left corner up and to the top middle and **235** backwards from the lower right corner up and to the middle.

3 5 3   Read Uranium **235** (twice) from the bottom starting at the two's (2)
—   —   forward and backward, the bomb had **two** Uranium 235 masses.
2   2

Now just shift the top row by putting the **5/2** first and add from top to bottom $(5 + 2) = 7$, $(3 + 2) = 5$.

5 3 3
— — —
2 2 2

7 5 5   (The time of the attack was **7:55** am.)

What was God's answer to Tora, Tora, Tora at Pearl Harbor?

How about the power of the 'Ark of the Covenant' with an 'H' added to (ToraH, ToraH, ToraH) on Hiroshima Japan on August 6, 1945 with a 235 Uranium nuclear bomb! Also all of the numbers of the Ark multiplied (3 x 5 x 3 x 2 x 2 x 2) = 360, like a *circle* or mushroom fireball cloud. These numbers added (3 + 5 + 3 + 2 + 2 + 2) = 17, God's victory number! All of these numbers squared (9 + 25 + 9 + 4 + 4 + 4) = 55, and there were 2 tablets of stone in the Ark with the (5 + 5) = 10: Ten Commandments written on them. The Ark of the Covenant had tremendous power in the Old Testament, and through *Jesus Christ* our modern day **Ark**, we still have the protection of a God who looks after those nations that love and fear Him, and the numbers *that don't lie* bear witness to this! 1st Samuel 4:5 "And when the ark of the covenant of the LORD came into the camp, all Israel shouted with a great shout, so that the **earth rang again**"; the earth actually rang, noticing also that this is a **45** verse. A fact of the nuclear bomb is that it splits the **atom** using fission and releases tremendous energy, like the energy of our creation fire in Psalm 29:7. The number **92**, as already stated, is the number of natural elements on the earth making a (**29 | 92**) mirror of energy and matter. In the nuclear bomb we are splitting the (**92nd**) element (*Uranium is the 92nd element*), to get the (**29**) fire of creation. We know that the nuclear bomb creates a tremendous *circular* fireball and the Arks measurements multiplied equal **360**. The Japanese surrendered in the (**9th month**) September 2nd (9/2)/1945, and this signing was on the deck of the Battleship U. S. S. Missouri BB **63**. The day that the Japanese signed the surrender (**92**) is the mirror to atomic creation fire (**29**); and the actual element (**92**) used in the bomb. The Battleship's hull number **63** is the mirror to the *circular* fireball: (**360 | 063**). The surrender was signed at **9:04** Tokyo time (**90 x 4**) = **360** again, or (**9 x 4**) = **36**; a (Time in history **36 | 63** Hull number) *mirror*. Like creation fire being 10^{29}, the Enola Gay that dropped the atomic bomb was a B-**29** Super-fortress airplane. It was **29** feet **7** inches high; now look again at Psalm **29:7** "The **voice of the LORD** divideth the **flames of fire**." The serial number of the Enola Gay was 44-86292; it has the **86** (August 6th date) and **292** mirror of (creation fire/elements) embedded in it. Oh, and by the way, our Battleship hull number of (**63**) + fire of (**29**) = **92**, the day of the signing!

2ⁿᵈ Chronicles 35:3 "And said unto the Levites that taught all Israel, which were holy unto the LORD, Put the holy (**ark**) in the house which Solomon the son of David king of Israel did build; it shall not be a burden upon your shoulders: serve now the LORD your God, and his people Israel." If we put all of these verse numbers in (2ⁿᵈ Chronicles 35:3) together that are talking about the '*Ark of the Covenant*', we get **235:3**. Here we have Uranium **235** and **353** connected; knowing that **353** is the top fraction numbers of the Ark's measurements of 3/2, 5/2, and 3/2 cubits. By dropping the 2 (in 2ⁿᵈ) below each 3 5 3 number we get the full measurement of 3/2, 5/2 and 3/2 cubits. It's amazing that these would be the verse numbers of a scripture talking about the **Ark**, noticing again that (3 x 5 x 3) = **45**.

Lets' talk about Noah's Ark for a moment: Genesis 6:15 "And this is the fashion which thou shalt make it of: The length of the ark shall be three hundred cubits, the breadth of it fifty cubits, and the height of it thirty cubits." Noah's Ark had for its measurements 300 x 50 x 30 cubits.

Just drop the zeroes of **300** x **50** x **30** cubits and we have 3 5 3 again, just like the Ark of the Covenants measurements.

$$
\begin{array}{ccc}
\textbf{3} & \textbf{5} & \textbf{3} \\
00 & 0 & 0
\end{array}
$$

This is **450,000** when multiplied (300 x 50 x 30) = 450,000 (450 x 1000 (God's Glory number)). Noah lived 950 years and (9 x 50) = **450**. In the first book of Kings 18:22 "Then said Elijah unto the people, I, even I only, remain a prophet of the LORD; but Baal's prophets are (**four hundred and fifty men**)." Later on in the first book of Kings 18:40 "And Elijah said unto them, Take the prophets of Baal; let not one of them escape. And they took them: and Elijah brought them down to the brook Kishon, and slew them there." Noah's Ark has a **450** in it for it's measurement as **8** people are preserved from the flood and likewise Elijah preserves Israel by slaying **450** prophets of Baal. The number forty-five (**45**) is the Bible's number of preservation, remembering that in **1945** America was preserved from its enemies of Japan and Germany. Also all of the natural elements power numbers (strong force (1), electromagnetic force (2), weak force (13), and gravity (38) = 54 when added together. So what are we preserved from? The natural realm of this world (**54**) of course, giving us a (**45 | 54**) mirror of preservation! We are saved by Jesus whose number is '8' (in the Greek His name numerically is '888'). Jesus (8) x 45 (preservation) = 360, like an eternal circle of 360 degrees. In the first book of Kings 18:22 is where we hear of the **450** prophets of Baal. The verse numbers multiplied (18 x 22) = 396 and (450 – 396) = 54! 1st Kings 18:25 "And Elijah said unto the prophets of Baal, Choose you one bullock for yourselves, and dress it first; **for ye are many**; and call on the name of your gods, but put no fire under." Notice in verse 18:25 it says *'for ye are many'* and (18 x 25) = **450**! The words '**Ark**' and '**covenant**' appear together in **45** scriptures of the Old Testament and just once in the New Testament in Hebrews 9:4. Hebrews **9:4** says: "Which had the golden censer, and the ark of the covenant overlaid round about with gold, wherein was the golden pot that had manna, and Aaron's rod that budded, and the **tables of the covenant**." Multiply verse numbers (**9** x **4** x **10** Commandments) = 360; just like the 'Ark of the Covenant's' total measurements of (3 x 5 x 3 x 2 x 2 x 2) = 360.

CHAPTER 4

Curtains folded in the
Eleventh Dimension

I had written a chapter on the Tabernacle of Moses in my previous book "The Unbroken Wholeness Power of God", but here I am going to add more facts concerning the Tabernacle of Moses. Modern day theory says that basically the universe has eleven dimensions. This would be one time dimension, three dimensions of space, and seven very tined curled up dimensions out of our common everyday experience. These tiny curled up dimensions are the size of the strings of string theory which is 10^-33 centimeters in length talked about in Psalm 33. In the book of Exodus chapter 25 verses 8 through 11 God said to Moses "And let them make me a sanctuary; that I may dwell among them, according to all that I shew thee, after the pattern of the tabernacle, and the pattern of all the instruments thereof, even so shall ye make it."

In the book of Exodus chapter 25 God instructs Moses to build a tabernacle with the Ark of the Covenant in it. God tells Moses to build it "after the pattern of the tabernacle." The pattern of these numbers for the tabernacle are amazing numbers that just seem to match the latest theories and facts of universe called **super string** theory and **M-theory**. The 'M' here can mean mystery or membrane. Some have also called this 'M' as the "Mother" of all theories or a theory of everything. Einstein spent the last 30 years of his life looking for this theory and didn't find it. Einstein called this his (Unified Field Theory). This theory of everything would tie together all of the forces and particles of the universe into a very tidy mathematical package, gravity included. Gravity up to this point has been the biggest mystery, but M-theory and string theory are unique in that they actually require gravity. String theory is a theory that is part of M-theory and is really five different string theories called Type I, Type IIA, Type IIB, Heterotic-O, and Heterotic-E. These **five** theories describe the five different kinds of strings such as closed and open loops of strings and the way the strings spin, and their symmetries. The incredible thing about all of these theories is, that out of all of the thousands of theories of the universe that could be, scientists seem to have broken them down to just **five** or **six** theories. Keep in mind these strings are incredibly small, the size of or a multiple of the Planck length, the smallest measurement that we know. About a billion atoms can fit on the period at the end of this sentence. Now imagine shrinking down from that point inside the atoms nucleus 10 to the 20th power times smaller, and that is the size of a string.

Later on it was discovered that these so-called five different theories were all connected together and possessed a duality to one another. Basically when one of these string theories is weak in energy, it exactly equals the same physics of the other theory, when the other dual theory is strong in energy. Also when one of these theories is large in its radius (such as the radius size of the whole universe), the other theory is the exact inverse of that size. Example: if one theory of the universe was 10 to the **$+61^{st}$** power in size; then the other dual theory is 10 to the **-61st** power in size, and yet they both lend to the same physical qualities; as long as they maintain this opposite or inverse symmetry. The duality or symmetry of these theories is indeed very mysterious. These **five** string theories are really just five different ways or **windows** to look at the same **universe**. The **sixth** theory (**M-theory**), which is called *eleven-dimensional* super-gravity, is the glue that is supposed to hold the other five string theories together. String theory deals with one-dimensional strings vibrating in ten dimensions (9 space and 1 time dimension). Eleven-dimensional super-gravity deals with two-dimensional (and more) membranes operating within 11dimensions (10 space and 1 time dimension). These two theories (string and M-theory are related). M-theory is the name used for all of these combined theories and is the glue that seeks to hold it all together in a theory of everything (**TOE**).

Whenever the Bible talks about curtains it's also referring to outer space (***the heavens***) and space-time dimensions. Remember that your spirit lives within these dimensions! Consider that Psalm 104:1 says "Bless the LORD, O my soul. O LORD my God, thou art very great; thou art clothed with honour and majesty. Who coverest thyself with **light** as with a garment: who **stretchest** out the heavens like a **curtain**." Also look at Isaiah 40:22 "It is he that sitteth upon the circle of the earth, and the inhabitants thereof are as grasshoppers; **that stretcheth out the heavens as a curtain**, and spreadeth them out as a tent to dwell in." Isaiah 44:24 "Thus saith the LORD, thy redeemer, and he that formed thee from the womb, I am the LORD that maketh all things; that **stretcheth forth the heavens** alone; that spreadeth abroad the earth by myself." Zechariah 12:1 "The burden of the word of the LORD for Israel, saith the LORD, which **stretcheth forth the heavens**, and layeth the foundation of the earth, and **formeth the spirit of man** within him." Job 9:8 declares: "Which alone **spreadeth out the heavens**, and treadeth upon the waves of the sea." Job 9:9-10 says "Which maketh **Arcturus**, Orion, and Pleiades, and the chambers of the south. Which doeth great things past finding out; yea, and wonders without number." Job 38:31 says "Canst thou bind the sweet influences of Pleiades, or loose the bands of Orion?" Job 38:32 proclaims: "Canst thou bring forth **Mazzaroth** in his season? or canst thou **guide Arcturus** with his sons?" The word **Mazzaroth** in Job 38:32 means the constellations. How could Job know about guiding ***Arcturus*** without a telescope? Job 38:22 "Hast thou entered into the treasures of the **snow**? or hast thou seen the treasures of the hail." How could Job know about the treasures of the ***snow*** without a microscope? Job 37:**6** "For he saith to the **snow**, Be thou on the **earth**; likewise to the small rain, and to the great rain of his strength." Snowflakes have **6** sides talked about on **6** numbered verses. Job **6**:16 "Which are blackish by reason of the ice, and wherein the **snow** is hid."

We begin at Exodus Chapter 26 verse 1.

Exo 26:1   Moreover thou shalt make the tabernacle with **ten curtains** of fine twined linen, and blue, and purple, and scarlet: with cherubims of cunning work shalt thou make them.

Exo 26:2   The length of one curtain shall be **eight and twenty cubits**, and the breadth of one curtain **four cubits**: and every one of the curtains shall have **one measure**.

In these first two verses Moses is instructed to make ten (10) curtains. The length of one curtain is twenty-eight cubits and the breadth or width is four (**4 x 28**), and there will be ten of these. It should be noted that by using these dimensions for the curtains we could say we have 4 x 10 to the 28th power, as there are ten curtains going through these (4 x 28) length and width numbers. This number (**4 x 10** to the **28th** power) just happens to be the number of particles (protons and neutrons), in the average human being.

Exo 26:3   The **five curtains** shall be **coupled** together one to another; and other **five curtains** shall be **coupled** one to another.

This verse is really amazing as these ten curtains are split into two sets of five curtains. Remember that there are **five** different string theories and that they all have a **duality** to one another. These two sets of five curtains must be coupled one to another. The terminology used in string theory that describes a string's strength is called the ***coupling strength***. Note the words "*coupled together one to another*" in the scripture above. In fact the strong coupling constant for any one of the five string theories is inversely proportional to the weak coupling strength of its partner. For example when the Type I string theory's coupling strength is strong, its duality partner theory Heterotic-O is weak by an exact inverse amount. If one string theory had a strength of **61** then the other's strength would be **1/61**, the inverse amount. This coupling constant is basically the strength of how strings interact when acted upon by the forces of nature. The number in physics associated with the string coupling constant is **137**; actually 1/137. It's called the dimensionless number and also the fine structure constant. The number 137 doesn't have a link to any other physical law of the universe. Another way to think of this number is that it's the probability that an electron will absorb a photon; we will talk about this mysterious 137 number later on in the book.

Exo 26:4	And thou shalt make loops of blue upon the edge of the one curtain from the selvedge in the coupling; and likewise shalt thou make in the uttermost edge of another curtain, in the coupling of the second.
Exo 26:5	**Fifty loops** shalt thou make in the one curtain, and **fifty loops** shalt thou make in the edge of the curtain that is in the coupling of the second; that the loops may take hold one of another.
Exo 26:6	And thou shalt make **fifty taches of gold**, and couple the curtains together with the taches: and it shall be one tabernacle.

In these last verses the loops take hold of one another and are coupled together to make one tabernacle. In string theory the strings are referred to as open and closed loops of string just like the scripture refers to them as loops here to couple the curtains. The theory of everything has a goal to put all of these theories into one theory just like the tabernacle shall 'be one tabernacle'. The number of fifty (**50**) loops here in the Bible means Pentecost and looks ahead to the day when the Holy Spirit will fall on the church. The number fifty also means jubilee and freedom. There is great freedom in God when there is oneness and wholeness and the people are coupled together as these curtains are within the church of Jesus Christ.

Exo 26:7	And thou shalt make curtains of goats' hair to be a covering upon the tabernacle: **eleven curtains** shalt thou make.

Exo 26:8   The length of one curtain shall be **thirty cubits**, and the breadth of one curtain four cubits: and the **eleven curtains** shall be all of one measure.

In Exodus 26:7 it says to make curtains of goats' hair and to make eleven (**11**) of them. Verse numbers (26 + 7) = **33** the Planck length 10^-33 centimeters from Psalm **33**. Ten (**10**) string dimensions from Psalm 33 + (**1**) of time = an (**11**) eleven-dimensional universe. In Bible terminology the scapegoat (referring to goats' hair) is the one who carries away our sins and is used as a sin offering. Leviticus **9:15** says "And he brought the people's offering, and took the **goat**, which was the **sin** offering for the people, and slew it, and offered it for **sin**, as the first." Verse numbers (**9 + 15**) = **24**, the Bible number (**24**) of the priesthood regarding **Jesus**; (8 + 8 + 8) = **24**. This is a picture of Jesus Christ and His sacrifice on the cross as our **sin** offering, the **scapegoat**. These **eleven curtains** are made of goat hair (strings). This is the extra eleventh dimension of our universe, entered into by Jesus Christ, just like there are eleven curtains here. Based on string theory the universe must have 11 dimensions total. In regards to this look at our mystery constant of **137** as (**1**) time dimension, (**3**) seen dimensions, (**7**) curled up dimensions for a total of **11** dimensions (1 + 3 + 7) = 11.

The number eleven in the Bible is always associated with judgment and disorder. As an example there were **eleven** apostles after the Last Supper until the day of Pentecost; also in Genesis **37** Joseph dreamed of **eleven stars** (his brothers) and was then sold by his brothers into slavery. Deuteronomy 1:2 says "There are **eleven days**' journey from Horeb by the way of mount Seir unto Kadeshbarnea." This eleven day journey took the children of Israel **forty years** in the wilderness because of their disobedience to God. Jesus Christ took on the heavy weight and gravity of our sins to secure our salvation and restore order to the universe. Maybe that is why the theory is called eleven-dimensional **super-gravity**. Gravity is 10^-38 power and (3 + 8) = 11. Isn't it amazing how string theory and M-theory have the same dimensions as the tabernacle and its curtains? God knew these secrets before time began and modeled the tabernacle after them as the numbers clearly show.

In Exodus 26:8 it says "The length of one curtain shall be **thirty** cubits, and the breadth of one curtain **four** cubits: and the eleven curtains shall be all of one measure." If you will also notice that our curtains first two measurements $(30 + 4) = $ **34**, just like our verse numbers $(26 + 8) = $ **34** and that 10-$\wedge 34^{th}$ power is the very important ***Planck's constant*** from Psalm **34**. Using these measurements again $(30 \times 4) = $ **120,** like the **120** people in an upper room in the book of Acts. For this curtain set of **eleven** the length is made to be **thirty cubits**, remembering that the first curtain set of ten had a length of **twenty-eight cubits**. This was the number of particles in a human: 4×10 to the 28th power. This thirty length curtain set has a length that is ***two more powers of ten*** than the twenty-eight set $(28 + 2 = 30)$. This thirty cubits length curtain set is a picture of none other than the Lord Jesus Christ, as two more powers of 10 are added, and these two powers are the **Father** and the **Holy Spirit**. The Bible says that in Jesus the fullness of the Godhead dwells bodily, Father, Son, and Holy Spirit. With these curtains being a length of thirty **(30)**, they distinguish Jesus from the (28) length curtain set, and of just being a man. In the thirty length curtain set the two extra dimensions of the Father and the Holy Spirit are added because the Lord Jesus Christ is God, the Holy Trinity Himself. Remember that Jesus stated, "I and my Father are one." Another interesting feature of the difference of the 28 and 30 length curtain sets is that $(4 \times 28) = $ **112**; just add **2** again, like we did with $(28 + 2) = $ **30** and you have $(112 + 2) = $ **114** of John **1:14** "And the Word was made flesh..." The number thirty is significant in the Bible as Jesus started His ministry when He was thirty years old and thirty in the Bible represents the blood of Christ and dedication. Using the same way that we measured the curtain set of ten would make this eleven curtains sets' measurements (4×11) to the 30th power or $(4 \times 11\wedge 30)$. Look at each side of these curtain measurements as $(4 \times 11 \times 30)$. If we multiply the (4×11) side we have 44. If we do the same to the other side we have $(11 \times 30) = $ 330. Now divide 44 by (1) time dimension and you get $(44 / 1) = $ **44**, the Planck time as in Psalm **44**. Also if we divide 330 by (10) space dimensions we get $(330 / 10) = $ **33**, the Planck length like Psalm **33**. We just accounted for one time dimension (44), and ten space dimensions (33), by dividing the eleven curtain set measurements by the number of (10) space and (1) time dimensions. Jesus is the master of space and time who lived 33 years on the earth!

This next scripture is the most amazing scripture as related to **M-theory**.

Exo 26:9   And thou shalt **couple five curtains** by themselves, and **six curtains by themselves**, and shalt **double** the **sixth** curtain in the forefront of the tabernacle.

Here we have five curtains by themselves, representing the five string theories and then six curtains by themselves representing M-theory. These are **five** string theories held together by a **sixth** theory that will be joined together to make the eleven curtains: (5 + 6) = **11**. This is a description of how **M-theory** works. Remember we said before that the sixth theory is eleven-dimensional super-gravity. Five curtains plus six curtains equals eleven curtains. M-theory is not fully understood yet, but seems to be the glue through which eleventh dimensional super-gravity is able to hold all of the other five string theories together. Here we have this demonstrated in the tabernacle with the five and six curtains. The amazing thing about M-theory is that when the **sixth** theory is added to **five** string theories, the **eleventh** dimension is said to be immediately **folded**, or **rolled up** within the other ten dimensions. As this eleven-dimensional membrane is rolled up, it is hidden, but still then acts like the strings in ten-string theory at low energies. It has also been said that a string at a much higher energy can grow into a two-dimensional membrane itself and create this eleventh space-time dimension. Notice that here in the scripture in Exodus 26:9 it says to "**double** the sixth curtain in the forefront of the tabernacle". This is utterly amazing and matches **M-theory**. If the sixth curtain, which is the eleventh curtain of the total set of (**5 + 6** curtains = **11**) is doubled over; (**folded**) in the forefront of the tabernacle for all to see, then we have described the basic structure of M-theory with the tabernacle curtains! Another way to look at the five and six curtain sets is that the six curtain set is the (sixth theory – eleven-dimensional super-gravity) going into the other five curtain set (five different string theories).

Referring to our '**coupling constant**' number of **137**, the word '**couple**' appears 10 times in the Bible. **Five (5)** of the '**couple**' words are referring to something being **joined together**, all in the book of Exodus. The other five are used to refer to a couple of things, a numerical amount. There are **5** string theories and the word '**couple**' appears **5** times in the Bible about **joining** something together. One of these 5 times is in Exodus **26:11** "And thou shalt make **fifty** taches of brass, and put the taches into the **loops**, and **couple** the tent together, that it may be **one**." Verse numbers (26 + 11) = **37**, like the mystery coupling constant 137. Here is the verse before Exodus 26:11: Exodus 26:10 "And thou shalt make **fifty loops** on the edge of the **one curtain** that is outmost in the **coupling**, and **fifty loops** in the edge of the curtain which **coupleth the second**." 50 loops + **50** loops = **100**; and **100** + verse numbers (26 + 11 = 37) = **137**, the mystery constant! This clearly shows that the 'Tabernacle of Moses' is a model of the universe even down to the smallest detail. The word '**coupled**' shows up exactly **11** times in the Old Testament all here in Exodus matching our **eleven** dimensional universe! The word '**coupling**' shows up in **8 different** scriptures, for a total of **10** times within those **eight (8)** scriptures. This matches the '**Eightfold Way**' of particle physics that we are going to talk about in a few moments. The Old Testament tabernacle **curtains** and **dimensions** are already patterned after what science now says the universe should look like, in all of its **eleven** space-time dimensions. One would be led to think that science is on the right track by seeing all of the pattern matching we find here. I hope that everyone can really appreciate the fact that these things were prophetically written **3,400** years ago, ***proof*** of our God! Can space really be rolled up in tiny string dimensions and membranes? Hebrews 1:10 "And, Thou, Lord, in the beginning hast laid the **foundation of the earth**; and the **heavens** are the works of thine hands." Hebrews 1:11 "They shall **perish**; but **thou remainest**; and they all shall **wax old** as doth a **garment**." Hebrews 1:12 "And as a vesture **shalt thou fold them up**, and they **shall be changed**: but **thou** art the same, and thy years shall not fail." Notice in Hebrews 1:12 "And as a vesture shalt thou **fold** them up"; like the folded dimensions that string theory talks about. Also notice that these begin in verses 10-12 of Hebrews, just like the 10 and 11 dimensional universe. Twelve (12) is the Bible number of divine government. Is this the coming **12th** dimension of the universe? A governmental chapter **12** dealing with one 'who was to **rule all nations**'; Revelation **12:5** "And she brought forth a man child, who was to rule **all nations** with a rod of iron: and her child was caught up unto God, and to his throne." Our verse numbers (12 x 5) = **60**, the size of the radius of the universe in Planck lengths: the 10^60th power of Psalm 60.

Isaiah 34:4 "And all the host of heaven shall be dissolved, and the heavens shall be **rolled together** as a **scroll**"; verse numbers (34 + 4) = **38** gravity. Revelation 6:14 "And the heaven departed as a **scroll** when it is **rolled** together; and every mountain and island were moved out of their places." Isaiah 34:4 (34 x 4) = 136, Revelation 6:14 (6 x 14) = 84, both added (136 + 84) = **220**; like the **22** letters of the Hebrew alphabet (building blocks of the universe) x **10** space dimensions (22 x 10) = **220**! We are talking about a scroll and scrolls have letters on them. We just covered space with (22 x 10 stringed dimensions); what happened to the (**44**) 'time' dimension? Go ahead and add 'time' (44) to our 220 number (44 + 220) = **264**. Jehovah is number (**26**)4 and there are 26(**4**) seen dimensions (**26 x 4**) = **104** like Psalm 104:2 "…who stretchest out the heavens like a curtain." These are the only two scriptures in the Bible with the words *rolled* and *scroll* together in them. Also (3 + 4 + 4 + 6 + 1 + 4) all verse numbers added equals **22**! The mystery constant of the universe (137) + anti-gravity (83) = **220**. Science says there is a total of **7** curled up dimensions; if we take our **22** letters of the Hebrew alphabet and divide by 7 we have (**22 / 7**) which equals pi (**3.1428**), the number used to compute the circumference of a circle, knowing that we live in a curved (circular) universe. Twenty-two plus seven (22 + 7) = 29 the creation fire number 10^29 power degrees from Psalm **29:7** (the 29 – 7) verse numbers = **22**. There are about **10^22nd** power stars in the universe and Genesis 22:17 says "…stars of the heaven…" Genesis **22**:17 proclaims: "That in blessing I will bless thee, and in multiplying I will multiply thy seed as the (**stars of the heaven**), and as the sand which is upon the sea shore; and thy seed shall possess the gate of his enemies." This is weird as the verse numbers (2217) sure look a lot like the division of (twenty-two divided by seven): (22/7). Keeping in mind that there are 10^{22nd} power as the number of stars: Deuteronomy **10:22** "Thy fathers went down into Egypt with *threescore and ten persons*; and now the LORD thy God hath made thee as the (**stars of heaven**) for multitude." Isn't this odd that verse numbers (10 x 22) = **220** and (threescore and ten persons) = **70**; **(220 / 70) = 3.1428** just like **(22 / 7)** does! This verse shows the number of stars, Hebrew alphabet, and curvature of the universe all in one! Job **22**:12 "Is not God in the height of heaven? and behold the height of the **stars**, how high they are!"

Going back to the tabernacle in Exodus 26:25 "And they shall be **eight** boards, and their sockets of **silver**, **sixteen** sockets; two sockets under one board, and two sockets under another board." **Silver** in the Bible always speaks of *redemption*. Moses is instructed to make eight (**8**) boards attached by sixteen (**16**) silver sockets; which again speaks of our redemption through the cancellation of our sin debt, just like string theory requires a cancellation of sixteen (**16**) dimensions. So then what is significant about the number of eight (**8**) boards here? It just so happens that one of the most promising string theories is the Heterotic-E string theory called E8 x E8. This **E8 x E8** is a symmetry group that can describe two completely different worlds actually living alongside the other. Any one side of the E8 group can be used to describe all of the symmetries and particles in our world, and (8 + 8 = **16**). The word heterotic here means that two different pairs of dimensions can run around the loop of a string. Twenty-six dimensions run counterclockwise and ten dimensions run clockwise, but **sixteen** of the twenty-six (counterclockwise dimensions) are cancelled out as stated earlier. This leaves ten dimensions running each way around the string and (26 - 16) = 10. Another fact of the number **eight** is that there is another major classification system of particles that was established in the early 1960's that's called the "**The Eightfold way**." This Eightfold way groups particles in patterns of eight (and others) according to their different characteristics such as spin, electric charge, and a thing called strangeness. Here is the 8 and 16 in 2nd Chronicles 29:**16** "And the priests went into the inner part of the house of the LORD, to **cleanse it**, and brought out all the

uncleanness that they found in the **temple** of the LORD into the court of the house of the LORD. Regarding the verse numbers (29:16); twenty-nine (**29**) deals with **fire** like Psalm 29 and here they are '*cleansing*' the temple; **16** is our sin debt cancelled and **uncleanness** done away with. And the Levites took it, to carry it out abroad into the brook Kidron. Now they began on the first day of the first month to sanctify, and on the **eighth (8th)** day of the month came they to the porch of the LORD: so they sanctified the house of the LORD in **eight (8) days**; and in the **sixteenth (16th)** day of the first month they made an end." In this scripture in 2nd Chronicles we have the 'eighth' and the 'sixteenth' day involved in the cleansing of the temple. Verse numbers (**29 + 16**) = 45 because now the temple is (**45**) preserved. Hebrews 12:**29** states: "For our God is a consuming **fire**." Eight and sixteen are core numbers in the Bible dealing with Jesus (8) and our sin debt (16), and core numbers describing the patterns and the particles of the universe.

What appears to be a different number of **six** theories here at low energies is really a picture of what a single M-Theory is at high energies, energy too high for us to probe physically at this time, but we can still predict (*probe*) mathematically. Do you think that God is involved at that higher energy level? Of course, as He is the oneness and wholeness being who dwells in unapproachable *light energy* as the Bible states! 1st Timothy **6:16** enlightens us with: "Who only hath immortality, **dwelling in the light** which no man can approach unto; whom no man hath seen, nor can see: to whom be honour and power everlasting. Amen." Verse numbers (6 + 16) = **22** the Bible number of light. Science understands that the whole universe exists in a broken symmetry and is trying to realize what the perfect symmetry is for all of these theories at higher energies. What else does the word of God also say about broken symmetry? 1st Corinthians 13:12 "For now we see through a **glass**, darkly; but then face to face: now I know in part; but then shall I know even as also I am known." This word glass here means *mirror*, we are looking into a dark broken mirror, but someday the *mirror symmetry* will be perfectly clear, as clear as crystal. Imagine knowing and seeing everything as you are now known of God. How do we see through this darkness into perfect symmetry? The answer is in the book of Matthew as said by Jesus; Matthew 5:8 "Blessed are the **pure** in heart: for they **shall see** God." A real interesting thing that top physicists say is that the average person, with a little knowledge of algebra and 2 hours at home can begin to find out the secrets of the universe. Why? Because of the mysterious duality and symmetry of the **5** string theories; if you know something about the small manageable part such as **1/61st**, then you can begin to understand the larger part at **61** (radius of the universe). String theory is a theory that they say was found 100 years before its time.

CHAPTER 5

The Torah Numbers: **304,805**

T he Torah is the first five books of the Bible: Genesis, Exodus, Leviticus, Numbers, and Deuteronomy, also known as the Pentateuch. The Jewish scribes were under strict orders to copy the Torah exactly as it had been handed down from the originals, they couldn't miss one character. Today we have the Torah and it still has exactly 304,805 characters (or individual letters in it). The first interesting thing about the Torah numbers is that the first four numbers (**3048**) are the numbers that we use to convert centimeters into feet. If you go to any reference book about measurement, it will say that to convert centimeters to feet use **30.48**. The number 30.48 centimeters is exactly one foot. This is the same as saying that there are **2.54** centimeters to one inch. This simply means that (2.54 x 12 *inches*) = **30.48** *centimeters*; which are first four Torah numbers! If you multiply the **30** part times the **.48** decimal of (30.48) you get **14.4**. 14 is the generational number and **144** (**14.4 x 10**) is the size of the man/angel from Rev. 21:17. Also notice that 2.54 broken into (**25 x 4**) = 100, and centimeters is a system based on 10's. If you multiply (**144 x pi**) you get **452** the mirror to 254: a (**254 | 452**) mirror. Let's add these mirrors to see what's inside: (254 + 452) = 706; now split the mirror in two (706 / 2) = **353**; our mysterious **353** number from the Ark of the Covenant, Noah's Ark, and the attack on Pearl Harbor. The Torah numbers divided by the number of the tribes of Israel (**12**) is (304805 / 12) = 25400, which brings us back to our 2.54 number x 10000. The word '**seed**' is found **254** times in the Bible; maybe this is what God uses to measure with, the ***mustard seed***! The number of characters (304805) in the Torah written about 3,400 years ago can be used to convert from the system of 10's ***centimeters or meters*** to our system of 12's (***feet and inches***). The World Trade Center attack of September 11, 2001 occurred on the **254**[th] day of the year. Read Isaiah 40:12 "Who hath measured the waters in the hollow of his hand, and meted out heaven with the span, and comprehended the dust of the earth in a measure, and weighed the mountains in scales, and the hills in a balance?" This is verse 40:12 of Isaiah and God is measuring and verse numbers 40 x 12 = **480**, the middle three Torah numbers: 30(**480**)5. If we multiply all of the Torah numbers together (3 x 4 x 8 x 5) they equal 480! Here is something important that happened in the **480**[th] year after the children of Israel were delivered out of the land of Egypt. 1st Kings 6:1 "And it came to pass in the ***four hundred and eightieth year*** after the children of Israel were come out of the land of Egypt, in the fourth year of Solomon's reign over Israel, in the month Zif, which is the second month, that he began to build the house of the LORD." The number 480 here also represents the **40** years in the wilderness for the **12** tribes of Israel as (40 x 12) = 480, knowing also that Israel became a nation again in 1948.

The Characters of the Bible 3,566,480

The total numbers of characters in the whole Bible Old and New Testaments is 3,566,480. We have our 480 here in the last three digits: 3566(**480**). Next comes the 66 books of the Bible 35(**66**)480; now the size of man above the Planck length at 10^35 power: (**35**)66480. All numbers added (3 + 5 + 6 + 6 + 4 + 8 + 0) = **32**, the Bible number of ***covenant***. The twenty-two letters of the Hebrew alphabet (22) + the Ten Commandments (10) = 32. If we take the first Torah number (**3**)04805 and multiply it by **48** (3 x 48) we get **144**, the size of the man or angel in Revelation 21:17 "And he measured the wall thereof, an (hundred and forty and four cubits), according to the measure of a man, that is, of the angel." Using **144** as 'square inches' converted to centimeters yields **929.0304** 'square centimeters' and there are **929** chapters in the Old

Testament; *notice that even the fraction is* **.0304**, the first three Torah numbers **304**. If we multiply the 3048 part of the Torah numbers by 30.48, the part that converts centimeters to feet, we get **92903.04**. This is **929** again with '0' and in the middle and then 3.04, the beginning 3 Torah numbers. The 929 chapters is like the **92** (elements) connected to **29** (creation fire) 9(2)9. If we take our last Torah number of **five** as in 30480(5) and multiply it by our (3 x 48) = **144** number we have (144 x 5) = **720**, which is the same as (3 x 48 x 5). This 720 number is really something, as we landed on the moon on 7/20/1969. In relation again to the moon and 720 see Psalm 72 verse 5 "They shall fear thee as long as the sun and **moon** endure, throughout all generations." Electrons that spin around the atom are called fermions; each fermion has to spin **720** degrees around the atom before returning to its original state of being. In relation to our 480 number Israel became a nation in 1948, and 4 x 8 = 32 the Bible number of covenant. Take the year Israel became a nation (**1948**) and add all of her numbers (**1 + 9 + 4 + 8**) = **22**; 22 is the Bible number of light in: Numbers 3:39 "All that were numbered of the Levites, which Moses and Aaron numbered at the commandment of the LORD, throughout their families, all the males from a month old and upward, were **twenty** and **two thousand**"; this is where God appoints **22,000** to serve in the sanctuary as **lights** unto the people. There are **22** bowls that hold the **oil** for the **candlestick** in the **Tabernacle**. There were **4** bowls on the center candlestick shaft and **3** bowls on each of the **6** branches coming from the candlestick (3 x 6) = **18 + 4 = 22** bowls. We also know that the Jews consider the **22** letters of the Hebrew alphabet the actual building blocks of the universe. Science says that there is our universe and a shadow universe; 2 **eleven** dimensional universes would be (**11 + 11**) = **22 dimensions**! The Hebrew alphabet also has (**5**) letters called finals, these finals add a prophetic sense to the word if they are used and (**22 + 5**) = **27**, our other number of light from Psalm **27**. Now in relation to 1948 look at (1 x 9 x 4 x 8) as it equals 288, the size of our two angels on the Ark (144 x 2) = **288**. These angels sit on the mercy seat of the Ark of the Covenant, see Psalm 80.

The Torah numbers and the *(Big One)* measuring
the whole universe!

This section is what I call the Big One, as it will show that the Torah numbers are the basis for all measurement in the universe. Take the Torah numbers 304,805 and drop the zeroes and you have 3485; this is just about the actual number of years ago that the Torah was written! Take these 3485 numbers and divide them by God's victory number **seventeen** (3485 / **17**) = 205, now multiply by 10 (205 x 10) = 2050; or just take 3485 and divide by **1.7** which is 2050. Remember the **150** Psalms and the fact that they show history from 1900 and that (1900 + 150) = 2050? Using the Torah numbers: **30** 480 **5** (**30** x **5**) = **150** Psalms. Now take 2050 and divide by the number of dimensions of the universe (2050 / 11) = 186.36; very close to our 186 base number for light speed and name of JeHoVaH squared. Now take 186 and multiply it by **pi** (186 x 3.14159) = **584.3**36, as the Torah numbers are now mirrored in this number in the first 4 digits; a (**5843 | 3485**) mirror. We used our light speed number in a curved universe and multiplied by **pi** to get the mirror of the Torah numbers. Notice that the mirror 5843 is close to 6,000 years, about how long ago since man was created! In fact just add our **150** number to 5843 and you have 5993 years, just 7 years short of 6,000 years. Using the actual exact speed of light in a vacuum (**186282.3976** miles per second) x pi = **585223.411**. Even this mirror is: (114.**322585 | 585223**.411) with the Torah numbers (5(**85**)22(**34**)11) embedded; and 411 and 114 connected to them. The Bible number of light (**22**) is right in the middle of this mirror (585**22**34) along with **5**, the number of books of the Torah. This is what happens when we divide natural light speed (186) with Bible light (22); we get (186 / 22) = 8.45, knowing that Jesus number is 8 and that 45 is the Bible number of preservation and exactly 1/8 of a circle; or how about another version of the Eightfold way of particle physics, Jesus. All of this in a circular universe with (8 x 45) equaling 360 as in a circle. Even (8 x .45) = 3.6, one 1/100 of a circle. This also looks a lot like Noah's Ark with 8 people onboard and the dimensions of (300 x 50 x 30 cubits) = **450,000**.

Billions of **light years**

Recall that we just talked about the Torah numbers 30.48 being the conversion factor from centimeters to inches and that 30.48 centimeters equals 1 foot or 12 inches. So whether we use inches, feet, or miles (as in 186,000 miles per / second) or centimeters/ meters with (300,000,000 meters per / second) as light speed doesn't matter, because the Torah numbers **30.48** are the actual conversion factor. Even our base number in meters for light speed (300 x pi) = **942**, just divide by ten space dimensions (942 / 10) = **94.2** and 94.2 is the exact figure from Psalm 90:4 where we used (2 x pi x 15 billion light year radius) to get a circumference of **94.2 billion** light years for the whole universe! We saw from before that the word '**Jesus**' appears **942** times in the Bible, all in the New Testament (942 / 10) = **94.2**. Here we have the two base numbers for light speed; 186 = miles, and 300 = meters and (300 – 186) = **114** (the Torah numbers squared: 9 + 16 + 64 + 25); and the 114 of John **1:14**; and the power of the quantum vacuum 10^{114}; and other important numbers in science as already discussed. The actual speed of light is **299,792,458** meters per second. Now we know why the Torah numbers, which are the actual number of letters in the first 5 books of the Bible relating to creation, are what they are. They are the numbers generated, *and the conversion factor itself*, when measuring the whole universe in size and time of years, using numbers of light (300 and 186). All of this happens while employing both major number scales (miles and meters), *amazing*! The square root of the Torah numbers (**3485**) is **59.033888**, and we know Jesus, whose number in the Greek is '**888**' lived **33** years on the earth. Here is an interesting one; take the 114 number and multiply it by pi (114 x 3.14159) = 358.14; we almost made a perfect circle of 360 degrees, we just need to add a little light (**1.86**) so that (358.14 + **1.86**) = 360! Using the first 4 Torah conversion numbers of **3048** / (**38 gravity**) = **80.2**, knowing that there are 10^{80} power particles in the universe: see **Psalm 80**. This number **80.2** is **2.08** backwards or the atomic weight of **Bismuth** (the 83rd element) divided by 100: (**208** / 100) = **2.08**. Science says that there must be 'right at', but no more than about 10^{80} power particles in the universe because of the gravitational constant; the Torah numbers divided by gravity strikes again!

The **2.54** gravity of the Element Table

If you add **22** (Bible number of light) to our base number for light speed (186 + 22) you get **208**, the atomic weight of our anti-gravity element Bismuth element no. 83 and (38 | 83) mirror to gravity in Psalm 38. We know that **2.54** is what we use to we convert centimeters to inches. Strangely enough, if you multiply our **254** number twice by itself like this; (25 x 4) = **100** and (2 x 54) = **108**, and add them you get (100 + 108) = **208**. We have talked a lot about the 83rd element Bismuth and its atomic weight of 208. What about the 38th element related to gravity because gravity is **10^38** power (times weaker) than the strong force? The **38th** element is Strontium and has a relative density or *specific gravity* of **2.54**! Now to be fair we must take the 83rd element Bismuth and use its relative density or *specific gravity* of **9.80** and multiply it (by itself twice) just like we did for the 2.54 number: (9 x 80) = **720** and (98 x 0) = 0; added together (720 + 0) = **720**. The value for 'gravitational acceleration' on earth is **9.80** meters! We know that all matter particles in the universe (called fermions) spin **720** degrees to get back to their starting positions; in other words matter is a trick of geometry. We have also stated that Einstein and science both say that *gravity* equals *acceleration* in a curved universe! It's very interesting to see the relationship that these two gravity/anti-gravity elements (38 | 83) have to each other when it comes to their numbers; especially knowing that (2.54 centimeters x 12 in.) = 30.48 centimeters, the first 4 Torah numbers. The Torah numbers (3 x 48 x 5) also equal **720**. It's like Strontium **38** (specific gravity **2.54**) points to Bismuth with atomic weight of **208**; and Bismuth **83** (specific gravity **9.80**) points to Strontium **38** as the gravity (spin **720** degrees) of all particles of matter. Bismuth's relative density divided by Strontium's relative density (9.80 / **2.54**) = **3.85**.

Let's look at the number **838,380**, the number of characters in the New Testament. Here we have anti-gravity and gravity with all of the eights and the threes. Look at the numbers (8 3 8 3 8 0) this way by dropping the threes down a row.

8 8 8 0   (Jesus name numerically in the Greek is '**888**'.)
3 3   (Jesus lived '33' years on the earth. All numbers
                 added $(8 + 3 + 8 + 3 + 8 + 0) = 30$;
                 Jesus number of blood and divine service is (30)
                 when He started His ministry.)

Another aspect of the Torah numbers is the fact that no matter how we arrange the Torah numbers, they equal very significant numbers. Look at the Torah numbers this way: $(30 + 48 + 05) = $ **83**, the number from Psalm 83 and science as anti-gravity. Now look at the Torah numbers reversed or mirrored: (50 84 03) because $(50 + 84 + 03) = $ **137**, the mystery constant of the universe called the dimensionless number and also known as the string coupling constant of string theory. This 137 is the strength of the electromagnetic force compared to the strong force; meaning 137 times weaker than the strong force. It might be noted that the odds in poker of getting **one pair** is 1.37, and the odds of an electron absorbing a photon is 1 out of 137. Even if you split the Torah numbers this way mirrored as in 508 and 403 they still equal $(5 + 8) = $ **13** and $(4 + 3) = $ **7**; 13 pasted to 7 equals **137**. It's also interesting to note that if we square and add together the numbers of 137 we have $(1 + 9 + 49)$ which equals 59, (**50 + 9**). The number 50 in the Bible always refers to the freedom of the Holy Spirit through Pentecost, like the day of Pentecost in the book of Acts in chapter 2. In the Old Testament (Numbers 28:26) for the feast called 'day of the first fruits', they were told to wait (49) days or (7 weeks). They then celebrated the feast on the very next day, the fiftieth (**50th**) day. You can see how this relates to our $(1 + 9 + 49) = $ **59**. If we add (1 day + 49 days) we have our **50 days**; with the 9 Holy Spirit (1 9 49) manifested in the middle. In relation to our (**1 + 9 + 49**) numbers; put them all together and you have the year **1949**.

1949

The year **1949** is the actual year of a tremendous move of the Holy Spirit in the United States and Canada called the 'latter rain' movement. Churches were having services 3 times a day 7 days a week for a 7 year period from about 1948-1955. I used to attend one of these churches that experienced this 'latter rain' in the 1960-1970's called "The Bethesda Missionary Temple" in Detroit, Michigan; which now is called the "The Bethesda Christian Church" located in Sterling Heights, Michigan. Many great ministers such as Billy Graham and Oral Roberts started their ministries during this time. The nine (9) refers to the fact that there are nine fruits and nine gifts of the Holy Spirit (1 **9** 4 **9**). The number nine (**9**) in the Bible also refers to the manifestation and completeness of something. The Holy Spirit was poured out and manifested to the world on the day of Pentecost fifty (**50**) days after Jesus' resurrection from the dead. Pentecost actually means '**fiftieth**'. In the Old Testament in Exodus 23:16 it was called "the feast of harvest". In Exodus 34:22 and Numbers 28:26 Pentecost is referred to as the "the day of the first fruits." Another fact about the number **137** is that it's the 33rd prime number, and we know by now that 10^-33 power is the Planck length, another dimensionless number where space and time merge together.

(1 x 3 x 7) and the Holy Spirit (21)

Because of the numbers we find within this **137** mystery number, it seems that the number 137 represents the **Holy Spirit of God** moving throughout the earth; this is why **137** is dimensionless and not connected to anything physical, just like the scientists say. Look at this very important scripture in John **3:7** "Marvel not that I said unto thee, Ye must be **born again**. The wind bloweth where it listeth, and thou hearest the sound thereof, but canst not tell whence it cometh, and whither it goeth: so is every one that is **born of the Spirit**"; noticing that this started in John **3:7**. Just put the one in front to get (1)37 and (3 x 7) = **21**. **Jesus** suddenly appears to the disciples in Luke 24:36 "And as they thus spake, **Jesus himself** stood in the midst of them, and saith unto them, Peace be unto you." The next verse: Luke 24:**37** "But they were terrified and affrighted, and supposed that they had seen a **spirit**"; verse numbers (24 x **37**) = '**888**', Jesus name in the Greek. Mark 15:**37** "And Jesus cried with a loud voice, and gave up the **ghost**." Relating this **137** number to the **Holy Spirit moving** throughout the earth: (**1 x 3 x 7**) = **21**. Look at the **21** of Acts **2:1** "And when the *day of Pentecost* was fully come, they were all with **one accord** in **one place**." There were **120** people in the upper room waiting for the Holy Spirit; God's victory number (**17**) + **120** people = **137**! God's victory number (**17**) squared and added (**1 + 49**) = **50**; and *fifty* means **Pentecost**! The words 'Holy' and 'Spirit' appear together in **21** scriptures of the Bible! All of the following scriptures have to do with the number (**21** and the **Holy Spirit:** (1 x 3 x 7) = **21**); or where the verse numbers are a multiple of the number **21**, even when (added or multiplied)! Revelation **21**:10 "And he carried me away in the **spirit** to a great and high mountain, and shewed me that great city, the holy Jerusalem, descending out of heaven from God." Matthew **1:20** "But while he thought on these things, behold, the angel of the **LORD** appeared unto him in a dream, saying, Joseph, thou son of David, fear not to take unto thee Mary thy wife: for that which is **conceived in her** is of the **Holy Ghost**"; verse numbers (1 + 20) = **21**. Luke 1:41 "And it came to pass, that, when *Elisabeth* heard the salutation of *Mary*, the **babe leaped in her womb**; and Elisabeth was filled with the **Holy Ghost**." We have the **Holy Ghost** and **two** pregnant women here now *Mary* and *Elisabeth* (1 + 41) = **42**; (**21 Holy Ghost x 2 women**) = **42**. Jude **1:20** "But ye, beloved, building up yourselves on your most holy faith, praying in the **Holy Ghost**"; (1 + 20) = **21**. 2nd Peter 1:**21** "For the prophecy came not in old time by the will of man: but holy men of God spake as they were moved by the **Holy Ghost**." Acts **21**:11 "And when he was come unto us, he took Paul's girdle, and bound his own hands and feet, and said, Thus saith the **Holy Ghost**, So shall the Jews at Jerusalem bind the man that owneth this girdle, and shall deliver him into the hands of the Gentiles." Hebrews **3:7** "Wherefore as the **Holy Ghost** saith, To day if ye will hear his voice, Harden not your hearts, as in the provocation, in the day of temptation in the wilderness:"; verse numbers (3 x 7) = **21**. Luke 11:26 "Then goeth he, and taketh to him **seven other spirits** more wicked than himself; and they enter in, and dwell there: and the last state of that man is worse than the first"; verse numbers (11 + 26) = **37**. Acts 19:2 "He said unto them, Have ye received the **Holy Ghost** since ye believed? And they said unto him, We have not so much as heard whether there be any **Holy Ghost**"; verse numbers (19 + 2) = **21**. Philippians **2:1** "If there be therefore any consolation in Christ, if any comfort

of love, if any fellowship of the **Spirit**, if any bowels and mercies."
Galatians 5:16 "This I say then, Walk in the **Spirit**, and ye shall not
fulfil the lust of the flesh"; $(5 + 16) = 21$. 2nd Corinthians 3:18 "But
we all, with open face beholding as in a glass the glory of the Lord,
are changed into the same image from glory to glory, even as by the
Spirit of the LORD"; $(3 + 18) = 21$. 1st Corinthians 12:9 "To
another faith by the same **Spirit**; to another the gifts of healing by
the same **Spirit**"; $(12 + 9) = 21$. Romans 8:13 "For if ye live after
the flesh, ye shall die: but if ye through the **Spirit** do mortify the
deeds of the body, ye shall live"; $(8 + 13) = 21$. Acts **21**:4 "And
finding disciples, we tarried there seven days: who said to Paul
through the **Spirit**, that he should not go up to Jerusalem." Acts
19:**21** "After these things were ended, Paul purposed in the **spirit**,
when he had passed through Macedonia and Achaia, to go to
Jerusalem, saying, After I have been there, I must also see Rome."
John 13:**21** "When **Jesus** had thus said, he was troubled in **spirit**,
and testified, and said, Verily, verily, I say unto you, that one of **you
shall betray me**"; **13** is the number of depravity and rebellion.
Luke 10:**21** "In that hour Jesus rejoiced in **spirit**, and said, I thank
thee, O Father, Lord of heaven and earth, that thou hast hid these
things from the wise and prudent, and hast revealed them unto
babes: even so, Father; for so it seemed good in thy sight." Luke
2:40 "And the child grew, and waxed strong in **spirit**, filled with
wisdom: and the grace of **God** was upon **him**"; we have **2** here with
"**God** was upon **him**" and $(2 + 40) = 42$ and $(21 \times 2) = 42$. 1st Peter
3:18 "For Christ also hath once suffered for sins, the just for the
unjust, that he might bring us to God, being put to death in the
flesh, but quickened by the **Spirit**"; $(3 + 18) = 21$. God's perfect
number **7** three times added: $(7 + 7 + 7) = 21$. We had stated that
Jesus is the number eight (**8**) of the Bible, and oxygen is number (**8**)
in the chemical table of elements. Relating this to breathing in the
Holy Spirit, the atmosphere (the air that you breathe) is **21%**
oxygen! Adding the Holy Spirit number (**(9)** to **21**) = 30; Jesus
number of blood and divine service. In relation to **Jesus**, He has the
Holy Spirit without **measure** in John **3:34** "For he whom God hath
sent speaketh the words of God: for God giveth **not** the **Spirit by
measure unto him**." Our verse numbers added $(3 + 34) = 37$, and
of course $(3 \times 7) = 21$. The number **37** in the Bible actually means

the (**Word** of the **Father**) and our verse also says "**speaketh the words of God.**" Also recall the important verses of John **3:7** and Hebrews **3:7** in relation to the **Holy Spirit**. John 20:22 says "And when he had said this, he **breathed** on them, and saith unto them, **Receive ye the Holy Ghost**"; verse numbers (20 + 22) = **42**; we have **2** again because "**He** breathed on **them**" and **42** = (**21 x 2**). Galatians 3:14 "That the blessing of Abraham might come on the **Gentiles** through *Jesus Christ*; that we might receive the promise of the **Spirit** through faith"; (3 x 14) = 42 and (**21 x 2**) = 42. These are really powerful and deal with the **Spirit** and "**resurrection from the dead.**" Luke 8:55 "And her **spirit** came again, and she arose straightway: and he commanded to give her meat;" (8 + 55) = 63 which is (**21** x 3) = **63**. This is right after Jesus resurrection in Luke 24:39 "Behold my hands and my feet, that it is I myself: handle me, and see; for a **spirit** hath not flesh and bones, as ye see me have"; (24 + 39) = **63**; (**21** x 3) = **63**. John 6:**63** "It is the **spirit** that quickeneth; the flesh profiteth nothing: the words that I speak unto you, they are **spirit**, and they are life"; (6 x **63**) = 378 or (**21 x 18**) = **378** also. Luke 9:42 "And as he was yet a coming, the devil threw him down, and tare him. And Jesus rebuked the **unclean spirit**, and healed the child, and delivered him again to his father"; (9 x 42) = 378 and (**21 x 18**) = **378** also. Matthew 12:28 "But if I cast out devils by the **Spirit of God**, then the kingdom of God is come unto you;" (12 x 28) = 336 (**21 x 16**) = 336 as well. Mark **1:26** "And when the **unclean spirit** had torn him, and cried with a loud voice, he came out of him"; 126 = (6 x **21**) a (1:26 | 6x21) mirror with **66** in the middle. Mark 6:49 "But when they saw him walking upon the sea, they supposed it had **been a spirit**, and cried out"; (6 x 49) = 294 and so does (**21** x 14) = 294. Luke **1:47** "And my **spirit** hath rejoiced in God my Saviour"; (7 x **21**) = **147**. Romans **8:4** "That the righteousness of the law might be fulfilled in us, who walk not after the flesh, but after the **Spirit**"; **84** = (**21 x 4**). Galatians **5:25** "If we live in the **Spirit**, let us also walk in the **Spirit**"; **525** = (**21** x 25). Hebrews **10:29** "Of how much sorer punishment, suppose ye, shall he be thought worthy, who hath trodden under foot the Son of God, and hath counted the blood of the covenant, wherewith he was sanctified, an unholy thing, and hath done despite unto the **Spirit of grace?**"; 1029 = (**21 x 49**). John

7:**39** "(But this spake he of the **Spirit**, which they that believe on him should receive: for the **Holy Ghost** was not yet given; because that Jesus was not yet glorified)"; (7 x **39**) = 273 or (**21** x 13) = 273. 1st Corinthians 14:15 "What is it then? I will pray with the **spirit**, and I will pray with the understanding also: I will sing with the **spirit**, and I will sing with the understanding also"; (14 x 15) = **210** and (**21** x 10) = **210** also. Hebrews 9:**14** "How much more shall the blood of Christ, who through the eternal **Spirit** offered himself without spot to God, purge your conscience from dead works to serve the living God?"; (9 x **14**) = 126 and (**21** x 6) = 126 also. 1st John **4:2** "Hereby know ye the **Spirit** of God: Every **spirit** that confesseth that **Jesus Christ** is come in the **flesh** is of God"; (**21** x 2) = 42. Revelation **4:2** "And immediately I was in the **spirit**: and, behold, a throne was set in heaven, and one sat on the throne"; (**21** x 2) = **42**. Romans **7:6** "But now we are delivered from the law, that being dead wherein we were held; that we should serve in **newness of spirit**, and not in the oldness of the letter"; (**7 x 6**) = 42 and (**21** x 2) = **42**. 1st Corinthians 4:**21** "What will ye? shall I come unto you with a rod, or in love, and in the **spirit** of meekness?" 1st Corinthians **2:10** "But God hath revealed them unto us by his **Spirit**: for the **Spirit** searcheth all things, yea, the **deep** things of God"; (**21** x 10) = **210**. Genesis **6:3** "And the LORD said, **My spirit** shall not always strive with man, for that he also is flesh: yet his days shall be an **hundred and twenty years**"; (**21** x 3) = **63** and 120 years is 021 backwards. Genesis **1:2** "And the **earth** was without form, and void; and darkness was upon the face of the deep. And the **Spirit of God** moved upon the **face of the waters**;" This is Genesis **1:2**, and **12** is the mirror of **21** (God's **Spirit**) reflecting off of the water, a (**12 | 21**) mirror.

137 and Creation

This **137** number is really called the inverse of the fine structure constant. The inverse of a number is the number 1 divided by the number such as 1 / 137.035989 = .007297353. Take this number (.007297353 x 1000 to get 7.297353 the real fine structure constant. Remember that this constant is the most mysterious number in physics, so let's look at its decimals. First look at the **.297** decimal part remembering Psalm **29:7** "The voice of the LORD divideth the **flames of fire**", and that this represented the 10^{29}th power heat of the creation event! Now the next decimals are **353** as in 7.297(**353**), recalling that **353** are the measurements of the Ark of the Covenant dealing with particle spin; the **3/2**, **5/2**, and **3/2** cubits numbers. In regards to the Ark again consider: 2nd Chronicles **35:3** "And said unto the Levites that taught all Israel, which were holy unto the LORD, Put the holy (**ark**) in the house which Solomon the son of David king of Israel did build; it shall not be a burden upon your shoulders: serve now the LORD your God, and his people Israel." This is pretty awesome that the most mysterious number would contain these Bible numbers of 'creation' and the basic structure of the particles. Just one more thing about 'creation', look at the connecting number **73** in 7.29(**73**)53 and the 1(**37**) number of **137**. Why are these 37 and 73 numbers special? Because the 'creation' sentence in Genesis 1:1 "In the beginning God created the heaven and the earth" in the Hebrew language numerically actually equals (**37 x 73**) = 2701. We will talk more about the creation sentence of Genesis 1:1 later. The last two digits in 7.2973(**53**) = **53**, the weight of the universe in kilograms 10^{53} power. This mystery number is loaded with what the Bible said 3,000 to 3,400 years ago in regards to creation and particles. As far as I can tell, the Bible mentions only these 3 important people who lived **137** years: Genesis 25:17 "And these are the years of the life of **Ishmael**, an **hundred and thirty and seven years**: and he gave up the ghost and died; and was gathered unto his people." Exodus 6:16 "And these are the names of the sons of **Levi** according to their generations; Gershon, and Kohath, and Merari: and the years of the life of **Levi** were an **hundred thirty and seven years**." Exodus 6:20 "And Amram took him Jochebed his father's sister to wife; and she bare him **Aaron and Moses**: and the years of the life of **Amram** were an **hundred and thirty and seven years**."

The **mezuzah** and **713**

The number **70** in the Bible always refers to the universality or restoration of Israel. Exodus 24:9 says: "Then went up Moses, and Aaron, Nadab, and Abihu, and **seventy** of the elders of Israel."

Numbers 11:16 also states: "And the LORD said unto Moses, Gather unto me **seventy men** of the elders of Israel, whom thou knowest to be the elders of the people, and officers over them; and bring them unto the tabernacle of the congregation, that they may stand there with thee." If you add the trinity of the Godhead (**3**) to 70 you get **73** our number related to the mystery constant and creation. Using the restoration of Israel (**70**) + Pentecost (**50**) we get (70 + 50) = **120** in an upper room waiting for the outpouring of the Holy Spirit in the book of Acts. Also if we look again at the Torah numbers the right way as in 304 and 805 they equal (3 + 4) = **7** and (8 + 5) = **13**; 7 + 13 pasted together is **713**. 713 is the number of characters in the '**mezuzah**'. The mezuzah is the segment of scripture starting in Deuteronomy chapter 6. This is a most important and sacred part of the scripture for the Jews to this day, because it is found on the doorpost of the home of every practicing Jew; it's also on all public buildings in Israel!

The **mezuzah** starting at Deut. 6:4.

Hear, O Israel: The LORD our God is one LORD: And thou shalt love the LORD thy God with all thine heart, and with all thy soul, and with all thy might. And these words, which I command thee this day, shall be in thine heart. And thou shalt teach them diligently unto thy children, and shalt talk of them when thou sittest in thine house, and when thou walkest by the way, and when thou liest down, and when thou risest up. And thou shalt **bind them for a sign** upon thine hand, and they shall be as **frontlets between thine eyes**. And thou shalt write them upon the **posts of thy house**, and on thy gates.

The **mezuzah**, second part starting at Deut 11:13.

And it shall come to pass, if ye shall hearken diligently unto my commandments which I command you this day, to love the LORD your God, and to serve him with all your heart and with all your soul, That I will give you the rain of your land in his due season, the first rain and the latter rain, that thou mayest gather in thy corn, and thy wine, and thine oil. And I will send grass in thy fields for thy cattle, that thou mayest eat and be full. Take heed to yourselves, that your heart be not deceived, and ye turn aside, and serve other gods, and worship them; And then the LORD's wrath be kindled against you, and he shut up the heaven, that there be no rain, and that the land yield not her fruit; and lest ye perish quickly from off the good land which the LORD giveth you. Therefore shall ye lay up these my words in your heart and in your soul, and bind them for a sign upon your hand, that they may be as **frontlets between your eyes**. And ye shall teach them your children, speaking of them when thou sittest in thine house, and when thou walkest by the way, when thou liest down, and when thou risest up. And thou shalt write them upon the **door posts of thine house**, and upon thy gates: That your days may be multiplied, and the days of your children, in the land which the LORD sware unto your fathers to give them, as the days of heaven upon the earth.

This is the *eleventh* commandment that holds the other Ten Commandments together and is the sum of them all, "Hear, O Israel: The LORD our God is one LORD." Other important lines are "they shall be as frontlets between thine eyes", and "thou shalt write them upon the door posts of thine house, and upon thy gates." The mezuzah is in the **FIFTH** book of the Bible, starting at the **SIXTH** chapter and ending at the **ELEVENTH** chapter. Do these numbers sound familiar? These are the numbers of the name of Jehovah and the dimensions of the Tabernacle of Moses related to string theory, **5 curtains, 6 curtains** for a total of eleven curtains (**11** space-time dimensions). The number of characters in the mezuzah is 713; this is the mystery constant (137) with the **7** switched around and put in the front as (**713**); "as frontlets between thine eyes." Remember **13** is the weak force from Psalm 13, so we need God (**7**) in front as our shield as we are weak and He is strong.

Five key numbers	186	(Light speed base number, Jehovah name squared)
from the Bible:	114	(Word made flesh John 1:14)
	144	(Size of the man/angel Revelation 21:17)
	119	(Victory number (**7 x 17** = 119), longest Psalm 119, Noah's Ark) Gen 8:4 "And the ark rested in the (**seventh** month), on the (**seventeenth**) day of the month, upon the mountains of Ararat." Genesis **7:17** "And the flood was forty days upon the earth; and the waters increased, and bare up the ark, and it was lift up above the earth."
	150	(Number of Psalms, size of universe, waters of the flood days). Gen 8:3 "And the waters returned from off the earth continually: and after the end of the hundred and fifty days the waters were abated."

713

All of these equal **713** the number of characters in the mezuzah from Deuteronomy chapter 6!

Genesis **7:13** "In the selfsame day **entered** Noah, and Shem, and Ham, and Japheth, the sons of Noah, and Noah's wife, and the three wives of his sons with them, **into the ark**." Matthew **7:13** "**Enter** ye in at the **strait gate**: for wide is the gate, and broad is the way, that leadeth to destruction, and many there be which go in thereat." Speaking of the *weak force* 7(**13**), (7 x 13) = **91**. There are 3 particles related to the weak force mentioned in **Psalm 13**, the W+ and W- particles and the **Z** particle. The **Z** particle is what carries the neutral current of the weak interaction at **91GeV**. If we add (**7 + 1 + 3**) they equal **11**. Now take our **91GeV** and minus the **11 (91 – 11) = 80**; and the other two particles W+ and W- come in at 80GeV in the weak interaction. We see again that the Bible agrees with science and nature, especially the fact that the Torah numbers as two sets **304** and **805** = (3 + 4) = **7** and (8 + 5) = **13**; pasted (**7** and **13**) = **713**.

The **Torah** and **Einstein**

Albert Einstein's father gave the young Albert Einstein a *magnetic compass* when he was a boy; this really inspired him and caused him to ask questions about the universe. In the year 1100 AD in China the first magnetic compass was used. In the year **1611** the King James Bible was published. In the year **1905** Einstein's 'Special Theory of Relativity' was published; he called 1905 his 'miracle year'. Take the year **1905** and minus the year **1100** (year of the compass) from it and you get (**1905-1100**) = **805** years. Take the year of Einstein's "General Theory of Relativity" which is **1915** and minus **1611** (year of the King James Bible) from it and we see that (**1915 – 1611**) = **304** years. Now we put **304** years together with **805** years and we have **304,805**; the exact number of characters in the Torah! Of course we also remember that Einstein was a Jew and that the good Lord had revealed some secrets to him. Do you think that maybe God is trying to tell us that the Bible is a *compass* to give our life *direction*? The year **1611** when the King James Bible was published is very interesting mathematically. If we add (16 + 11) we get **27**, the number of books in the New Testament. If we square all of the numbers in **1611** we get (1 + 36 + 1 + 1) = **39**, the number of books in the Old Testament. If we multiply (1 x 6 x 11), they equal sixty-six (**66**), the total number of books in the Bible as (39 + 27) = **66**! If we multiply (1 x 6 x 1 x 1) we get six (**6**), the number of man who the Bible was written for. If we square and add all in 1611 then we have the double operation of squaring with (1 + 36 + 1 + 1) = **39** and adding with (1 + 6 + 1 + 1) = **9**; in adding these we have (39 + 9 = **48**), and in **1948** Israel became a nation.

The **Torah**, Noah, Abraham, and **17**

If you take the zeroes out of the Torah numbers 304, 805 you have 34 and 85 both of which are exactly divisible by **17** (God's victory number) as (**17** x 2) = 34 and (**17** x 5) = 85. The Torah numbers (304,805 / **17**) = **17929.705** we have the 17 again and there are 929 chapters in the Old Testament (17(**929**)). Here is why (**17 x 7**) = **119** is powerful referring to God talking to Abraham: Genesis **17:7** "And I will establish my **covenant** between me and thee and thy seed after thee in their generations for an everlasting **covenant**, to be a God unto thee, and to thy seed after thee." Using our **119** number as (11 x 9) = **99**; Genesis **17:1** "And when Abram was (**ninety years old and nine**), the LORD appeared to Abram, and said unto him, I am the Almighty God; walk before me, and be thou perfect." Here is '**17**' and covenant with Noah in Genesis 9:**17** "And God said unto **Noah**, This is the token of the **covenant**, which I have established between me and all flesh that is upon the earth." Genesis **7:17** "And the flood was forty days upon the earth; and the waters increased, and bare up the ark, and it was lift up above the earth." Here is the result of God making a covenant with Noah and some more (**7 and 17** numbers) in Genesis 8:4 "And the ark rested in the (**seventh month**), on the (**seventeenth**) day of the month, upon the mountains of Ararat." We are talking about covenant and verse numbers (8 x 4) = **32**, the Bible number of covenant. A **17** of the New Testament: Luke **17**:27 "They did eat, they drank, they married wives, they were given in marriage, until the day that **Noe** entered into the ark, and the flood came, and destroyed them all." This **17** scripture says 'until the day' and (**17 + 27**) = **44** the Planck time of **Psalm 44**; their **time** was up! The book of Hebrews only has 13 chapters but still manages to do this (1(**17**): Hebrews **11:7** "By faith **Noah**, being warned of God of things not seen as yet, moved with fear, prepared an ark to the saving of his house; by the which he condemned the world, and became heir of the righteousness which is by faith." We know that our flood numbers of (**7 x 17**) = **119** and that our last scripture in Hebrews about Noah equals (**11 x 7**) = **77**; (**119 − 77**) = **42** the size of the (flooded) earth in Planck units. A few more **77** Noah's Ark scriptures: **Genesis 7:7** "And **Noah** went in, and his sons, and his wife, and his sons' wives with him, into the ark, because of the waters of the flood." **Genesis 7:11** "In the six hundredth year of **Noah's** life, in the second month, the (**seventeenth day**) of the month, the same day were all the fountains of the great deep broken up, and the windows of heaven were opened." Using our famous 17 and 7 again: (**17 + 7**) = **24** the weight of the (**flooded**) earth in kilograms, or 10^24 power as stated in

Psalm 24:1 "The earth is the LORD's..." So if this is all about Bible covenant (8 x 4) = **32** and the number 17, what is the connection regarding the flood? Genesis **7**:20 "**Fifteen** cubits upward did the waters prevail; and the mountains were covered"; (**32 – 17**) = **15**. All of God's numbers have a rhyme and reason and are tied together by their meanings. Do you get the feeling that **17**, (**7 x 17**) = **119**, and (**7 x 11**) = **77** are here on purpose related to Abraham and Noah's Ark regarding God's covenant promises? Why is the number **17** involved with Noah, water, and the flood? Because the mirror of **17** is **71** a (**17 | 71**) mirror; and the earth is **71%** water!

CHAPTER 6

A Man named **Fibonacci**

L eonardo da Pisa, was born in 1175 AD in Pisa, Italy. Later on he was called Fibonacci. He is responsible for introducing to the Latin world, the decimal number system. Fibonacci is most well known for introducing in his book called Liber abaci the 'Fibonacci numbers'. This number series uses the simple rule: add the last two numbers to get the next number starting with the number 0.

Example: 0, 1, (0 + 1) = 1, (1 + 1) = 2, (1 + 2) = 3, (2 + 3) = 5, (3 + 5) = 8, (5 + 8) = 13.

Here is the Fibonacci number series up to number 17711, the first 23 Fibonacci numbers.

(0, 1, 1, 2, 3, 5, 8, 13, 21, **34, 55, 89**, 144, 233, 377, 610, 987, 1597, 2584, 4181, 6765, 10946, 17711)

The amazing thing about this number set is that these numbers actually appear everywhere in nature. An example would be that some plants branch out in a way that they always have a Fibonacci number of growing points. Flowers such as the daisy have a Fibonacci number of petals, such as **34, 55**, or **89** petals, and these are Fibonacci numbers. Sunflowers have this arrangement in their seeds where they **spiral** outwards both from the left and the right using a Fibonacci number of **spirals**! Many other types of flowers have these Fibonacci number patterns, so do pine cones and pineapples. One of the main features of this number set is the spirals that are created everywhere in nature as a result of the Fibonacci numbers. The nautilus shell is an example of a Fibonacci number spiral, the nautilus shell is on the cover of my first book called *"The Unbroken Wholeness Power of God."* The tip of a growing plant is called the apex. Around the apex of plants grow little bumps called primordia. As these primordia spread out they are pushed out farther and farther apart from the apex, and they grow into the features of the plant, like a flower or leaf or fruit. If you take the angle that these primordia grow, using the center of the seed head as a reference, then one gets an angle of **137.5** degrees. This is very strange that the angle would be this number of **137** as 137 is also our mystery constant of the universe and dimensionless number talked about earlier. The only other angle possible (opposite side) is (360 – 137.5) = **222..5** degrees, and **22** is the Bible number of light and number of characters in the Hebrew alphabet.

Let's take a look at the 13th and 14th Fibonacci numbers **144** and **233**.

Reversing these numbers we have **332** and **441** or how about **33:2** and **44:1** as in Psalm numbers! We know from the Psalms that Psalm **33:2** is about an "Instrument of **10 strings**" and that Psalm **44: 1** is about "**time**"; and that these numbers 33 and 44 are the Planck length (10^{-33}) centimeters and the Planck time 10^{-44} seconds, the smallest measurements in physics. The Fibonacci numbers appear to be the *most key* scriptures backwards or *mirrored*; especially the fact that we found these two main Psalms; 33 and 44 that describe space and time **exactly** on their verse numbers! Now let's look at the **8**[th] Fibonacci number which is **13** and the two numbers on each side of it in the set: (8 and 21). Forwards we would have **81321** and reversed **12318**. Dropping the '1' but keeping the rest of the set intact we have (**2318**). In 1957 in a physics experiment it was discovered, that during certain interactions of the weak force (Psalm **13** is the weak force), that parity or *mirror symmetry* was violated in the universe because of an ultra-tiny particle called a **neutrino**. This is because the neutrino only spins to the left. This is the equivalent of looking into the mirror and seeing your *'same image'* and not your mirror or opposite image; pretty bizarre stuff. There was a book written about this appropriately called **'The God Particle'**. Remember that **10^-13** power is this same weak force that we are talking about for this violation of mirror symmetry, and this is the **8**[th] Fibonacci number which is **13**. So keeping in mind the **8**[th] Fibonacci number is **13**, let's go to the **8**[th] book of the New Testament, which is the 2nd Book of Corinthians, to our mirrored number (**2:318**) and use them as verse numbers: **2**[nd] **Corinthians 3:18** "But we all, with open face beholding as in a **glass** the glory of the Lord, are changed into the *same image* from glory to glory, even as by the **Spirit** of the LORD." Here in this scripture it says "beholding as in a glass" (this word glass is **mirror**); "are changed into the *same image*" just like the parity violation discovered in 1957 from the weak force (**13**) in seeing the *'same image'* in the mirror. To quickly recap for simplicity: the **8**[th] book of the New Testament (**2**[nd] Corinthians) in chapter **3** verse **18** (a **2:318** mirror of the Fibonacci numbers **8132**) contains the answer to the mirror parity violation ("changed into the *same image*"); and the **8**[th] Fibonacci number is **13**, the weak force (of Psalm **13**) where this violation actually occurs in nature! From this we see that God has ingrained His principles in nature, and in His Word, and that they both agree in physical law and number.

Next we have the Torah numbers after the 8, 13, and 21 of our Fibonacci numbers with 34, 55, and 89. The Torah numbers (numbers of letters in the first five books of the Bible: Genesis, Exodus, Leviticus, Numbers and Deuteronomy) are 304805; without the zeroes 34 and 85.

Fibonacci numbers: **34, 55, 89**
Torah numbers: **34** (**5**) **58**, with the (**5**) in the middle as the five books of the Torah, and the 58 reversed from the actual 85 of the Torah numbers 34 85, but all of the Torah numbers are here.

Here are the first 14 Fibonacci numbers with the next numbers to look at in parenthesis.

Forwards:
(0, 1, 1, (**2, 3, 5**), 8, 13, 21, 34, 55, 89, 144, 233)

Backwards: Psalm **33:2**; Psalm **44:1**; Torah numbers **85, 43** or **34, 58**; **2ⁿᵈ** Corinthians **3:18**; Ephesians **5:32**.

(**33:2, 44:1**, 9(**8, 55, 43**), 1(**2, 31, 8**), (**5, 3, 2**), 1, 1, 0)

The 6ᵗʰ Fibonacci number is 5; going backwards from 5 we have (**5 3 2**). Let's look at Ephesians **5:32**.

After the book of Acts in the New Testament there is only one scripture with a chapter number of **5** with a verse number that goes as high as **32**, it's in the book of Ephesians. Ephesians **5:32** "This is a great **mystery**: but I speak concerning Christ and the church." This is another one of those very key mystery scriptures that contains the Fibonacci numbers 2, 3, 5 backwards as **5:32**.

There are two special numbers associated with the Fibonacci sequence called the *golden mean*, they are **.618** and **1.618**; this is because each Fibonacci number divided by the previous one equals this golden mean. An example is (89 / 55) = **1.618** or (144 / 89) = **1.618** or (89 / 144) = **.618**. When a set of (constantly getting smaller) rectangles are drawn within each other using this golden mean as a ratio for the length of their sides, a line can be traced out in a **spiral** pattern that resembles the nautilus shell. Many things in nature such as flowers, plants, fruits, and even galaxies have this pattern. With 1.618 in mind and this being the *'golden'* mean look at **1ˢᵗ Samuel 6:18** "And the (*golden*) mice, according to the number of all the cities of the Philistines belonging to the five lords, both of fenced cities, and of country villages, even unto the great stone of Abel, whereon they set down the **ark of the LORD**: which stone remaineth unto this day in the field of Joshua, the Bethshemite." This is even (**1ˢᵗ** Samuel) chapter **6** verse **18**, as in **1618**; referring to the golden mean mentioning *'golden'* in the third word. The word *'golden'* was found **61** times in the Bible, and we find the number 61 here in 1.(**61**)8 or .(**61**)8 the golden mean. Known also is the fact that the universe is **10^61ˢᵗ** powers in size above the Planck length. Exodus **16:18** "And when they did (**mete**) it with an omer, he that gathered much had nothing over, and he that gathered little had no lack; they gathered every man according to his eating." Exodus **16:18** is measuring (**mete**) as in a meter. The word '**gold**' was found **361** times in the Bible. Our electromagnetism number (19) from Psalm **19** is **61** upside down; and (19 x 19) = **361**. Gold is actually element number **79** in the periodic (chemistry) table and (61 + 18) = **79** as in (.618) joined together by the (**1**). Also gold being found 361 times multiplied out is (3 x 6 x 1) = **18** as in (.6(**18**)). Gold as number **79** added is (7 + 9) =**16** as in (1.6)18. Our '**79**' *chemical number of gold* multiplied as (**7 x 9**) = **63**, and our 79 added as (**7 + 9**) = **16**; both sums yield (**63 + 16**) = **79** (**gold**) again. Nehemiah **7:72** "And that which the rest of the people gave was twenty thousand drams of **gold**, and two thousand pound of **silver**, and threescore and seven priests' garments"; verse numbers (**7 + 72**) = '**79**'. Job 22:25 "Yea, the Almighty shall be thy defence, and thou shalt have plenty of **silver**"; verse numbers (22 + 25) = **47** and **SILVER** is number **47** in the chemical **element** table. The word **SILVER** shows up **282** times in the Bible, a number evenly divisible by 47 (6 x 47) = **282**. Haggai **2:8** "The **silver** is mine, and the **gold** is mine, saith the **LORD of hosts**." Gold (**79**) + Silver (**47**) = **126** and JEHOVAH is **26**.

CHAPTER 7

The Eightfold way a (821 | 128) mirror, and Creation

⟨✦⟩

Genesis 1:1 "In the beginning God created the heaven and the earth." This is what this looks like in Hebrew (יִמֹ וֹאֵת הֹאֹרֵץ בֹּרֹאשֹׁית בֹּרֹא אֹלה יֹמֹ אֹת הֹשֹׁמֹ). Hebrew reads backwards so this would start from your right side. Each Hebrew letter is assigned a value. For instance the word 'God' (אֹלה יֹמֹ) in Hebrew has a value of 86 when all of its letters are added. If you add all of the Hebrew letter values for each word in Genesis 1:1, the first verse of the Bible regarding creation, they equal **2701** (913 + 203 + 86 + 401 + 395 + 407 + 296), which is also the same as the 'mirror multiples': (**37** x **73** = **2701**). In the Bible thirty seven (**37**) numerically means 'Word of the Father' and we are talking about God the Father speaking the universe into existence. The word '**light**' (אֹוֹר יֹוֹם) has 6 characters in the Hebrew language and is encoded in this creation sentence at **2701** skip characters between each letter matching the **2701** value of the creation sentence itself. This means that there are exactly 2701 characters from each letter to letter in the word '**light**', and this is known as an **ELS** or Equidistant Letter Sequence in the Bible. Psalm 27.01 or rather stated Psalm **27:1** says "The Lord is my **light** and my salvation!" We know that the word Jehovah in Hebrew when added equals 26 and this word 'light' in the creation sentence starts on the 26th character from the beginning of the Bible! Finding these kinds of equidistant words in groups of related words shows a pattern. Many words are encoded this way in the Old Testament like crossword puzzles, and many historical events that have related words, appearing close together have been found. Even whole sentences have been found at (ELS) in the Bible. Here is a sample sentence "Gushing from above, Jesus was my mighty name, and the clouds rejoiced"; this whole sentence is encoded in the book of Isaiah chapter 53 at only **20** skip characters between each letter. The mathematical odds of finding this sentence encoded in any book at that low of an equidistant skip code of (20), is about 286 billion times 1 trillion to one!

Another interesting thing about the creation sentence being (37 x 73) = 2701, are the numbers squared that would make these numbers. I have found that squaring numbers and adding them brings out the meaning of the number. We saw this in the name of Jehovah (JHVH) where each character 5, 6, 5, and 10 when all squared and added equal 186, our base number for light speed. If we take the radius size of the whole universe this is 10^{61}power in Planck units; in squaring **(61)** with 6 we get **(36)** and squaring 1 we get **(1)** and (36 + 1) = **37** our left side of the creation mirror **(37 x 73)**. If we take the gravity power number (see Psalm 38) which is 10^{-38} power and square it, we have 3 squared = **(9)** and 8 squared = **(64)** and (9 + 64) = **73**, the right side of the **(37 | 73)** mirror. Using the radius size of the universe **(61)** and gravity **(38)** and squaring and adding them we get **37** and **73**, the multiples of the creation event sentence. Think also of the mystery constant of the universe 137 as a (1 x **37** | **73** x 1) mirror, or (**137** | **731**) mirror of creation. We are also aware of how many scriptures we found related to the **Holy Spirit** and (1 x 3 x 7) = **21**. The mezuzah of Deuteronomy 6 contains **713** characters a (**713** | **317**) mirror; this kind of looks like the weak force (13) and the mass of the electron (31).

More Bible Equidistant Letter Sequence codes (**ELS**)

With this set of ELS codes, we are making them more difficult to find because the word(s) coded must equal what is being talked about in the Bible at that place, and the actual skip code or verse numbers must be significant also! Can other books do this too?

George Bush is found as an ELS code at a continuous sequence as **Bush, George** in Hebrew: (גורגבוש). This is 7 characters in the Hebrew and is found in the book of Nehemiah **12:38** at **4350** skip characters. If you will notice that the code for Bush, George is **4350** skip codes, and that George Bush is the **43rd** president of the fifty **(50)** United States. What an amazing coincidence, don't you think? Even the verse numbers **(12 + 38) = 50**. But wait there is more, right where this code starts for Bush in Nehemiah it talks about *two towers*. It even mentions the *tower of the furnaces*, relating of course to the World Trade Towers. Nehemiah **12:38**-39 "And the other company of them that gave thanks went over against them, and I after them, and the half of the people upon the wall, from beyond the **tower of the furnaces** even unto the broad wall; And from above the gate of Ephraim, and above the old gate, and above the fish gate, and the **tower** of Hananeel, and the **tower** of Meah, even unto the sheep gate: and they stood still in the prison gate." The number **12** in the Bible means government and **38** is gravity or something heavy from Psalm 38; the gravity or burden of the government is on George Bush's shoulders! If you remember that we talked before about Psalm 144 and that 144 was the measure of the man or the angel. Starting at Psalm 144:10 is the word JESUS in Hebrew: (יהושע) ; and it's encoded at **888** skip characters, and we know from the Greek language that His name is '888' numerically. Psalm 144:10 says "It is **he** that giveth salvation unto kings: who delivereth David his servant from the hurtful sword." The "It is **he** that giveth salvation..." here in Psalm 144:10 is Jesus, the '**888**'.

Encoded in the book of Deuteronomy chapter 19:6 is the word **(AMERICA)** at **7613** skip characters between each letter; in Hebrew it looks like this (אמר יקה). In the text two verses away at 19:8 it says "And if the LORD thy God **enlarge thy coast**, as he hath sworn unto thy fathers, and give thee all the **land which he promised to give unto thy fathers.**" Just like the founding fathers of our country and the land God promised to those who came to America for religious freedom; 1776 and **13** colonies (7613 skip code). If we combine the Bible chapter and verse number of Deuteronomy (19:6) where the word America is found (196), with the skip code of (7613) for America, and paste them together we would have (196 + 7613) = (1967613). This is unusual, as the first four numbers of ((**1967**)613) are the year that Israel had their Six Day War, in 1967. Also the last three numbers (**613**) of 1967(**613**) are the exact number of laws for the Jews in the Old Testament. We have the Spirit of '**76**' which represents America; right in the middle of the number set helping and supporting the nation of Israel with the numbers (196(**76**)13). Look what happens if we mirror (1967613 | **3167691**). This mirror number starts out with (**316**)7691; like John **3:16**, the most well known scripture in the **world**, "For God so loved the **world**, that he gave his only begotten Son, that whosoever believeth in him should not perish, but have everlasting life." Next we have the spirit of America '**76**' again in the middle with 316(**76**)91. Finally there is the number **91** as the last two digits of the number 31676(**91**). We all know that **1991** was the year of the Gulf War with Iraq, and that America protected Israel from scud missiles with our patriot missiles. Now look at Psalm **91** again with verses 5-6 "Thou shalt not be afraid for the **terror by night**; nor for the **arrow that flieth by day**; Nor for the pestilence that walketh in darkness; nor for the destruction that wasteth at noonday." Here we have reference to the '**terror** by night' and the '**arrow** that flieth by day'. Terrorism and missiles (**arrows**) in the Psalm number of the same year as these attacks, **1991**. Remember that God promised the Jews the land of Israel as an inheritance forever, which is just like in the scripture above that says "and give thee **all the land** which he promised to give **unto thy fathers**." There is a double meaning here for **America** and **Israel** with the 'land that was promised', and we see the support of America helping God's chosen people, the nation of Israel. The word **ISRAEL** in Hebrew: (**ישראל**) is encoded in Deuteronomy **19:9** at **1359** skip codes (just 3 verses where we started this in Deuteronomy 19:6). Now like we did before for AMERICA, put the verse number for Deuteronomy (**19:9**) where **ISRAEL** is found with the skip code of **1359** and we have (**1991359**). As you can see we have the full year ((**1991**)359) spelled out of the Gulf War, right where the word **ISRAEL** is encoded. Using our verse 19:9 and **1359** skip code we have (1991**359**); the modern day Jewish calendar began in **359** A. D. by Rabbi Hillel. In reference again to the number 359: document #**359** dated January 8, 2002 for the (The

Washington Institute for Near East Policy) named Peace-Watch, is about Israel called: "The Seizure of **Gaza-Bound** Arms: Military Implications." This **1359** skip code is really loaded with relevant information about Israel. Mohammed died in **632** AD and for whatever symbolic reason this may convey **(632 + 1359) = 1991,** the year of the Gulf war. We know from **Psalm 87** that Saddam Hussein restored the old Babylonian Empire and that he that was defeated in **1991.**

Another example of a Bible code is the word **EINSTEIN,** which is found in the book of Daniel 2:21 at 9120 skip characters. In the old Hebrew text at exactly 9120 skips between the letters spells out the word E I N S TE I N in Hebrew: (נ י י נשטנ י י א). This is particularly interesting as the real Bible text at Daniel 2:21-22 says "And he changeth the **times** and the seasons: he removeth kings, and setteth up kings: he giveth **wisdom** unto the wise, and **knowledge** to them that know understanding: He revealeth the **deep and secret things**: he knoweth what is in the darkness, and the **light** dwelleth with him." Is this a coincidence that where Einstein appears at a 9120 ELS skip code, that *time and deep and secret things* are in the scriptures? We all know the mysteries about light, gravity, time, and relativity that Einstein discovered. . The words **ATOMIC** skip (6107) and **SCIENTIST** skip (7240) are both encoded in Daniel **2:22**. The word EINSTEIN, which is the longest way to spell his name in the Hebrew (**9** characters), only shows up *twice* in the whole Old Testament at an ELS skip code. The only other place for EINSTEIN is at a skip code of -16498; and this is in the book of Exodus 21:29 "But if the ox were wont to push with his **horn in time past**"; notice the statement *'horn in time past'* as Einstein, of course was all about **time** and relativity. The word **Albert** is also found in this same verse in Exodus 21:29 at a skip code of 24441, just 5 spaces away from the word **EINSTEIN.**

In Psalm 67:4 encoded at only **-17** skip characters are the words **ATOMIC WEAPON** (כל י אט ומ) in the Hebrew. Psalm 67 only has 7 verses; 5 verses from Psalm 67:4 is Psalm 68:2 "As smoke is driven away, so drive them away: as *wax melteth before the fire*, so let the wicked perish at the **presence of God.**" Where ATOMIC

WEAPON is encoded it says "...as wax **melteth** before the **fire**..." In Psalm 67:6 is the word **URANIUM** encoded at -4228 skip codes and **FIREBALL** is encoded in Psalm 67:3 at 2276 skip codes. The word **NUCLEAR** is encoded in Psalm 67:5 at -16916 skip codes.

The word **ELECTRON** (אלקטרון) at an ELS skip code is found just 25 times in the Old Testament. One of these places where it is encoded is in Genesis **31:4** at **8827** skip codes. We know that the electron's job is to absorb and send out photons of light. There are 10^{88} power photons of light and 10^{27} power is the light of Psalm 27, and look at our skip code again (**8827**). We know that the mass of the ELECTRON is 10^{-31} power, noticing that this ELS code is found in Genesis **31:4** and that Psalm **31:4** says "Pull me out of the **net**..." It might also be noted that the electron has **4** basic different kinds of **orbitals**.

In Genesis **31:2** the word **ORBITAL** is encoded twice, and the word ORBIT is encoded once at **10480** skip codes. A very strange skip code, because Psalm **104** talks about stretching the heavens ((**104**)80); and there are 10^{80} power particles in the universe (104(**80**). Psalm **31:2** says "**Bow down** thine ear to me; deliver me **speedily**..." all about our orbiting *speedy* **ELECTRON**. The words **SPIN** and **WAVE** are also encoded in Genesis 31:4. Also notice that our orbiting ELECTRON is found in verse 31:4 and that 3.14 is **pi**. Recall also from Psalm 31 that the word 'speed' in all its forms is **found 31** times in the Bible.

The word **ELECTRON** is encoded at Exodus 40:**22** at -**18622** skip codes; notice that this skip code is **186** (light speed) and (**22**) Bible light together. Just a few verses later in Exodus 40:24 "And he put the (**candlestick**) in the tent of the congregation..." Exodus 40:25 "And he lighted the (**lamps**) before the LORD; as the LORD commanded Moses." As stated before in regards to Psalm 31; these Exodus verse numbers (40 x 25) = **1000**. The words (**lighted**) and (**lamps**) from our Exodus 40:25 scripture are found together in only 2 scriptures in the whole Bible. The word lamps appears **31** times in the Bible, the word lamp appears **13** times in the Bible, a (13 | 31) mirror of the weak force and the electron. We have the **186** skip code and (**186 x 1000**) = 186,000 miles per second (light speed). We also have the -186(**22**) skip code and (**22 x 1000**) = 22,000, the number the Lord appoints to the sanctuary to administer light to the people in Numbers 3:39. What are the odds that the word ELEC-TRON would be encoded at -**18622** skip codes in a verse talking about 'lamps and light' where the verse numbers (40 x 25) make **1000**, and can be multiplied by the skip code to make sense? Consider also that this started on *light* with the number **22** in Exodus 40:**22**. (40 x 22) = **880** or (10 x 88), or how about 10^**88** power photons of light in the universe. Now consider another 40:22 scripture: Isaiah 40:**22** "It is he that sitteth upon the **circle of the earth**, and the inhabitants thereof are as grasshoppers; that **stretcheth out the heavens as a curtain**, and spreadeth them out as a tent to dwell in." Now lets just add '*Jesus*' as an '**8**' to the skip code of 18622: 1862(**8**)2; now we have the exact (**186,282**) speed of light in miles per second. By the way, all of our verse numbers (4 + 0 + 2 + 2) = **8**.

The Hebrew word for **TITANIC** is: (ק י טנ י ט) and this word is encoded at an ELS code in the Old Testament just 37 times. One of those places is Psalm **124:4** "Then the **waters** had overwhelmed us, the stream had gone over our soul." There are over 23,000 verses in the Old Testament; this would make our odds about 620 to 1 that one of the 37 encoded TITANIC words would land here. The word Titanic is encoded at **12140** skip codes and starts exactly on Psalm **124:4**. The Psalm number **124** holds the year 19(**12**) and month (**4**) April that she hit the iceberg. The skip code **12140** holds the year again (**12**) and the day (**14**) fourteen that the ship hit the iceberg; and the Psalm is talking about "**Then the waters had overwhelmed us...**" The skip code could have been any number from 2 to 65,000 skips for any of these ELS codes. The Hebrew word **SANK** (שקע) is encoded in Psalm **124:7** at **1912** skip codes! **SUNKEN** (שקו ע) is encoded at only **34** skip codes. The word **ICEBERG** (קרח ו נ) is encoded **twice** in this same Psalm **124:7** verse at -5904 and 13835 skip codes. In Psalm **124:7** just four characters from the word 'iceberg' at -5904 skips, is the Hebrew word **HIT** (לקל ו ע) at 10061 skip codes; and 3 characters from the word 'iceberg' is the word **STRUCK** (מושבנת) at 3535 skips. Found as well in Psalm **124:7** is the word **FLOODED** (שׁטוף) at only **66** skip characters. The month and day "**April 14th**" (נ י ס נ ב ו) as one continuous 6 character date, is encoded here at 3283 skip codes in Psalm **124:3**. The year '**1912**' (תרעב) is also here in Psalm 124:3 at only **172** skip codes; the year '**1912**' is also encoded here in Psalm **124:4** at oddly enough -**1249** skip codes. Psalm **124:5** says "**Then the proud** *waters* **had gone over our soul**"; encoded here is the Hebrew word for **DROWNED** (מ וטבע) at 5329 skip codes. The word **RIPPED** (פר ום) is in Psalm 124:7 at **344** skips and the word **HULL** (מכסה) is just **2** characters away at 1482 skip codes; the word **RAMMED** (בט וש) at only -**41** skips is in Psalm **124:6**. In regards to this Psalm number (**124**), remember Psalm (**12:4**) "Who have said, With our tongue will we prevail; our lips are our own: who is lord over us?", and how this fit into our **1912** Psalm of the matching Psalms for 1901– 2050?

In my previous book called: "**The Unbroken Wholeness Power of God – Bible Secrets Revealed**" there is an ELS Bible code matrix of the World Trade Center attack of September 11, 2001. This Bible code contains the most unusual aspects in an ELS code that I have seen. The skip code for the matrix is **2,818** right at the actual death toll; the words **SEPT2001**, INFAMY, BUSH, DEATH, BLOOD SPILLED, **TRADE** (and more) in Hebrew stand up straight like **towers in the code** at **2,818** skip characters. The words 'terror' and 'terrorist' are also found many times in the matrix. The Hebrew word for **Jet** which is 5 characters goes through the word **SEPT2001** at the top of the word (where the first jet hit), and another **Jet** word goes through the word **TRADE** at -54 skips in the spot where the second plane hit! All of the exact Bible positions and a matrix in English are provided from my book "The Unbroken Wholeness Power of God." The main purpose of this book isn't the Bible codes; however I just wanted to let you know that I have found many historical events in the Bible at ELS codes that are unique, in that the main terms and dates can only be found in one spot, and many other people have found unique ELS codes also. Can other books do what we have just shown here with the Bible codes? Especially using verse numbers and specific meaning-ful skip codes, and land on verses describing the meaning of the code in the book as well? Using the WTC matrix attack, I was able to predict about 7 months ahead of time, what the death toll was going to be.

The Bible Codes and the magnificent **Eightfold** Way of **821**

The first five books of the Bible are Genesis, Exodus, Leviticus, Numbers, and Deuteronomy and are called the Torah. In the first book of the Torah called Genesis in the very first verse (Genesis 1:1), the word Torah is encoded at **50** skip characters. In the second book of the Torah called Exodus in the first verse (Exodus 1:1) the word Torah is also encoded at **50** skip characters. In the last book of the Torah called Deuteronomy near the end of the book in Deut. 32:3 is the word Torah again, only this time at **-50** skip characters. In the book of Numbers 34:9 near the end of the book is the word Torah also at **-50** skip characters. Words can be spelled forwards or back-wards with the Bible codes. In the middle of the Torah in the book of Leviticus 13:10 is the word **Jesus at 8** skip characters! The name Jesus is associated with the number eight (**8**) as stated before, Jesus in the Greek language is '888' numerically, and 8 in the Bible means new beginnings and resurrection. This is what this looks like:

Genesis	Exodus	Leviticus	Numbers	Deuteronomy
Torah 50	Torah 50	**Jesus 8**	-50 haroT	-50 haroT

The last two books of the Torah, Numbers and Deuteronomy (at **-50 skip**) mirror the first two books of Genesis and Exodus with the word Torah (at **+50 skip**) and they all point to the *center* of the book of Leviticus chapter 13, where the name of Jesus is encoded at only eight (**8**) skip characters. The lower the skip code the more difficult a word is to find. As just previously stated this means there must be exactly 8 'letters' between each letter of the name **Jesus**. This knowledge had been known before this book was written, however I have found more **ELS skip code** words here next to the name of Jesus in the book of Leviticus. The position number is how many characters from the very beginning of the Bible, in the book of Genesis that a word starts out at. Position number 158954 means 158, 954 characters from Genesis 1:1 where the "In the beginning

God created..." verse starts. It's also interesting to note that the word 'Torah' and 'theory' are interchangeable in the Hebrew language.

This next amazing segment of ELS codes is the 'main segment' of words found in the *very center* of the five (5) books of the Torah. This amazing and important segment is also just five (5) words.

English	Verse	Position	Skip	Hebrew word
offering	Leviticus 13:10	158592	882	מתנה
priest	Leviticus 13:10	158593	-882	גלח
Jesus	Leviticus 13:10	158594	8	ישוע
Levitical	Leviticus 13:10	158594	-821	לוי י
symmetry	Leviticus 13:10	158595	821	תואם

As you can see there are five words all contained within the same verse in Leviticus 13:10; (offering and priest) at **882 and -882** skip codes as a positive/negative pair, and the words (Levitical and symmetry) at **-821 and 821** skip codes as a positive/negative pair. The word **Jesus** fits in right between them at a skip code of just eight (**8**) in the middle at position of 158594. Observe how tight these words are (offering, priest, Jesus, Levitical, symmetry) at only one position away from each other; spanning positions 158592-158595, a range of just *4 characters*! What are the chances that these mirror counterpart Hebrew words at (882 and 821) skip codes are all in the same verse in the middle of the Torah, when the word Torah itself is mirrored (at +50 and -50 skip codes) pointing to this book of Leviticus? It appears that we have these five words mirroring the five books of the mirrored Torah, right smack in the **center** of the **Torah**. Also consider the fact that related words, such as (Levitical **-821** and symmetry **821**) are mirror partners (a negative and a positive) skip code, right next to each other (one character away) in the very same verse; and that the negative skips are the inner ones, right next to the eight! These words point to the day when Jesus, as our Levitical priest and king, would shed His blood as an offering for our sins. In a few moments we will also see why these numbers **882 and 821** are important in the world of physics and how they describe some of the most important forces of our universe.

When I had first discovered these symmetry pairs I didn't realize the significance of the numbers 882 and 821, the skip codes right next to Jesus name in Leviticus 13:10. Keep in mind that the Tabernacle of Moses, as we have said and shown is a pattern of the universe and space time dimensions, and the earthly model of the heavenly model. Hebrews 8:5 "Who serve unto the example and **shadow** of **heavenly things**, as Moses was admonished of God when he was about to make the tabernacle: for, See, saith he, that thou make all things **according to the pattern** shewed to thee in the mount." As we had mentioned before in a previous chapter, that the Eightfold way, which is a system of the classification of particles, was introduced to the world in the early 1960's. The Eightfold way is a classification system for all of the elementary particles in physics, and was presented to the world in **1961**. All of the protons and neutrons that make up the center of the atom are made of yet smaller particles called **quarks**. There are three quarks that make up every proton and neutron in the universe. These three quarks that make up these particles are never separated, they always stick together as a set. They are like a **(holy trinity)** that can't be separated. Quarks have strange properties, in that they get weaker when they get closer to one another and stronger the farther away that they get from one other! The only verse in the Bible where '**threefold**' appears is in Ecclesiastes **4:12** "And if **one** prevail against him, **two** shall withstand him; and a **threefold cord** is not quickly broken." Divide verse numbers (**412 by 3** quarks) = **137**. 3, the mystery constant! If you remember the dog in the movie "Honey I shrunk the kids" was named Quark. **Two** up quarks and **one** down quark make up a proton and **two** down quarks and **one** up quark make up a neutron. There are six (6) different kinds of quarks named: up quark, down quark, top quark, bottom quark, charm quark, and strange quark. These six (6) quarks are the foundation of all the particles and the forces that interact between the particles in the universe.

The **Eightfold way** system is explained by the arrangement of quarks within the particles that are forming the patterns of the

Eightfold way. This system was a great success and helped the classification of all particles as well as predicting the existence of new particles. The symmetry used to measure this system is called SU(**3**) x SU(**2**) x SU(**1**) gauge symmetry. Gauge symmetry is simply a way to measure something. It's like saying: how can I do some operation to a field of particles and the symmetry still remains the same? Think of a ball, no matter which way you rotate the ball it still looks the same as far as its shape is concerned; whereas if you rotated a cardboard box, its shape would look different from other angles. The important thing to know here is that in the SU(**3**) part of the gauge symmetry, (SU means 'special unitary group'), is that there are **eight** possible transformations. This means that all **eight** of the particles can be transformed into the others. This is also like saying that the particles rotate in an eight-dimensional mathematical space, although not the same thing as the 10 dimensional universe space. These eight (**8**) particles are called **gluons** and mediate the *color force* which operates between the quarks. This color force isn't like what we think of as the color of an object, such as red, but has to do with the three (3) ways, as the name 'SU(**3**)' implies; that the quarks can be pointed in any direction at 120 degrees from each other. A full circle is 120 degrees x 3 (quarks) which is 360 degrees. There are then **eight** transformations possible for the SU(**3**) part of the gauge theory for the particles. The SU(2) part of the theory only has **two** possible dimensions or transformations, having to do with neutrons and protons called *isotopic spin*. Isotopic spin is like an up or down internal pointer for neutrons and protons, where they both exist in a different 'quantum state', but are the same particle!

The SU(**1**) part of the theory has only **one** possible transformation, and this has to do with electromagnetism. What we have here in this gauge symmetry are (**8**) transformations, (**2**) transformations, and (**1**) transformation, and (**821**) is the same **main skip code number** found in the center of the book of Leviticus for the words Levitical and symmetry. Remember, this is how all of the particles in the universe work using this **821 Eightfold Way**, also considering that **Jesus** is always associated with the number **8**. Another consideration for the **821** number dealing with nature and transformation is: Romans **8:21** "Because the creature itself also shall be **delivered** from the *bondage of corruption* into the glorious **liberty** of the children of God." This is why the **821** skip code is in the middle of the Torah, it's looking to the day when the saviour **Jesus** will die on the cross and actually deliver the 'creation' from **bondage**; totally awesome and the numbers match the scripture! The number **21** in the Bible (according to scholars) represents the '**exceeding sinfulness of sin'**; so this makes sense that Jesus (**8**) would die for our sinful **nature** (**21**), **8** and **21** together. We also talked about the number **21** being (1 x 3 x 7) = **21**; and how this related to the **Holy Spirit**. How can this number **21** be both the "Holy Spirit" and the "exceeding sinfulness of sin?" This is because God's Spirit got messy and involved with us at the deepest level in this scripture: Romans **8:16** "The **Spirit** itself beareth witness **with our spirit**, that we are the children of **God**." Notice that this says "**with** our spirit." This forgiveness for **sin** takes '*grace*' and **5** in the Bible is the number of grace (816 + 5) = **821**. Using our verse numbers again from Romans **8:16** (8 x 16) = **128** the mirror to 821: (**128 | 821**). Relating this to our **old nature**, the word 'flesh' appears **128** times in the New Testament. Two of these particles that we are talking about in the Eightfold way are actually called the (lambda) as in the Lamb of God, and the (omega-minus) as in Jesus the Omega. The first paper of this theory was sent in during the year **1961**, and **1961** is very important so hang on to that year.

There are just **5** string theories. The heterotic string theory called **E8 x E8** talked about before has to do with this very same SU(3) x SU(2) x SU(1) gauge symmetry of the *Eightfold Way*. In fact, *everything* in particle physics is included in one of the (E8) parts of this E8 x E8 symmetry group. Keep in mind that we have the skip codes of (offering at **882** and priest at -**882**) right next to the word Jesus at eight (**8**) skip codes in the book of Leviticus. The **E8 x E8** string theory is actually *two worlds of eight* living right next to each other; as the skip code of (**882**) suggests. The other string theory (of the **5**) that offers the most hope is the SO(32) symmetry group; this group removes the infinities encountered with the other string theories. This is interesting also, because in using our **882** number we have: (**8 + 8 = 16**) and (**16 x 2**) = **32** as in

SO(32). The number **32** means 'covenant' in the Bible, and this would certainly be like the duality of joining different string theories together; just like God's desire is to join Himself with man in a covenant bond. Both of these **E8 x E8** and **SO(32)** string theories deal the with the extra **16** dimensions or **cancellations** we talked about earlier in the Tabernacle of Moses. The number **16** in the Bible means **love**. The amazing thing is that when you take **882** (E8 x E8) and minus **821** (our gauge symmetry transformation number) from it, you get the number **61**, the year (**1961**) in which the **Eightfold way** was discovered! If you turn **61** upside down you get **19**, the electromagnetism number from Psalm **19**. Now paste (19 + 61) together and you get the year (**1961**), the actual year of the theory. Now we have up and down symmetry as (19 is 61 upside down) just like the quarks have up and down symmetry that make up the particles. Just as a side note; Roger Maris (a New York Yankee) hit 61 home runs in 1961 and Yankee stadium is on 161st Street. In the year **1961** the first man went into space, his name was Yuri Gagarin.

Here are these **882** and **821** codes again:

English	Verse	Position	Skip	Hebrew word
offering	Leviticus 13:10	158592	**882**	מת נה
priest	Leviticus 13:10	158593	-882	גלח
Jesus	Leviticus 13:10	158594	**8**	ישׁוע
Levitical	Leviticus 13:10	158594	-821	לוויי
symmetry	Leviticus 13:10	158595	**821**	תואם

Here is the simple math (882 – 821) = **61**

It's now known that the size of the radius of the universe is 10 to the **61**st power times the Planck length, which equates to about 15 billion light-years. Again we see the importance of the number **61**; it's also the radius size of the whole universe! This also means that a universe that has the reciprocal of this value in size, (like a tiny circular dimension) which is 10 to the -61st power, has the same physical qualities as the large universe, as long as the symmetry remains. This power number of **61** (times the Planck length), is just one number bigger than 60 and puts it very close to our Psalm 60 number of the broken universe, especially considering the fact that the universe is being stretched, it's getting bigger! Science even says that if the universe is being stretched and getting bigger, then the symmetry of *string theory* says that it also means that the Planck length must be getting smaller. This is because the large/small symmetry must remain.

The main issue here is that the number 61 is the number that we get when we take 882 and minus 821 from it. This is incredible because of the fact, that in the middle of the symmetry of the Torah, we would find these power symmetry numbers (882 and 821); numbers that describe the size and symmetry theories of the *whole universe*! If 61 is the radius size of the universe, then let's flip the number 61 over and we get 19, which we know from Psalm 19, is all about electricity and electromagnetism. The number nineteen (**19**) in the Bible also represents faith. With the 1961 number we have electromagnetism next to the symmetry of size, and it doesn't matter if we turn the universe upside down because (19 = 61 upside down) and (61 = 19 upside down) and the symmetry remains the same. Consider also that our 1961 numbers multiplied out (1 x 9 x 6 x 1) = **54** which is all of our four forces of the universe numbers when added together: (1) = Strong force, (2) = Electromagnetic force, (13) = Weak force, (38) = Gravity: (1 + 2 + 13 + 38) = 54. It's said also of the real universe, that if (in theory), we changed all positive particles to negative ones, and changed all negative particles to the positive ones, that the universe wouldn't care as its symmetry was not affected. Is symmetry a dimension all of its own? Mirror symmetry sure is a mysterious quality of the universe. I really think that this 'mirror symmetry' deals with the invisible '**inner** spirit universe' that lives within us; and the realms of the 'seen' **outer** space-time dimensions. Maybe the difference in symmetry, and the fact that we live in a broken symmetry is the actual holographic reflection that makes up our universe. Keep in mind that God and heaven would have a perfect symmetry. In this sense, we are just a fraction or fractal of the real reality of God's true light. Symmetry is awesome, but what lives on the edge of the mirror in between the symmetry is even more mysterious. The study of membranes and holographic surfaces is a big part of M-theory and string-theory.

Some more interesting facts about the number **1961** are that if you add these power numbers together (19 + 61) you get **80** and 10 to the 80th power is the number of particles in the universe. If you subtract 19 from 61 you get forty-two (**42**), and we know that the **earth** is 10 to the 42nd power times larger than the Planck length. Also forty-two (42) is the: ***power number of light wave cycles*** from Psalm **42**. The earth's mass is 10^{24th} power kilograms as we have seen in Psalm 24 "The **Earth** is the Lord's, and the fullness thereof". The number (24) is a mirror of the number (42), the size of Earth times the Planck length. Look at what I call the Matthew mirror: Matthew **24:42** "Watch therefore: for ye know not what (**hour**) your Lord doth come." Here we are warned about the hour (**24 *hours*** in a day) that Jesus will return to the earth (size of **earth** being **42** times the Planck length) in verse 24:42 of the book of Matthew; a (**24 | 42**) mirror. If you add the light of Jesus at eight (8) skip characters to our 1961 with the numbers (19 + 61 + 8), then you get **88**; and 10 to the 88th power is the number of light particles (photons) in the universe. We also know that Jesus, always associated with the eight's as in (88), is the light. You remember before in chapter five how we talked about the mystery number and dimensionless coupling constant of string theory, the number **137**. If we add all the numbers of 137 then we have (1 + 3 + 7) = **11**. If we square the individual numbers in 137 and then add them together we have (1 + 9 + 49) = **59**. If you will recall, the square root of the Torah numbers (**3485**) is **59**.033888. If we just pasted these two together next to each other we have (11 and 59) = **1159**. It just so happens that our symmetry numbers when multiplied together (**19 x 61**), equal **1159** also.

Keep in mind that **70** means 'the restoration of Israel' and also 70 is God's perfect number (7 times 10), a magnification of His power. We get **70** from just adding (**11 + 59**) together. There really seems to be a lot within this 137 number. Also be advised that maybe God is trying to tell us something with the number 1159.

When the time is **11:59 pm**, there's just one minute until *midnight* and the day is over. Matthew **25:6** "And at *midnight* there was a cry made, Behold, the bridegroom cometh; go ye out to meet him." Be aware of what day you live in and what time it is in history and God's timetable. I noticed something incredible here as this scripture in Matthew **25:6** says: "...at *midnight* there was a cry made..." This is the end time when Jesus comes for the bridegroom. Remember all of those Psalms that have the meanings of the same year as the Psalm number, and the fact that there are only **150** Psalms? What happens after these **150** years are over, which would be the year **2050** because our Psalms started in 1901? These verse numbers for Matthew 25:6 are (**25 x 6**) = **150**! Exodus **25:6** says "**Oil** for the light, spices for anointing **oil**, and for sweet incense." Just prior to this is: Matthew **25:3-4** "They that were foolish took their **lamps**, and took no **oil** with them. But the wise took **oil** in their vessels with their **lamps**." You are going to need *Holy Spirit* **oil** and **power** in the last days. Don't think that you can wait until **2049** to get right with God because of this: **Luke 12:20** "But **God** said unto him, **Thou fool**, this **night** thy **soul** shall be required of thee: then whose shall those things be, which thou hast provided?" I am not really trying to make a prediction here because the Lord will move according to His own timetable. Rather the idea is to make us aware of when things could happen, and just how accurate the scriptures are when it comes to verse numbers and years.

There is another very important fact of the mystery number 137, because it's the fine structure constant value, but only at very low energies. This 137 constant becomes a changing or running constant as the energy gets higher. At higher energies and short distances this fine structure constant number of physics is the number 128. This very important **128** 'constant' is derived from a measurement of the mass of the W boson particle (mentioned in the weak force of Psalm 13). The only place in the whole Bible where the word *'constant'* shows up is in: **1st Chronicles 28**:7 "Moreover I will establish his kingdom for ever, if he be (*constant*) to do my commandments and my judgments, as at this day." This is Chronicles the **1st** book verse **28:7** or **128**:7 just using the numbers; subtle and truly awesome. Even the word '**constantly**' shows up just three times in the whole

Bible, and look what we find embedded in Proverbs **21:28** "A false witness shall perish: but the man that heareth speaketh (**constantly**)." Speaking of the **128** constant being a measurement; the word 'measure' as the root word in: measure, measures, or measured shows up **128** times in the Bible. Any form of the word constant and measurement seems to be related to the **128** number. This 128 constant is related to the mass of the W boson particle at about 80 GeV (GeV = Giga electron Volts); Giga means billion. Our **821** transformation number of the Eightfold Way found in Leviticus **13:10** (words: Levitical and symmetry) is the mirror of the mystery constant at high energy **128**; a (**128 | 821**) mirror. Isn't this also interesting that this is Leviticus chapter **13:10** and that **10^13** power is the weak interaction as in **Psalm 13**. The fact is that this whole symmetry exists because Jesus Christ became weak and died as the *Lamb of God* for our sins so that we could become strong and be saved. What an incredible symmetry of the weak and the strong forces that we see in all of these verses.

The **128** physics constant is a mirror to the 821 transformation number (**821 | 128**), and they both are the most core numbers that describe the particles and forces of the universe. If we add all of the numbers in 128 we get $(1 + 2 + 8) = 11$, which is just like the fact that the $(1 + 3 + 7$ mystery number added$) = 11$, as in the eleven dimensions of the universe. If we add the sums of the squares of 128 $(1 + 4 + 64)$ we get **69**; now add both and $(11 + 69) = 80$. We know that 10 to the **80th** power is the number of particles in the universe, and that the weak interaction of the W boson particle is around **80** GeV dealing with this 128 number. We also know that Psalm 80 is where spirit and matter come together because Psalm 80 is talking about God, and says "...thou that dwellest between the cherubims..."; referring to the Ark of the Covenant. The two angels at size 144 on the Ark of the Covenant $(144 + 144) = 288$, the mirror to our **882** number (from Leviticus 13:10); a (**288 | 882**) mirror of two worlds (like the **E8 x E8** string theory). The Ark of the Covenant is two worlds coming together where God met man! Remembering from before that $(882 - 821) = 61$. If we take our 882 number (skip code for priest and offering) in Leviticus 13:10 and multiply it by all its numbers, we have $(8 \times 8 \times 2) = 128$, the fine structure constant and mirror to our **821** number! If we multiply our 821 number the same way, we get (8 x 2 x 1) = **16** (our cancellation number) and the mirror to our **61** (universe radius size): a **(16 | 61)** mirror. If we divide our 128 by 16 (cancellation number) we get (128 / 16) = **8**; the skip code for **Jesus** in between these 882 and 821 numbers. Even if we use the mirrors of 882 and 821 we would have (288 – 128) which is 160, which is the mirror to 061, or drop the zero and we have 61 again. If we take our 821 number and break it up and multiply it like this: **(8 x 21)** then we have **168**. This 168 number is the total number of (photons **10^88** power and particles **10^80** power) in the universe as: (88 + 80) = **168**. Also we know that within this 168 number is (16 x 8) = 128; the mirror to our 821 or (8 x 21) number where we started. Now just spin (6) quarks in the Eightfold way (8) and reverse the 6 and 8 in our **168** number and we have **186**, our base number for light speed! Is this cool or what? All of these most important numbers for the universe and their factors describe the most important number constants and they are encoded in the very center of the Torah along with Jesus **(8)** who of course made it all! These are among the tightest and most magnificent **ELS** codes found in the Bible, especially where they are found!

If we divide **19** into **61** we get **3.21**, which are the same numbers as in SU(3) x SU(2) x SU(1) gauge symmetry where it all started. Philippians **3:21** says "Who shall change our **vile body**, that it may be fashioned like unto his **glorious body**, according to the working whereby he is able even to subdue all things unto himself." In relation to the **821** number: Romans **8:21** "Because the creature itself also shall be delivered from the **bondage of corruption** into the **glorious liberty** of the children of God." The 3.21 is incredible because it relates to the 821 gauge symmetry and we have these two scriptures (Phil 3:21 and Romans 8:21) talking about us *being changed*. If we divide 61 into 19 we get the decimal .3114. The **(114)** part of this decimal repeats over and over again, and just doesn't seem to end. Here is a sample of just five rows of (61divided into **19**) as .3114754098360...etc. The **114** part is at the beginning of every row for easy viewing/counting. Here's (61 divided into 19) with a sampling of its repeating decimals as we leave the .3 on the first row for clarity.

.3
11475409836065573770491803278688524590163934426229508196721 3
11475409836065573770491803278688524590163934426229508196721 3
11475409836065573770491803278688524590163934426229508196721 3
11475409836065573770491803278688524590163934426229508196721 3
11475409836065573770491803278688524590163934426229508196721 3

We know that the number 114 is the number that science uses to measure the energy of the quantum vacuum. This number is the energy density of the zero-point fluctuations in empty space and is 10 to the **114th power**. This is a number with 114 zero's in it and that is a whole lot of energy. Zero point fluctuations means that the energy of the quantum vacuum (so-called empty space) is never at rest. It's never zero, it always has some energy, otherwise it would disobey the *uncertainty principle*, and we would know where the particle is and this isn't allowed in quantum physics. This 114 power number is actually the measurement of the energy of a cubic meter of empty space using the joules measurement system. A joule is a unit of energy required to lift something weighing one pound about nine inches. If you will notice by counting the characters in our row display of the decimal (61 divided into 19 = .3114), that the number **114** repeats every **61st character**! Here we have the quantum vacuum energy of the universe (**114**) power number; repeating itself exactly every **61st number**, and we know that 61 is the size/symmetry (10 to the 61st power) radius size of the universe found in the center of the Torah: (882 − 821 = **61**). This 114 power number, *in our decimals*, just keeps circling the universe at a circular radius of size 61 when (energy (19) is divided by the universal size of (61)).

As stated before the first five books of the Bible called the Torah (Genesis, Exodus, Leviticus, Numbers, and Deuteronomy) have exactly 304,805 characters in them. If we take these numbers (304,805) and square and add them all together we have (9 + 0 + 16 + 64 + 0 + 25), and they all equal **114**, the vacuum energy number! Could this be any more incredible? The Torah, which holds the mystery symmetry numbers in the center by the ELS skip codes (882 and 821), also equals the energy of the quantum vacuum number 114 when squared and added together. This is just like in Einstein's formula of E=MC squared, in that when we square C, the speed of light, the true hidden power is released, just like in squaring the Torah numbers. Remember also, that the inches measurement of the **Ark of the Covenant** (2 ½ x 1 ½ x 1 ½ cubits) converted is (52 + 31.2 + 31.2) inches equals **114**. We also know that Psalm **114** matches our power number of 114 with Psalm 114 "… **Tremble, thou earth**, at the presence of the **Lord**, at the presence of the **God of Jacob**." If you recall we had previously stated that science is now saying that the universe is made out of information. Now consider how much information would be in the quantum vacuum of so-called empty space because the vacuum holds such incredible power; even within an incredible tiny area. This means that in the small area of empty space the size of a proton, there is more energy than all of the matter in the whole universe! If we turn our 114 (power of the quantum vacuum) number around and mirror it then we have 411 as in (**114 | 411**); the number that we all know as being (**411 = information**). If you want to (call **411**) on God for information, He has the power (**114**) to answer you! Also remember that the new element Ununquadium is an island of stability and has an atomic number of **114**. The Higgs boson has already been stated to probably come in with the energy of 114 GeV. The Higgs boson is the force field that gives mass to everything in the universe; without the Higgs field all of the elements in your body would just fly apart! There is a secret about the Higgs boson that will be revealed at the end of the book, so hang on for a while and the secret will be unveiled.

The symmetry of the **Elevens** in Creation

Let's look at another example of some symmetry that is related to creation. We are going to look at a progression of multiples of the number eleven, as if it were creation to see what happens. We will look at the numbers (1 x 1) = 1

$$(1 \times 11) = 11$$
$$(2 \times 11) = 22$$
$$(3 \times 11) = 33$$
$$(4 \times 11) = 44$$

This is five (5) levels of a progression of elevens starting from the number one. We are doing this knowing that we live in an eleven (11) dimensional universe with five (5) string theories. It will look like this below starting with the number one.

    1. Oneness and beginning.
  11. Disorder.
  22. Light.
  33. Space.
  44. Time.

The number 1   Geneses 1:1 "In the **beginning** God created the heaven and the earth."

This is the beginning coming out of the oneness (**1**) and wholeness of God causing the creation event.

The number 11   Geneses 1:2 "And the earth was **without form**."

Here we have the eleven (**11**) dimensional universe and the fact that the number eleven actually means disorder, and notice that the earth was **without form** and is in disorder!

The number 22   Genesis 1:3 "And God said, Let there be **light**: and there was **light**."

We know that the number (**22**) in the Bible means light. There are also 22 characters in the Hebrew language.

The number 33   Genesis 1:4 "And God saw the light, that it was good: and God **divided** the light from the **darkness**."

We also know that (**33**) is 10^-33 centimeters as in the Planck length, which represents a base

128

measurement of space and the heavens, as God divides the light from the darkness and creates **space**.

The number 44 — Genesis 1:5 "And God called the light **Day**, and the darkness he called Night. And the Evening and the morning were **the first day**."

God has just created everything in space and now **time** has gone forth as the 'evening and the morning of the first day', recalling that (**44**) is $10^\wedge$ -44 seconds, the Planck time.

Looking at this progression of elevens (11's) and seeing how it relates to creation is awesome because each verse of the Bible in Genesis is actually is related in meaning to the numbers 1, 11, 22, 33, and 44, our Bible and physics numbers. However let's look at all of these numbers if we add their squares. An example of this is the number 22 by squaring and adding the two's (2 squared = (4) + 2 squared = (4)) = 8; which is the same as (4) + (4) = 8.

1	1 squared (1)	= **1**
11	1 squared (1) + 1 squared (1)	= **2**
22	2 squared (4) + 2 squared (4)	= **8**
33	3 squared (9) + 3 squared (9)	= 18
44	4 squared (16) + 4 squared (16)	= 32

Now starting at the bottom with the number 32 we will list all of the numbers together, going from the bottom to the top (32, 18, 8, 2, 1), which as two sets is (**321**) and (**8821**). All of our symmetry numbers from Leviticus are now here again, only this time in the creation event as we have '321' as coming from (19 divided into 61 = 3.21) and as '321' with SU(3) x SU(2) x SU(1) gauge symmetry. Also we have the numbers '**8821**'. These are the same numbers as in our (882 and 821) symmetry numbers again from the book of Leviticus. This time however, the 882 and 821 are now connected by a common number eight (8) and are embedded within each other as ((**882**)1) or the same numbers as (8(**821**)).

Take a look at them like this: 8(8)2
(8)21

8(8)21

You can see the connection with the beginning eight of (8)21, and the middle eight of 8(8)2, as the common eight (8) among them within the 8(8)21 sequence. We are recalling also that the E8 x E8 string theory is two worlds living next to each other (**882**). Also the fact that Jesus is both God and man and is literally the bridge between these two worlds (heaven and earth), as the number eight (8)! Jesus can float and move between these two worlds. Look at Matthew 28:18 "And Jesus came and spake unto them, saying, All power is given unto me in heaven and in earth." Matthew **28:8** "And they departed quickly from the **sepulchre** with fear and great joy; and did run to bring his disciples word"; an (**882 | 288**) mirror of two worlds (heaven and earth) and the resurrection of the dead! Acts 1:9-11 "And when he had spoken these things, while they beheld, he was taken up; and a cloud received him out of their sight. And while they looked stedfastly toward heaven as he went up, behold, two men stood by them in white apparel; Which also said, Ye men of Galilee, why stand ye gazing up into heaven, this same Jesus, which is taken up from you into heaven, shall so come in like manner as ye have seen him go into heaven." Jesus can come and go from earth to heaven and heaven to earth at His own will as these scriptures say. Let's see why this extra floating eight is important.

Looking back at the center of the book of Leviticus to our main code segment we have the following:

English	Verse	Position	Skip	Hebrew word
offering	Leviticus 13:10	158592	882	מתנה
priest	Leviticus 13:10	158593	-882	גלח
Jesus	Leviticus 13:10	**158594**	**8**	ישוע
Levitical	Leviticus 13:10	**158594**	**-821**	לויי
symmetry	Leviticus 13:10	158595	821	תואם

The floating eight is the name of Jesus at eight (8) skip characters in the middle of the mirrored Torah. Notice that the words (Jesus and Levitical) start on the exact same Bible position number, which is: 158,594. Keep in mind, that these words as Hebrew words, can share some of the same characters. Even here we see that the eight (8) in Jesus skip code is embedded within the -821 skip code of the Levitical symmetry number (-821); it's on the very same position (158,594)! This is absolutely incredible and matches our sequence of eleven numbers for creation (8821); knowing that we live in an **eleven** dimensional universe. Remember also that concerning creation is John **1:1** "In the beginning was the Word...", with Jesus as the Word who also is the eight (8) that created all things. Computer words are also based on the number eight; computers are an octal system with evenly banked memory divisible by eight such as 64, 128, 256, 512, or 1024 bytes and on and on. With a computer eight bits equals one byte. One byte or (eight bits) is what is takes to define just one character typed in from your keyboard to the computer screen, or one character stored in a document. Now back to our 321 8821 number sets from creation, if you will also notice that (8 + 8 + 2 + 1) even equals 19; our 61 number if turned upside down. Also if we include the '321' part then (3 + 2 + 1) = 6. If we paste them together (like we did with the 19 + 61) we have (**6 + 19**) which is now 619, and this (**619**) number has the same (symmetry), even if we turned it upside down, just like 1961. Also we have retained our 61 (size) and 19 (electromagnetism) numbers by making them one in (619) by joining the middle ones as in (**6(1)9**). Now just like our number (8) for Jesus, which was imbedded within another (8) within the -821 skip code, the number one (1) is embedded between the 6 and the 9 and is shared by them both. We can now read our power numbers of the universe as 61 or 19 with a shared one (1) in the middle: 6(1)9. Look at the number **619** in the scripture in Hebrews **6:19** "Which hope we have as an anchor of the soul, both sure and stedfast, and which entereth into that **within the veil**." Talk about power and oneness as this **6:19** goes right from the **earth** to within the veil of **heaven**! Another 619 verse: 1st Corinthians **6:19** "What? know ye not that your body is the temple of the Holy Ghost which is in you, which ye have of God, and ye are not your own?" Now 619 in Ephesians: Ephesians

6:19 "And for me, that utterance may be given unto me, that I may open my mouth boldly, to make known the mystery of the gospel." Matthew **6:19** "Lay not up for yourselves treasures upon earth, where moth and rust doth corrupt, and where thieves break through and steal." John **6:19** "So when they had rowed about five and twenty or thirty furlongs, they see Jesus walking on the sea, and drawing nigh unto the ship: and they were afraid." Also 619 in Luke **6:19** "And the whole multitude sought to touch him: for there went virtue out of him, and healed them all." Here we have the unbroken wholeness power of Jesus as pure virtue coming out and healing everyone who touches Him. We have all of these power scriptures in **6:19** numbered verses. Hang on a moment and we'll see what this 619 number is all about.

A prime number is any positive integer number that can be divided by itself or the number one only. Here are the first 18 prime numbers 2, 3, 5, 7, 11, 13, 17, (**19**), 23, 29, 31, 37, 41, 43, 47, 53, 59, (**61**). You can see that the numbers **19**, (8th in the set) and **61**, (18th in the set); are also prime numbers. If we took which prime numbers that 19 and 61 represented, and added them, then (8 + 18) = **26**, the total number of dimensions of the universe and name of Jehovah (5 + 6 + 5 + 10) = 26! If we multiplied these prime numbers (8 x 18) then we have **144**; the size of the man or the angel from Revelation 21:17. The number '619' also is a prime number; in fact the number '**619**' is the **114th** prime number! As a matter of fact (**6 x 19**) also equals **114**. We know by now how powerful our 114 number is, with all the places in nature and the Bible it shows up. As well we know how it (114) relates to both forms of our symmetry numbers of **1961** and **619**, which both look the same even when turned upside down.

CHAPTER 8

Codes, Bible words, and the English language

W hat about the English language, does it contain codes? These are not directly related to the Bible, but I thought that you would find these very interesting and fun. Here is a grid of values assigned to the English language, these are numbers 1 – 26 covering A – Z and the numbers above these are the numbers squared. We talked before how that simply squaring numbers seems to bring out the essence of the number, such as in squaring: J=10, H=5, V=6, H=5 in JeHoVaH to make (100 + 25 + 36 + 25) = 186 our light speed number.

1	4	9	16	25	36	49	64	81	100	121	144	169
1	2	3	4	5	6	7	8	9	10	11	12	13
A	B	C	D	E	F	G	H	I	J	K	L	M

196	225	256	289	324	361	400	441	484	529	576	625	676
14	15	16	17	18	19	20	21	22	23	24	25	26
N	O	P	Q	R	S	T	U	V	W	X	Y	Z

133

Let's add up the name of Jesus to see what it equals J=**10**, E=**5**, S=**19**, U=**21**, S=**19** for a total of **74**. Jesus equals **74** in English. For three years, just recently, scientists did an experiment in a particle accelerator to come up with a whole new mathematical constant. Eighty-eight (**88**) million particle collisions later they came up with a new number that represents the difference between **matter** and **anti-matter** in the universe, and yes you guessed it, *or came close*, as the number is **.74**!

JESUS = **74**. All of the name of Jesus in English squared and added (J=100 + E=25 + S=361 + U=441 + S=361) = **1288**. The mirror to 1288 is a (**1288 | 8821**) mirror; this brings us right back to our numbers from the center of the Torah and the progression of elevens in the creation event (**8821**), matching the 821 and 882 numbers of particle physics. With the **74** number also consider that (**7 + 4**) = **11** and that (**7 x 4**) = 28; just add the ones (**11**): (128 | 821). The 49th element is called Indium; it has an atomic mass of **114** (Word made flesh) and a relative density or *specific gravity* of **7.4**.

Here is the word **FAITH** in English with its numerical values.

F   A   I   T   H

6   1   9   20   8   (**619 208**)

We didn't even have to add this one; it's our power number (619) and (208) atomic weight of anti-gravity from Psalm 83; what a power word! Remember also that **26** (JeHoVaH) x Jesus (**8**) = **208**. The word **FAITH** just added (6 + 1 + 9 + 20 + 8) = 44 having to do with time; see Psalm 44. Only one scripture in the whole Bible has the word 'faith' and 'time' together in the King James version of the Bible: 1st Peter 1:5 "Who are kept by the **power** of God through (**faith**) unto salvation ready to be revealed in the last (**time**)." This is a real power word: **FAITH**, as the words 'kept by the power of God' are in this faith scripture.

F   A   I   T   H   F   U   L

6   1   9   20   8   6   21   12 (6 + 1 + 9 + 20 + 8 + 6 + 21 + 12) = **83**. This is our anti-gravity number again from Psalm 83. Your faithfulness lifts you above the natural realm with anti-gravity.

P   R   A   Y   E   R

16 18   1   25   5   18   (16 + 18 + 1 + 25 + 5 + 18) = **83**.

G   O   D

7   15   4   (7 + 15 + 4) = **26**; just like JHVH in Hebrew = (10 + 5 + 6 + 5) = **26**.

Now we are going to square and add all of the values in the words **JESUS CHRIST** to see the power of squaring. The English language seems to contain codes for scientific numbers. This one really blew my mind when I squared them and added them for each name.

Remember we are using the squares of the alphabet numbers such as H=8, which equals 64 when squared.

J   E   S   U   S   C   H   R   I   S   T

100 25 361 441 361 = **1288**   9   64 324 81 361 400 = **1239**

Now we put these squared and added numbers (1288 and 1239) together **12881239**.

Now look into the mirror: (**12881239** | 93218821) or (93218821| **12881239**). Here we have the mirrored number **9** first as the Holy Spirit (***Christ***) and then we have 321 **8821** which is right back to our (3 2 1) gauge symmetry numbers and 8821 numbers from the center of the Torah; and the progression of elevens squared from the creation event in Genesis. All of this comes from the name of **Jesus Christ**. You know this 93,218,821

(93 million) mirror number also looks very close to the distance to the sun (**Son**) in miles.

Peter Higgs is the scientist who first investigated the idea of a Higgs boson; the field that holds the whole universe together. This is the (field or particle) would complete the standard model of particle physics. We also talked about the Higgs boson coming in at the energy of about (**114 GeV**). This fact needs to to confirmed, and maybe will be confirmed in three or four years at the new particle accelerator in Cern. This is because more energy is required than our present day accelerators can deliver to fully discover it.

Using the normal English alphabet conversion for Peter Higgs and adding the numbers; is this a coincidence?

P	E	T	E	R		H	I	G	G	S	
16	5	20	5	18		8	9	7	7	19	= (**114**) 114 GeV is where the Higgs boson is expected.

H	I	G	G	S		B	O	S	O	N	
8	9	7	7	19		2	15	19	15	14	= (**115**) If the words were HIGGS BOSOM they would equal 114 as we get a little closer to the secret.

Here are the words 'Only Son' referring to Jesus Christ.

O	N	L	Y		S	O	N	
15	14	12	25		19	15	14	= (**114**)

A powerful 114 verse: John **1:14** "And the **Word** was made **flesh**, and dwelt among us..."

John 3:16   "For God so loved the world, that he gave (his

	only begotten Son)…"
John 1:18	"No man hath seen God at any time, the (only begotten Son), which is in the bosom of the Father, he hath declared him."

We are getting closer to the secret to be revealed at the end of the book! Remember that the Higgs boson is the field that gives mass to everything (all matter) in the universe in the weak interaction at 10^-13 power; see Psalm 13. Look at this 1:3 scripture: Hebrews 1:3 "Who being the brightness of his glory, and the express image of his person, and (**upholding** all **things** by the **word** of his power), when he had by himself purged our sins, sat down on the right hand of the Majesty on high." In this scripture we have a hint in: "…upholding all things by the word of his power…"

The word BEGOTTEN added together using numbers of the English alphabet.

```
B   E   G   O    T    T    E   N
2   5   7   15   20   20   5   14 = (88)
```

Jesus is the eight's (**88**) in new beginnings, and there are 10^88 power photons in the universe. See also Psalm 88 and **waves** like Photon waves of light, knowing that Jesus is the light!

G O D (**26**) + B E G O T T E N (**88**) = (**114**)

```
J    E   S    U    S         C   H   R    I   S    T
10   5   19   21   19        3   8   18   9   19   20   = (151)
```

```
H   O    L    Y         S    P    I   R    I   T
8   15   12   25        19   16   9   18   9   20        = (151)
```

```
L    O    R    D        O    F         H   O    S    T    S
12   15   18   4        15   6         8   15   19   20   19   = (151)
```

```
J    E   S    U    S         I   S         L    O    R    D         = (151)
10   5   19   21   19        9   19        12   15   18   4
```

L	I	G	H	T		O	F		J	E		S	U	S		= (**151**)
12	9	7	8	20		15	6		10	5		19	21	19		

P	R	A	Y	I	N	G		T	O		G	O	D		= (**151**)
16	18	1	25	9	14	7		20	15		7	15	4		

C	R	E	A	T	I	O	N		E	V	E	N	T		= (**151**)
3	18	5	1	20	9	15	14		5	22	5	14	20		

John 1:51	"And he saith unto him, Verily, verily, I say unto you, Hereafter ye shall see **heaven open**, and the angels of God ascending and descending upon the **Son of man**."
John 15:1	"I am the **true vine**, and my **Father** is the husbandman."
Luke 1:51	"**He hath shewed strength** with his arm; he hath scattered the proud in the imagination of their hearts."
Luke 15:1	"Then drew near unto him all the publicans and sinners for **to hear him**."

The power number 114 is the "Word made flesh" of John 1:14 and we know that 37 is the number in the Bible also meaning the "Word of the Father" and part of our creation sentence numbers (37 x 73). The expression "**In the beginning**..." in English = **137**, the mystery constant. Knowing this: (Word of the Father = **37**) we add (**114 + 37**) to get **151** and Luke **15:1** says about words "...for to **hear** him." Look also at **Jesus** and the **Father** in John **15:1** "I am the **true vine**, and my **Father** is the husbandman"; knowing again that Jesus is the 114 and the Father is the 37 (114 + 37) = **151**, the verse numbers of John **15:1**.

Genesis 1:1 "In the beginning God created the heaven and the earth." = **411** in English; our information number and the mirror to '114' a (411 | 114) or (**114 | 411**) mirror. Don't forget John **1:1** "In the beginning was the Word, and the Word was with God, and the Word was God." Genesis **1:14** "And God said, Let there be (**lights**) in the firmament of the heaven to divide the day from the night; and let them be for signs, and for seasons, and for days, and years." John **1:4** "In him was life; and the life was the (**light**) of men." We got plenty of **1's** and **4's** here and lots of creation **light** going on.

Mark **15:2** "**And Pilate asked him,** Art thou the (**King of the Jews**)? And he answering said unto them, Thou sayest it." This is Mark **15:2** and we are relating these in English to the crucifixion that equal **152**. All of the following phrases when added in English = **152**. Jesus number of blood and divine service is **30** and (**15 x 2**) = **30** and (1 + 5 + 2) = **8**.

KING OF THE JEWS = (**152**) From Mark **15:2**.

AND PILATE ASKED HIM = (**152**) From Mark **15:2**.

JESUS CRUCIFIED = (**152**)

JESUS ON A TREE = (**152**)

GOLGOTHA'S TREE = (**152**)

LORD DIED FOR SIN = (**152**)

LORD AT CALVARY = (**152**)

SAVED BY JESUS = (**152**)

The **133** Cessium Atomic Clock

Eventually it was realized that the planet's rotation is not actually uniform. That is to say, each day is not the same length. This makes the Earth a rather poor clock. The duration of a second was eventually re-defined in 1960 at the Eleventh General Conference on weights and measures to be 1/31,556,952.9794 of an ephemeris year. An ephermeris year is determined by taking astronomical observations and applying to them the laws of motion to determine the orbital period of the Earth around the Sun. This became known as the ephemeris second. Later work with atomic energy yielded another curiosity: 9,192,631,770 of the state transitions of the radiation emitted from a Cessium (**133**) atom coincidentally is the same length as the 1960 ephemerous second. This became the modern definition of the length of a second, and is the basis for atomic clocks.

CESSIUM CLOCK = **133**. This is the Cessium **133** atom that keeps time.

MAN = **28**. Man has $10^{28\text{th}}$ power particles in his body (**4 x $10^{28\text{th}}$**) power from the Tabernacle curtains.
Genesis 1:27 "So God created **man** in his own image, in the **image of God** created he him; male and female created he them." Verse numbers $(1 + 27) = $ **28**. Jesus = **74** (7 x 4) = **28**.

CURVED UNIVERSE = **186**. The base number for light speed (186 x 1000) = 186,000.

GRAVITY ACCELERATION = **208**. The atomic weight of Bismuth element no. 83 (the anti-gravity element) see Psalm 83. Einstein says that gravity equals acceleration in a curved universe. See also Psalm 90:4.

AMERICA = **50**. This is the **50** United States of America.

FLORIDA = **65**. Many go here at this age to retire.

CALIFORNIA = **88**. There are 10^{88} power photons of **light** making this *Sunny California*.

TEXAS = **69**. Houston, Texas was the control center for the moon mission in **1969**.

HOUSTON = **112**. The first two missions that landed on the moon were Apollo **(11)**2 and 1**(12)**. Apollo **12** was launched at **11:22** EST time November 14, 1969. Apollo **11** and **12** were retrieved by the aircraft carrier U.S.S Hornet CVS **12**. HOUSTON, TEXAS = **181**, is this **181** the 'command module' or 'the eagle has landed'?

MICHIGAN = **64**. The most popular car in this states' history was introduced in **1964**, the ***Ford Mustang***. The Ford Mustang sold 418,812 units in its first year.

DETROIT, MICHIGAN = **155**. Watch your speed in your **Mustang**, keep is at **(1 x 55)** = **55** mph while on **(15 x 5)** = **75** (Interstate **75**), which goes through the heart of **Detroit**.

NEVADA = **47**. This is about when all of the big hotels started in Las Vegas (1946-**1947**) by Bugsy Siegel. Bugsy Siegel was killed in his Beverly Hills, CA. home June 20, **1947**. This is the year that Boulder Dam was renamed to the Hoover Dam in Nevada (**1947**).

ARKANSAS = **84**. Bill Clinton wins his second term as Governor in this state in **1984**.

COLORADO = **83**. There is less gravity up higher in the mountains; **83** is anti-gravity see Psalm 83:18.

NEW YORK = **111**. We have a lot of tall buildings here. THE BIG APPLE = **101**. Just take a bite out of the apple in the middle of the buildings.

WASHINGTON DC = **137**. This place is always a mystery; ***the mystery constant is 137***.

MAKE CENTIMETERS TO INCHES = **254**. There are **2.54** centimeters per inch.

WASHINGTON MONUMENT IS FIVE HUNDRED FIFTY FIVE FT. HIGH = **555**.

WORLD TRADE TOWERS = **220**. Two **110** story buildings (110 x 2) = **220**.

DOWNTOWN MANHATTAN = **220**.

OSAMA BIN LADEN = **110**. He is a 110 story building terrorist.

NINE ONE ONE = **110**. This was the fate of a 110 story building.

World Trade Towers terrorist attack September eleventh in the year two thousand one = **(911)**.

A DECEMBER SEVENTH NINETEEN FORTY ONE = **(353)**. The number of planes in the attack **(353)** on Pearl Harbor December 7,1941.

ATOMIC BOMB HIROSHIMA JAPAN = **(235)**. The atomic bomb dropped on Hiroshima actually was a Uranium **235** device.

ON JULY SIXTEENTH NINETEEN FORTY FIVE THE FIRST ATOMIC BOMB EXPLODED = **(716)**. July is the 7th month and this happened on the 16th day **7/16/1945**.

APOLLO ELEVEN LANDS ON THE MOON JULY TWENTI-ETH NINETEEN SIXTY NINE = **(720)**. July 20 is 7/20 as July is the 7th month, and on **7/20** we landed on the moon. See also Psalm 72.

PRESIDENT JOHN F KENNEDY WAS SHOT AND KILLED ON A NOVEMBER THE TWENTY SECOND, NINETEEN SIXTY THREE IN DALLAS TEXAS = **(1122)**. November is the 11th month and he was shot on the 22nd day of November: **11/22/1963**.

MOHAMMED THE ISLAMIC PROPHET DIES IN SIX HUNDRED AND THIRTY TWO = **(632)**. Mohammed died in **632** A. D.

THE TITANIC SANK = **(154)**.
The Titanic sank on the fifteenth day **(15)**4 of the 15**(4)** month:
April 15, 1912.

RMS TITANIC SANK AFTER COLLIDING WITH ICEBERG =
(415). Now we have **4** (**4th** month=April) on the **(15)** fifteenth day:
4/15/1912.

DAVID BLAINE = **(83)**. He is the famous magician who levitates a
few inches off of the ground, and we know that **83** is the number of
anti-gravity, Bismuth the 83rd element in Psalm 83.

Here is the one (**Jesus Christ**) who walks on the water.

John **1:14** "And the Word was made flesh…"
"AND THE **WORD** WAS MADE FLESH…" = **(228)**, an exact
multiple of 114 (**114 x 2**) = **228**. There are **22** letters in the Hebrew
alphabet and Jesus' number is **8**!

John 1:14 "…and dwelt among us…"

DWELT AMONG = **(114)**

As just stated above: Genesis 1:1 "In the beginning God created the
heaven and the earth." "In the beginning God created the heaven
and the earth" = **(411)** the information number; the mirror to John
1:14 a (**411 | 114**) mirror.

The Wisdom and the weight of the Proverbs

Famous (**weighed**) events that happen in the proverbs (1100, 1611)
of the same year.

* Proverbs 11:1 "A false **balance** is abomination to the LORD: but
a just **weight** is his delight."

The year is **1100** AD and in China the first **magnetic** compass
was used. This is as close as we can get to 1100 with a verse

number (11:1) as there are no 11:00 verses. Electro**magnetism** is the **balance** of the **two** powers of positive and negative forces at 10^19 power; see Psalm 19. (19 x 2) = 38 the **weight** of gravity in Psalm 38.

* Proverbs 16:11 "A just **weight** and balance are the LORD's: all the **weights** of the bag are his work."

The year is **1611** and the King James Bible is published; a very just **balance** and spiritual **weight**.

It looks like the devil is judged by the **weight** of God's **Word** in John **16:11** "Of judgment, because the prince of this world is **judged**."

We talked before about significant years dealing with Einstein, science, and the Bible for the years 1100 and 1611 in chapter 5. Take the year of the King James Bible **1611** and minus the year of the first use of the (**electro**)magnetic compass (1611 – 1100) = **511**. The mass of the **ELECTRON** in GeV (**G**iga electron Volts) is . **511**. Allow the *magnetism* of God's **Word** to *point* you toward Him.

The only other place in the Proverbs where the word **weight** or **weights** is found is in Proverbs 20.

Proverbs 20:10　"Divers **weights**, and divers **measures**, both of them are alike abomination to the LORD."

Proverbs 20:23　"Divers **weights** are an abomination unto the LORD; and a false **balance** is not good."

If these four Proverbs all deal with **weight** and **balance** and coincide with the years (1100, 1611) as very significant events, then what happens in 2010 and 2023?

Proverbs 20:**10**　would coincide with Psalm **110** as far as the years go for the year **2010**.

Psalm **110**:6   "He shall **judge** among the **heathen**, he shall fill the places with the dead bodies; he shall **wound** the heads over many **countries**."

Proverbs 20:**23**   would coincide with Psalm **123** as far as the years go for the year **2023**.

Psalm **123**:1-4   "Unto thee lift I up mine eyes, O thou that dwellest in the heavens. Behold, as the eyes of servants look unto the hand of their masters, and as the eyes of a maiden unto the hand of her mistress; so our eyes wait upon the LORD our God, until that he have mercy upon us. Have mercy upon us, O LORD, have mercy upon us: for we are exceedingly filled with **contempt**. Our soul is exceedingly filled with the scorning of **those that are at ease**, and with the **contempt of the proud**."

Proverbs 20:**23**   talks about "...**a false balance is not good**" and Psalm **123** talks about "...**scorning of those that are at ease**, and with the contempt of the proud"; and both would be related to the year **2023** if we follow this yearly pattern in the Proverbs and Psalms.

CHAPTER 9

New Testament Scriptures and Power numbers

We are going to take a look mainly at the New Testament scriptures and some from the Old Testament to see how their verse numbers equal what the verse is talking about. Obviously we can't expect the word 'light' to show up in every verse numbered **22 or 27**. However, we are looking for the *tendency* of certain scientific subject matter to show up in the most 'key numbered' scriptures and match their meanings when the opportunity arises. We are going to look at the Bible on a large scale to see if the verse numbers are magnetic to the meanings that they portray in nature. We are going to look for patterns in **groups** of related science data by their scripture numbers, even when they are added or multiplied to equal the number. Scripture numbers having to do with the weight of the universe and the heavens seem to be in the **52-54** range; the universe is estimated to weigh about **10^53** kilograms. Gravity numbers **38** and **39** are found when encountering things falling or heavy and Jesus walking on the water. Phrases like **'KING OF THE JEWS'** have to do with **38** and His heavy cross. The numbers **27** and **22** show up in many key scriptures that talk about **light** and 'blind men' being healed. The number **22** shows up in a lot of scriptures talking about 'words and letters' because there are **22** letters in the Hebrew alphabet. Time as **24** (hours), **44** Planck time, and **133** dealing with the Cessium atom appear in these key

147

numbered scriptures. Seeds and things rising or springing up (**offspring**) are within **31** numbered scriptures because 31 is the Bible number of **offspring** and **increase**. The number **31** (mass of the electron) shows up when talking about the **world** and the fleshly **elements**. The number **45** shows up for preservation and scriptures having the words 'saved' or 'salvation'. We are also going to look at the numbers *66, 666*, and **18** related to the satanic kingdom. Most major scriptures dealing with *measurement* seem to equal their meaning with their scripture numbers. There are about **400** scriptures listed by their scientific and biblical numerical **groupings**.

* This first set of scriptures deals with the numbers of light (**22** and **27**) and (**28** the body).

Matthew **10:27** "What I tell you in darkness, that speak ye in (**light**): and what ye hear in the ear, that preach ye upon the housetops." Remember Psalm **27:1** "The LORD is my (**light**) and my salvation; whom shall I fear" and that $10^{-27\text{th}}$ power is the number for the minimum energy of a photon of (**light**) in erg seconds? This is also called Planck's constant and is one of the most important constants in physics.

Jeremiah 4:23 "I beheld the (**earth**), and, lo, it was without form, and void; and the **heavens**, and they had no (**light**)." Verse numbers (4 + 23) = **27** and Jeremiah is talking about having no (**light**). Verse numbers (4 x 23) = 92, the number of natural elements found on *earth*. Verse numbers (4 x 2 x 3) = 24 and we know the Earth is $10^{24\text{th}}$ power in kilograms of weight and "I beheld the **earth**..." is in this scripture. Verse numbers (23 – 4) = 19 like our electricity Psalm 19 "The **heavens** declare the glory of God..."

Matthew **6:22** "The **light** of the **body** is the eye: if therefore thine eye be single, thy whole body shall be full of **light**." We know from the Bible that '**6**' is the number of man. The number **22** is also a Bible number of light and Matthew 6:22 says "The (**light**) of the (body) is the eye: if therefore thine eye be single, thy whole (**body**) shall be full of (**light**)." Note that this scripture is talking about light and the body, and the verse numbers (6 + 22) = **28**. We know from the Tabernacle of Moses and curtain sizes that the body (average human being) has **4 x 10^28th** power particles in it! We also have the 4 and 10 here as (2 + 2) = 4 and (6 + 2 + 2) = 10 as in 4 x 10^28 power.

* The number **28** as it relates to man, the body, soul, and eternal life.

Matthew **10:28** "And fear not (them) which kill the (**body**), but are not able to kill the **soul**: but rather fear him which is able to destroy both **soul** and (**body**) in hell." Again a 10 to the 28th power scripture number dealing with the number of particles in the body.

John **10:28** "And I give unto them (**eternal life**); and they shall never perish, neither shall any (**man**) pluck them out of my hand." We know that 10^28th power is the number of particles in a 'man'. The phrase "eternal life" is in this scripture, and **28** is actually the Bible number meaning '**eternal life**'.

Acts **10:28** "And he said unto them, Ye know how that it is an unlawful thing for a (**man**) that is a **Jew** to keep company, or come unto one of another nation; but God hath shewed me that I should not call any (**man**) common or unclean."

Deuteronomy **28:4** "Blessed shall be the fruit of thy **body**, and the fruit of thy ground, and the fruit of thy cattle, the increase of thy kine, and the flocks of thy sheep." We have the **28** and the **4** here for 4 x **10^28** power with the "fruit of the **body**."

Deuteronomy **28:11** "And the LORD shall make thee plenteous in goods, in the fruit of thy **body**, and in the fruit of thy cattle, and in the fruit of thy ground, in the land which the LORD sware unto thy fathers to give thee."

Deuteronomy **28:18** "**Cursed** shall be the fruit of thy **body**, and the fruit of thy land, the increase of thy kine, and the flocks of thy sheep." 18 is the number of bondage and consider the **Cursed** word.

Deuteronomy **28**:53 "And thou shalt eat the fruit of thine own **body**, the flesh of thy **sons** and of thy daughters, which the LORD thy God hath given thee, in the siege, and in the straitness, where-with thine enemies shall distress thee." We will see in a few pages why the **53** number deals with fathers and **sons**.

Romans 7:4 "Wherefore, my brethren, ye also are become dead to the law by the **body** of Christ; that ye should be married to another, even to him who is raised from the dead, that we should bring forth fruit unto God." Marriage and body (7 x 4) = **28**.

1st Corinthians 7:4 "The wife hath not power of her own **body**, but the husband: and likewise also the husband hath not power of his own **body**, but the wife." Talking about wife, husband, and body (7 x 4) = **28**.

Lamentations 4:7 "Her Nazarites were purer than snow, they were whiter than milk, they were more ruddy in **body** than rubies, their polishing was of sapphire." (4 x 7) = **28**.

Ephesians 5:23 "For the husband is the head of the wife, even as Christ is the head of the church: and he is the saviour of the **body**." Husband and wife dealing with the **body** again and (23 + 5) = **28**.

1st Thessalonians 5:23 "And the very God of peace sanctify you wholly; and I pray God your whole **spirit** and **soul** and **body** be preserved blameless unto the coming of our Lord Jesus Christ." Body again and (5 + 23) = **28**.

1st Corinthians 12:16 "And if the ear shall say, Because I am not the eye, I am not of the **body**; is it therefore not of the **body**?" More **body** and (12 + 16) = **28**.

James 2:26 says: "For as the **body** without the spirit is dead, so faith without works is dead also." Body again mentioned and (2 + 26) = **28**.

Isaiah 10:18 "And shall consume the glory of his forest, and of his fruitful field, both **soul and body**: and they shall be as when a standard-bearer fainteth." **Body** and **soul, 28** is eternal life (**soul**) and $(10 + 18) = \mathbf{28}$.

2nd Peter **2:8** "(For that righteous **man** dwelling among them, in seeing and hearing, vexed his righteous **soul** from day to day with their unlawful deeds)."

Gen 1:27 "So God created **man** in his own image, in the image of God created he him; male and female created he them." We (**man and woman**) are created in God's image and $(1 + 27) = \mathbf{28}$.

Genesis **2:8** "And the LORD God planted a garden eastward in Eden; and there he put the **man** whom he had **formed**." He formed a (**28**) man's body.

Leviticus 7:21 "Moreover the **soul** that shall touch any unclean thing, as the uncleanness of **man**, or any unclean beast, or any abominable unclean thing, and eat of the flesh of the sacrifice of peace offerings, which pertain unto the LORD, even that **soul** shall be cut off from his people." $(7 + 21) = \mathbf{28}$.

Leviticus 17:11 "For the life of the **flesh** is in the **blood**: and I have given it to you upon the altar to make an atonement for your **souls**: for it is the blood that maketh an atonement for the **soul**." $(17 + 11) = \mathbf{28}$.

Leviticus 22:6 "The **soul** which hath touched any such shall be unclean until even, and shall not eat of the holy things, unless he wash his **flesh** with water." $(22 + 6) = \mathbf{28}$.

Numbers 15:**28** "And the priest shall make an atonement for the **soul** that sinneth ignorantly, when he sinneth by ignorance before the LORD, to make an atonement for him; and it shall be forgiven him."

Job 33:**28** "He will deliver his **soul** from going into the pit, and his **life** shall see the light."

Psalms 24:4 "He that hath clean hands, and a pure heart; who hath not lifted up his **soul** unto vanity, nor sworn deceitfully." (24 + 4) = **28**.

Psalms 119:**28** "My **soul** melteth for heaviness: strengthen thou me according unto thy **word**."

Lamentations 3:25 "The LORD is good unto them that wait for him, to the **soul** that seeketh him." (3 + 25) = **28**.

* More of the **light** numbers **22** and **27**.

Acts **22**:6 "And it came to pass, that, as I made my journey, and was come nigh unto Damascus about noon, suddenly there shone from heaven a great (**light**) round about me." The mirror scripture to Matthew 6:22 is Acts 22:6, a (6:22 | 22:6) mirror of lights and **22** is the Bible number of light.

Acts **22**:8 "And I answered, Who art thou, Lord? And he said unto me, I am Jesus of Nazareth, whom thou persecutest." Paul had just gotten zapped by the **light** and knocked off of his horse by Jesus (the light **22**) and (22 + 8) = 30 Jesus number of divine service; Jesus number of new beginnings is **8**.

Acts 9:3 "And as he journeyed, he came near Damascus: and suddenly there **shined** round about him a **light** from heaven", and verse numbers (9 x 3) = **27** a number of light; see Psalm **27**:1 and Matthew **10:27**.

Mark 9:3 "And his raiment became **shining**, exceeding **white as snow**; so as no fuller on earth can white them." Shining **bright** raiment and (9 x 3) = **27** light!

Matthew 17:5 "While he yet spake, behold, a **bright cloud** overshadowed them: and behold a **voice** out of the cloud, which said, This is my beloved Son, in whom I am well pleased; hear ye him." A **bright** cloud appeared (**22** as light) and the voice of God (**22**) letters in the Hebrew alphabet; (17 + 5 = **22**).

Matthew 24:**27** "For as the lightning cometh out of the east, and shineth even unto the west; so shall also the coming of the **Son of man** be." The Son of man is here and **24** is the number of Jesus related to the priesthood and $(8 + 8 + 8) = 24$; and **27** is light (lightning). The word lightning(s) appears **27** times in the Bible.

Deuteronomy **27**:16 says "Cursed be he that setteth (**light**) by his father or his mother. And all the people shall say, Amen."

Exodus **27**:20 "And thou shalt command the children of Israel, that they bring thee pure oil olive beaten for the (**light**), to cause the **lamp** to burn always."

Ezekiel 1:**27** "And I saw as the colour of **amber**, as the appearance of **fire round about** within it, from the appearance of his loins even upward, and from the appearance of his loins even downward, I saw as it were the **appearance of fire**, and it had **brightness** round about." Here is fire and brightness of **light** in a **27** verse.

2nd Samuel **23:4** "And he shall be as the (**light**) of the morning, when the (**sun**) riseth, even a morning without clouds; as the tender grass springing out of the earth by (**clear shining**) after rain." $(23 + 4) = 27$.

Job **18:6** "The **light** shall be dark in his tabernacle, and his **candle** shall be put out with him." Light speed is **186,000** miles per second. $(18 \times 6) = 108$ so does $(27 \times 4) = 108$.

Proverbs 4:18 "But the path of the just is as the **shining light**, that **shineth** more and more unto the perfect day." $(4 + 18) = 22$.

Exodus **10:22** "And Moses stretched forth his hand toward heaven; and there was a **thick darkness** in all the land of Egypt three days." Somebody turned the lights (**22**) out! They saw no stars and there are 10^{22} power stars in the universe.

Acts **2:20** "The **sun** shall be turned into **darkness**, and the moon into blood, before the great and notable day of the Lord come." (2 + 20) = **22**.

Acts **22**:9 "And they that were with me saw indeed the **light**, and were afraid; but they heard not the **voice** of him that spake to me."

Acts **22**:11 "And when I could not see for the glory of that **light**, being led by the hand of them that were with me, I came into Damascus."

1st Timothy **6:16** "Who only hath immortality, dwelling in the **light** which no **man** can approach unto; whom no man hath seen, nor can see: to whom be honour and power everlasting. Amen." Verse numbers (6 + 16) = **22**, the Bible number of light. This also says "…whom no man (**6**) hath seen..."

Revelation **22:5** "And there shall be no night there; and they need no **candle**, neither **light** of the **sun**; for the Lord God giveth them **light**: and they shall reign for ever and ever." We have **22** as the chapter and **5** as the verse numbers and (**22 + 5**) = **27**, the number for **light** in Psalm **27**.

Revelation **22**:16 says "I Jesus have sent mine angel to testify unto you these things in the churches. I am the root and the offspring of David, and the **bright and morning star**." Bright as in bright light (**22**) and morning star as in 10^22 stars in the universe.

2nd Samuel **22**:29 "For thou art my **lamp**, O LORD: and the LORD will **lighten** my darkness." The word **lighten** (here in a **22** numbered verse) shows up in the King James Version of the Bible just 7 times. One of those seven times is in Psalm 13:3 "Consider and hear me, O LORD my God: **lighten** mine eyes, lest I sleep the sleep of death"; our Psalm describing the weak force of the universe that involves particles of **light** with mass called bosons.

2nd Samuel **22**:13 "Through the **brightness** before him were **coals of fire** kindled."

154

Job 10:**22** "A land of darkness, as darkness itself; and of the shadow of death, without any order, and where the **light** is as darkness."

Job 12:**22** "He discovereth deep things out of darkness, and bringeth out to **light** the shadow of death."

Job **22**:28 "Thou shalt also decree a thing, and it shall be established unto thee: and the **light** shall shine upon thy ways."

Daniel **2:22** "He revealeth the deep and secret things: he knoweth what is in the darkness, and the **light** dwelleth with him."

Luke **10:22** "All things are delivered to me of my Father: and no man knoweth who the Son is, but the Father; and who the Father is, but the Son, and he to whom the Son will (**reveal**) him." If you don't have a **revelation** of God then you have no **light**; the book of *Revelation* has **22** chapters.

Ezekiel **22**:7 "In thee have they set **light** by father and mother: in the midst of thee have they dealt by oppression with the stranger: in thee have they vexed the fatherless and the widow."

Matthew **2:2** "Saying, Where is he that is born **King of the Jews**? for we have seen his **star** in the east, and are come to worship him." This verse **2:2** says "...we have seen his **star**" and there are $10\wedge22$ power **stars** in the universe that send us their light (**22**). **2** squared + **2** squared = (4 + 4) = **8**; **Jesus!**

John 3:19 "And this is the condemnation, that **light** is come into the world, and **men loved darkness** rather than **light**, because their **deeds were evil**." Verse numbers (3 + 19) = **22**, the Bible number for light. On October 11, 2001 President George Bush announced that he was going to expose **22** terrorists to the **light**! The 11th is a multiple of **22** (11 x 2) = 22. Also verse numbers (3 x 1 x 9) = **27** as in the **light** of Psalm 27.

Revelation 21:23 "And the city had no need of the **sun**, neither of the **moon, to shine in it**: for the glory of God did **lighten it**, and the **Lamb is the light** thereof." (21 + 23) = **44** (**Did time stop?**); (**22** x 2) = 44 also.

* **Blind** men and the **light** of **22** and **27**.

John 9:13 "They brought to the Pharisees him that **aforetime was blind**." Now he sees **light** (9 + 13) = **22**.

Matthew 12:**22** "Then was brought unto him one possessed with a devil, **blind**, and dumb: and he healed him, insomuch that the blind and dumb both spake and **saw**." He was healed and saw the (**22**) light. (12 + 22) = **34**; 10^-34 power is one photon of **light** see **Psalm 34**.

Psalms 146:8 "The LORD **openeth the eyes** of the **blind**: the LORD raiseth them that are bowed down: the **LORD** loveth the righteous." (146 + 8) = 154; 154 = (**22** x 7).

Isaiah 56:10 "His watchmen are **blind**: they are all ignorant, they are all dumb dogs, they cannot bark; sleeping, lying down, loving to slumber." (56 + 10) = 66; **66** = (**22** x 3).

Exodus 4:11 "And the LORD said unto him, Who hath made man's mouth? or who maketh the dumb, or deaf, **or the seeing**, or the **blind**? have not I the LORD?" (4 x 11) = 44; 44 = (**22** x 2).

Leviticus **22:22** "**Blind**, or broken, or maimed, or having a wen, or scurvy, or scabbed, ye shall not offer these unto the LORD, nor make an offering by fire of them upon the altar unto the LORD."

Job 29:15 "I was eyes to the **blind**, and feet was I to the lame." (29 + 15) = 44; 44 = (**22** x 2).

Mark 8:**22** "And **he** cometh to Bethsaida; and they bring **a blind man** unto **him**, and besought him to touch him." He being Jesus the number (**8**) cometh to Bethsaida to touch the **blind** man and give him (**22**) *sight!*

Luke 4:18 "The **Spirit of the Lord** is upon me, because he hath anointed me to preach the gospel to the poor; he hath sent me to heal the brokenhearted, to preach deliverance to the captives, and recovering of **sight to the blind**, to set at liberty them that are bruised." (4 + 18) = **22**.

Luke 7:**22** "Then Jesus answering said unto them, Go your way, and tell John what things ye have **seen** and heard; how that the **blind see**, the lame walk, the lepers are cleansed, the deaf hear, the dead are raised, to the poor the gospel is preached."

Matthew 9:**27** "And when Jesus departed thence, **two blind men followed him**, crying, and saying, Thou son of **David**, have mercy on us." Psalm **27** "The Lord is my **light**..." This one is **27** not 22 because **David** wrote the Psalms and these two are crying out to the **son of David** for sight. Verse numbers (9 + 27) = **36**; the number of man is **6**, and **2** men are **(6 x 6) = 36**.

Luke 14:13 "But when thou makest a feast, call the poor, the maimed, the lame, **the blind**." (14 + 13) = **27**.

John 9:6 "When he had thus spoken, he spat on the ground, and **made clay of the spittle**, and he anointed the **eyes of the blind man** with the **clay**." This time Jesus uses the 'clay' **elements** (9 x 6) = **54** (all of the forces of nature combined = 54); 54 = **(27 x 2)**.

John 9:**18** "But the Jews did not believe concerning him, that he **had been blind**, and received his **sight**, until they called the parents of him that had received his **sight**." (9 + 18) = **27**. The Jews did not believe because they were in bondage (**18**). Verse numbers put together: **918 = (27 x 34)** both quantum power numbers of **light** in **Psalm 27** and **Psalm 34**! Verse numbers multiplied (9 x 18) = 162 and so does (6 x **27**) = 162.

* This next set of scriptures deals with **gravity**, things **heavy**, and things **falling**, using the number **38**, see also Psalm **38**.

Mark 13:25 "And the stars of heaven shall **fall**, and the powers that are in heaven **shall be shaken**." The verse numbers $(13 + 25) =$ **38**; the force of gravity in relation to our stars of heaven **falling**.

Isaiah **3:8** "For Jerusalem is ruined, and Judah is **fallen**: because their tongue and their doings are against the LORD, to provoke the eyes of his glory." The word **fallen** appears $(38 \times 2) =$ **76** times in the Bible.

Psalms 18:**38** "I have wounded them that they were not able to rise: they are **fallen** under my feet."

Proverbs **28:10** "Whoso causeth the righteous to go astray in an evil way, he shall **fall** himself into his own pit: but the upright shall have good things in possession." $(28 + 10) =$ **38**.

2ⁿᵈ Samuel 3:**38** "And the king said unto his servants, Know ye not that there is a prince and a great man **fallen** this day in Israel?"

Leviticus 11:**38** "But if any water be put upon the seed, and any part of their carcase **fall** thereon, it shall be unclean unto you."

Jeremiah **38**:19 "And Zedekiah the king said unto Jeremiah, I am afraid of the Jews that are **fallen** to the Chaldeans, lest they deliver me into their hand, and they mock me."

1ˢᵗ Samuel **26:12** "So David took the spear and the cruse of water from Saul's bolster; and they gat them away, and no man saw it, nor knew it, neither awaked: for they were all asleep; because a deep sleep from the LORD was **fallen** upon them." $(26 + 12) =$ **38**.

2ⁿᵈ Chronicles 29:9 "For, lo, our fathers have **fallen** by the sword, and our sons and our daughters and our wives are in captivity for this." $(29 + 9) =$ **38**.

Ezekiel **38**:20 "So that the fishes of the sea, and the fowls of the heaven, and the beasts of the field, and all creeping things that creep upon the earth, and all the men that are upon the face of the earth, **shall shake at my presence**, and the **mountains shall be thrown**

down, and the steep places shall **fall**, and every wall shall **fall** to the ground."

Luke 20:18 "Whosoever shall **fall** upon that stone shall be broken; but on whomsoever it shall **fall**, it will grind him to powder." (20 + 18) = **38** and 18 is bondage.

Isaiah 34:4 "And all the host of heaven shall be dissolved, and the heavens shall be rolled together as a scroll: and all their host shall **fall** down, as the leaf **falleth** off from the vine, and as a **falling** fig from the fig tree." (34 + 4) = **38**.

Job **38**:4-6 "Where wast thou when I laid the **foundations of the earth**? declare, if thou hast understanding. Who hath **laid the measures** thereof, if thou knowest? or who hath **stretched the line upon it**? Whereupon are the **foundations thereof fastened**? or who laid the **corner stone thereof**." All in a **38** numbered verse talking about the foundations of the universe and **10^-38** power is gravity.

Speaking of **38:4**; now look at our gravity Psalm **38:4** "For mine iniquities are gone over mine head: as an **heavy** burden they are too **heavy** for me." This is the only place in the Bible where the word (**heavy**) is found twice in the same verse. The word **heavy** is found in **38** different verses of the Bible!

Hebrews 12:26 "Whose voice then **shook the earth**: but now he hath promised, saying, Yet once more I shake not the earth only, but also heaven." Here the earth and heaven is **shaking** and verse numbers (12 + 26) = **38** which is *gravity*.

Deuteronomy 25:13 "Thou shalt not have in thy bag divers **weights**, a great and a small." Our (25 + 13) verse numbers = **38** (gravity) with 'divers **weights**' in this important verse; the word '**weights**' is only in the whole Bible 6 times.

Numbers 7:31 "His offering was one silver charger of the **weight** of an hundred and thirty shekels, one silver bowl of seventy shekels, after the shekel of the sanctuary; both of them full of fine flour mingled with oil for a meat offering." (7 + 31) = **38**.

Ezra 8:30 "So took the priests and the Levites the **weight** of the **silver**, and the **gold**, and the vessels, to bring them to Jerusalem unto the house of our God." (8 + 30) = **38**.

Leviticus 19:36 "Just **balances**, just **weights**, a just ephah, and a just hin, shall ye have: I am the **LORD** your **God**, which brought you out of the land of Egypt." We have 'just **weights,** a just ephah' and (19 + 36) = **55**. This is the *just weight* of the 'Ten Commandments' on 2 tables of stone (5 + 5) = **10**. Verse numbers (19 x 36) = 684 which is evenly divisible by **38** (gravity); (**38 x 18**) = **684**. In relation to **684** is: Psalm **68:4** "Sing unto God, sing praises to his name: extol him that **rideth upon the heavens** by his name JAH, and rejoice before him." In relation to gravity/anti-gravity and the number **18**: Psalm 83:**18** "That men may know that thou, whose name alone is **JEHOVAH**, art the **most high** over all the earth."

* This next set deals with numbers in the **52-54** range of the weight and forces of the universe and the *heavens* and also the earth at 10^42 power in size of Planck units.

Matthew 24:29 "Immediately after the tribulation of those days shall the sun be darkened, and the moon shall not give her light, and the **stars shall fall from heaven**, and the **powers of the heavens** shall be shaken." In this scripture it's talking about the whole universe with the (powers of the heavens shall be shaken) and the verse numbers (24 + 29) = **53**. The weight of the universe is about **10^53** power in kilograms.

Isaiah 45:8 "Drop down, ye (**heavens**), from above, and let the skies pour down righteousness: let the earth open, and let them bring forth **salvation**, and let righteousness spring up together; I the LORD have created it". Our verse numbers (45 + 8) = **53**; also (45 x 8) = **360** as in a circle.

Isaiah 40:12 "Who hath measured the waters in the hollow of

his hand, and **meted out heaven** with the span, and comprehended the dust of the **earth in a measure**, and **weighed the mountains in scales**, and the hills in a balance?" Verse numbers (40 + 12) = **52**, close to the estimated weight 10^52-53 kilograms of the universe.

Isaiah **45:7** "I **form the light**, and **create darkness**: I make peace, and create evil: I the LORD do all these things"; and (45 + 7) = **52**.

Job 28:25 "To make the **weight** for the winds; and he **weigheth** the waters by measure." We just talked about the weight of the universe being near 10^53 kilograms and verse numbers (28 + 25) = **53**.

Leviticus 19:35 "Ye shall do no unrighteousness in judgment, in **meteyard**, in **weight**, or in **measure**." Here is a major scripture from the Old Testament dealing with measurement and (19 + 35) = **54**, all of our four forces of the universe.

* Here are more **54** numbers about heaven and the elements.

Luke 12:33 "Sell that ye have, and give alms; provide your-selves bags **which wax not old**, a treasure in the (**heavens**) that faileth not, where no thief approacheth, neither moth corrupteth." These verse numbers (12 + 33) = **45** the number of preservation and in this scripture we are talking about "...bags which wax not old, a treasure.." The number 45 is a mirror to 54, our number of the heav-ens, a (**45 | 54 mirror**) of preservation from the natural elements.

Luke 21:33 "Heaven and earth shall pass away: but my words shall not pass away." All of **heaven** and **earth** are involved here and the verse numbers (21 + 33) = **54**, which is all of our forces of the universe added together: (1) = Strong force, (2) = Electromagnetic force, (13) = Weak force, and (38) = Gravity; which when added (1 + 2 + 13 + 38) = **54**.

Matthew 24:30 "And then shall appear the sign of the **Son of man** in **heaven**: and then shall all the tribes of the earth mourn, and they shall see the Son of man coming in the **clouds of heaven** with power and great glory." We are talking about heaven and earth again and (24 + 30) = **54**. The number 24 is the number of the priesthood in the Bible and 30 is Jesus' number of blood, service, and dedication, and this scripture is talking about the **Son of man**.

Ephesians 6:9 "And, ye masters, do the same things unto them, forbearing threatening: knowing that your Master also is in **heaven**; neither is there respect of persons with him." Heaven again and (9 x 6) = **54**.

Luke 9:**54** "And when his disciples James and John saw this, they said, Lord, wilt thou that we command fire to come down from **heaven**, and consume them, even as Elias did?" The disciples wanting to command fire to come down from **heaven** in a verse with **54** in it.

Matthew 18:3 "And said, Verily I say unto you, Except ye be converted, and become as little children, ye shall not enter into the **kingdom of heaven**." The kingdom of heaven again and (18 x 3) = **54**.

Matthew 16:19 "And I will give unto **thee** the keys of the **kingdom of heaven**: and whatsoever thou shalt bind on earth shall be bound in heaven: and whatsoever thou shalt loose on earth shall be loosed in heaven." Talking about the keys of the kingdom and heaven and all individual verse numbers (1 x 6 x 1 x 9) = **54**. (16 + 19) = **35** (man) or '**unto thee**' the one who received the keys.

Mark 16:19 "So then after the Lord had spoken unto them, he was received up into **heaven**, and sat on the right hand of God." This one says 'received up into heaven' and (1 x 6 x 1 x 9) = **54**.

Luke 9:16 "Then he took the five loaves and the two fishes, and looking up to **heaven**, he blessed them, and brake, and gave to the disciples to set before the multitude." We have 'looking up to heaven' and (9 x 1 x 6) = **54**.

Matthew 6:9 "After this manner therefore pray ye: Our Father which art in **heaven**, Hallowed be thy name." In this scripture is "Our Father which art in heaven"; heaven again and 6 x 9 = **54**.

Hebrews 6:19 "Which hope we have as an anchor of the soul, both sure and stedfast, and which entereth into that **within the veil**." Here we are within the veil, which would certainly be heaven and (6 x 1 x 9) = **54**.

John 6:19 "So when they had rowed about **five and twenty** or thirty furlongs, they see Jesus **walking on the sea**, and drawing nigh unto the ship: and they were afraid." Jesus with command over all of the elements (**54**) and (6 x 1 x 9) = **54**. **Five and twenty furlongs** equals our verse numbers (6 + 19) = **25**. 6 x 19 = **114** "The **Word** made flesh."

Isaiah 45:12 "I have made the earth, and created man upon it: I, even my hands, have stretched out the **heavens**, and all their host have I commanded." Remember that God stretches out the heavens and that there are 10 total space dimensions; our verse numbers (45 x 12) = 540 or (**54 x 10**) = **540**.

Job 9:6 "Which **shaketh the earth** out of her place, and the pillars thereof tremble." (9 x 6) = **54**. Just put the '**0**' round **earth** in the middle of 96 with '**906**' because the word 'earth' is found **906** times in the Bible!

Judges **5:4** "LORD, when thou wentest out of Seir, when thou marchedst out of the field of Edom, the earth trembled, and **the heavens** dropped, the clouds also dropped water." This is just plain **54** and talking about the heavens.

Ezra 9:6 "And said, O my God, I am ashamed and blush to lift up my face to thee, my God: for our iniquities are increased over our head, and our trespass is grown up unto the **heavens**." (9 x 6) = **54**.

Nehemiah 9:6 "Thou, even thou, art LORD alone; thou hast

made heaven, the **heaven of heavens**, with all their host, the earth, and all things that are therein, the seas, and all that is therein, and thou preservest them all; and the host of **heaven** worshippeth thee." (9 x 6) = **54**.

Psalms 50:4 He shall call to the **heavens from above**, and to the earth, that he may judge his people. (50 + 4) = **54**.

* The Planck size of the **Earth** and the number **42**. There are many more **42's** than shown this is just a sampling.

Genesis **7:6** "And Noah was **six hundred years** old when the flood of waters was upon the **earth**." This is talking about 'the waters upon the **earth**' and verse numbers (7 x 6) = **42** the size of **earth** above the Planck length.

Hebrews **6:7** "For the **earth** which drinketh in the rain that cometh oft upon it, and bringeth forth herbs meet for them by whom it is dressed, receiveth blessing from God." (6 x 7) = **42**.

Zechariah **6:7** "And the bay went forth, and sought to go that they might walk to and fro through the **earth**: and he said, Get you hence, walk to and fro through the **earth**. So they walked to and fro through the **earth**." (6 x 7) = **42**.

Genesis **6:7** "And the LORD said, I will destroy man whom I have created from the face of the **earth**; both man, and beast, and the creeping thing, and the fowls of the air; for it repenteth me that I have made them." (6 x 7) = **42**.

Genesis 19:23 "The sun was risen upon the **earth** when Lot entered into Zoar." (19 + 23) = **42**.

Genesis 28:**14** "And thy **seed** shall be as the dust of the **earth,** and thou shalt spread abroad to the west, and to the east, and to the north, and to the south: and in thee and in thy **seed** shall all the families of the **earth** be blessed." (28 + 14) = **42** and **14** is the generational (**seed**) number of Psalm 14.

Genesis **42**:6 "And Joseph was the governor over the land, and he it was that sold to all the people of the land: and Joseph's brethren came, and bowed down themselves before him with their faces to the **earth**."

Exodus 34:8 says: "And Moses made haste, and bowed his head toward the **earth** and worshipped." $(34 + 8) = $ **42**.

Job **38:4** "Where wast thou when I laid the foundations of the **earth**? declare, if thou hast understanding." God is talking about the foundations of the **earth** and verse numbers $(38 + 4) = $ **42**. Also **38** is gravity and there are **4** basic forces of the universe; strong force, weak force, electromagnetism, and gravity. There are also **4** seen dimensions of the universe: length, width, height, and time.

Hosea 2:21 "And it shall come to pass in that day, I will hear, saith the LORD, I will hear the heavens, and they shall hear the **earth**." The **earth** is mentioned in this scripture and $(2 \times 21) = $ **42**.

Haggai 2:21 "Speak to Zerubbabel, governor of Judah, saying, I will shake the heavens and the **earth**"; $(2 \times 21) = $ **42**.

Acts 16:26 "And suddenly there was a great **earthquake**, so that the foundations of the prison were shaken: and immediately all the doors were opened, and every one's bands were loosed." This was an *earthquake*, and the earth is $(16 + 26) = $ **42**.

Matthew 12:**42** "The queen of the south shall rise up in the judgment with this generation, and shall condemn it: for she came from the **uttermost parts of the (earth)** to hear the wisdom of Solomon; and, behold, a greater than Solomon is here."

Luke 11:31 "The queen of the south shall rise up in the judgment with the men of this generation, and condemn them: for she came from the **utmost parts of the (earth)** to hear the wisdom of Solomon; and, behold, a greater than Solomon is here." $(11 + 31) = $ **42**.

Revelation 18:**24** "And in her was found the **blood of prophets**, and of saints, and of all that were slain upon the **earth**." (18 + 24) = **42**, and the earth is 10^**24**th power kilograms of weight like Psalm **24** and we know that **18** is bondage.

Revelation 14:3 "And they sung as it were a new song before the throne, and before the four beasts, and the elders: and no man could learn that song but the hundred and forty and four thousand, which were redeemed from the **earth**." (14 x 3) = **42**.

Matthew 17:25 "He saith, Yes. And when he was come into the house, Jesus prevented him, saying, What thinkest thou, Simon? of whom do the **kings of the earth** take custom or tribute? of their own children, or of strangers?" (17 + 25) = **42**. (17 x 25) = **425**.

* The numbers **35 and 53** that mirror the size of **man** and our **heavenly father** is coming up next. These have to do with a **Father** and **Son** relationship and the measure of a **man**. The universe weighs **10^53** kilograms and man is **10^35** powers size greater than the Planck length (**35 | 53**).

John **10:35** "If he called them **gods**, unto whom the word of God came, and the scripture cannot be broken." Jesus is talking about men being God's and man is actually **10^35** powers greater than the Planck length in **size**. Here is the verse before: John 10:34 "Jesus answered them, Is it not written in your law, **I said, Ye are gods**?"

Matthew **10:35** "For I am come to set a (**man**) at variance against his (**father**), and the daughter against her mother, and the daughter in law against her mother in law." This scripture is talking about a man and his father and man actually is **10^35** magnitudes in size above the Planck length. To get a comparison the earth is 10^42 magnitudes above the Planck length, a difference of (42 − 35) = 7 or 10^7th powers magnitude.

Matthew 18:**35** "So likewise shall my heavenly **Father** do also unto you, if ye from your hearts forgive not every one his **brother** their trespasses." We have **man** again with the words 'his brother' as the **35** and verse numbers (18 + **35**) = **53**, the number that seems to turn up as the **Father** a (**35 | 53**) mirror.

Matthew **5:48** "Be ye therefore perfect, even as your **Father** which is in heaven is perfect." This scripture is talking about the Father, and us being perfect (or a reflection) of Him and (5 + 48) = **53** (weight of the universe). This is man at 10^35 powers in size above the Planck length, a (**35 | 53**) mirror or reflection of the **Father**.

Luke 12:**53** "The **father** shall be divided against the **son**, and the **son against the father**; the mother against the daughter, and the daughter against the mother; the mother in law against her daughter in law, and the daughter in law against her mother in law."

Revelation **5:3** "And no **man** in **heaven**, nor in earth, neither under the earth, was able to open the book, neither to look thereon." Here we have the expression '**no man**' and man is size 10^35 power, which is the opposite of **53** a (**53 | 35**) mirror. We just saw in Matthew 5:48 (5 + 48) = **53**, was about the Father.

John **3:5** "Jesus answered, Verily, verily, I say unto thee, Except a (**man**) be born of water and of the Spirit, he cannot enter into the **kingdom of God**."

Ephesians **3:5** "Which in other ages was not made known unto the (**sons of men**), as it is now revealed unto his holy apostles and prophets by the Spirit."

John 12:23 "And Jesus answered them, saying, The hour is come, that the (**Son of man**) should be glorified." (12 + 23) = **35**.

Acts 13:22 "And when he had removed him, he raised up unto them **David** to be their king; to whom also he gave their testimony, and said, I have found **David** the (**son of Jesse**), a **man** after mine own heart, which shall fulfil all my will." (13 + 22) = **35**.

Matthew 23:**35** "That upon you may come all the righteous **blood shed** upon the earth, from the blood of righteous Abel unto the **blood** of Zacharias (**son of Barachias**), whom ye **slew** between the temple and the altar." We have **35** and the '**son of Barachias**' and **23** is the Bible number of **death**.

Matthew 12:23 "And all the people were amazed, and said, Is not this the (**son of David**)?" (12 + 23) = **35**.

Mark 10:**35** "And James and John, the (**sons of Zebedee**), come unto him, saying, **Master**, we would that thou shouldest do for us whatsoever we shall desire."

Mark 12:**35** "And **Jesus** answered and said, while he taught in the temple, How say the scribes that **Christ** is the (**son of David**)?"

Mark 14:21 "The (**Son of man**) indeed goeth, as it is written of him: but woe to that **man** by whom the (**Son of man**) is betrayed! good were it for that **man** if he had never been born." (14 + 21) = **35**.

Luke 1:**35** "And the angel answered and said unto her, The Holy Ghost shall come upon thee, and the power of the **Highest** shall overshadow thee: therefore also that holy thing which shall be born of thee shall be called the (**Son of God**)."

Luke 9:**35** "And there came a **voice out of the cloud**, saying, This is my (**beloved Son**): hear him."

John 1:34 declares: "And I saw, and bare record that this is the (**Son of God**)." (1 + 34) = **35**.

John 3:**35** "The **Father** loveth the **Son**, and hath given all things into his hand."

John 4:**53** "So the **father** knew that it was at the same hour, in the which **Jesus** said unto him, Thy **son** liveth: and himself believed, and his whole house."

John 6:**53** "Then Jesus said unto them, Verily, verily, I say unto you, Except ye eat the flesh of the (**Son of man**), and drink his blood, ye have no life in you."

John 8:**35** "And the servant abideth not in the house for ever: but the (**Son abideth**) ever."

John 9:**35** "**Jesus** heard that they had cast him out; and when he had found him, he said unto him, Dost thou believe on the (**Son of God**)?"

Hebrews 7:28 "For the law maketh men high priests which have infirmity; but the word of the oath, which was since the law, maketh the (**Son**, who is consecrated for evermore)." (7 + 28) = **35**.

Hebrews 11:24 "By faith Moses, when he was come to years, refused to be called the (**son of Pharaoh's daughter**)." (11 + 24) = **35**.

* The **153** *'great fishes'* number and the "Sons of God."

Adding up (100 + 53) = 153. John 21:11 "Simon Peter went up, and drew the net to land full of great fishes, an (**hundred and fifty and three**): and for all there were so many, yet was not the net broken." Matthew 4:19 "And he saith unto them, Follow me, and I will make you **fishers of men**." The number **153** in the Bible means the "manifestation of the **Sons of God**" and deals with the disciples catching **men** in the net of salvation for Jesus. Romans **8:19** declares "For the earnest expectation of the creature **waiteth** for the manifestation of the (**sons of God**)." We are 'waiting' for the mani-festation of the 'sons of God' and verse numbers (8 x 19) = **152**; just add the oneness (**unity**) of the church (**152 + 1**) = **153**. Ephesians **4:13** "**Till we all come** in the (**unity**) of the faith, and of the knowledge of the **Son of God**, unto a perfect **man**, unto the **measure** of the stature of the fulness of Christ." We are still waiting (**till we all come**) and verse numbers (**4 x 13**) = **52**, just add unity

(1) again (52 + 1) = **53**. The word '**unity**' is only in the Bible 3 times. Here is the term '***great fish***' again in Jonah 1:**17** "Now the LORD had prepared a (**great fish**) to swallow up Jonah. And Jonah was in the belly of the fish three days and three nights." This is a **17** verse and **17** is an exact multiple of **153**; **9** is the number of **manifestation** in the Bible and (**17 x 9**) = **153**. Matthew 12:41 "The men of Nineveh shall rise in judgment with this generation, and shall condemn it: because they repented at the preaching of (**Jonas**); and, behold, a greater than Jonas is here"; verse numbers (12 + 41) = **53**. Matthew 12:39 "But he answered and said unto them, An evil and adulterous generation seeketh after a sign; and there shall no sign be given to it, but the sign of the prophet (**Jonas**)." The verse numbers here are (12 + 39) = **51**, considering that **Jonas** was **3** days and **3** nights in the belly of the fish, makes this (**3 x 51**) = **153**. Psalms 144:**9** "I will sing a **new song** unto thee, O God: upon a psaltery and an instrument of (**ten strings**) will I sing praises unto thee." **144** is the size of the **man**/angel from Revelation 21:17; verse numbers (**144 + 9**) = **153**!

* These are scriptures about time using the numbers **24, 44, and 133** (The cesium atom that tracks time).

Mark **13:31** "Heaven and earth shall pass away: but my words shall **not pass away**." Jesus' words are timeless "...shall not pass away" and verse numbers (**13 + 31**) = **44** the Planck **time** from Psalm 44. Also look at our (**1331**) all together; knowing that all time in the universe is kept by the cesium **133** atom and (**133 x 1**) = **133**.

Mark **13:32** "But of that **day and that hour** knoweth no man, no, not the angels which are in heaven, neither the Son, but the Father."

Nehemiah **13:31** says "And for the wood offering, at (**times**) appointed, and for the firstfruits. Remember me, O my God, for good." (**133** and (13 + 31) = **44**).

Jeremiah **13:3** "And the word of the LORD came unto me the (**second time**), saying." The mirror to the last verse is: Jeremiah **33:1** "Moreover the word of the LORD came unto Jeremiah the (**second time**), while he was yet shut up in the court of the prison, saying." A (**133 | 331**) mirror of Jeremiah, and both verses are about **time** and both say the (**second** time).

Matthew **13:30** "Let both grow together until the harvest: and in the (**time**) of harvest I will say to the reapers, Gather ye together first the tares, and bind them in bundles to burn them: but gather the wheat into my barn."

Mark **13:33** "Take ye heed, watch and pray: for ye know not when the (**time**) is."

Luke **13:33** "Nevertheless I must walk **to day**, and **to morrow**, and the **day following**: for it cannot be that a prophet perish out of Jerusalem."

Luke **13:35** "Behold, your house is left unto you desolate: and verily I say unto you, Ye shall not see me, until the (**time**) come when ye shall say, Blessed is he that cometh in the name of the Lord."

Acts **13:33** "God hath fulfilled the same unto us their children, in that he hath raised up Jesus again; as it is also written in the second psalm, Thou art my Son, this (**day**) have I begotten thee."

Psalm **133:3** "As the dew of Hermon, and as the dew that descended upon the mountains of Zion: for there the LORD commanded the blessing, even life **for evermore**." This is talking about life evermore, beyond **time**.

Psalms 115:18 "But we will bless the LORD from this (**time**) forth and **for evermore**. Praise the LORD." (115 + 18) = **133**.

Jeremiah **51:33** "For thus saith the LORD of hosts, the God of Israel; The daughter of Babylon is like a threshing floor, it is (**time**) to thresh her: yet a little while, and the (**time**) of her harvest shall come."

Galatians **4:4** "But when the fulness of the (**time**) was come, God sent forth his Son, made of a woman, made under the law." This important scripture mentions **time** again in a **4:4** verse; the Planck time from Psalm **44**.

Psalm **44:1** "We have heard with our ears, O God, our fathers have told us, what work thou didst in their days, in the (**times**) of old."

Psalms 22:2 "O my God, I cry in the **day** (**time**), but thou hearest not; and in the **night season**, and am not silent." (22 x 2) = **44**. (22 + 2) = **24 hours** (the **day** time and **night** season).

Isaiah **44:8** "Fear ye not, neither be afraid: have not I told thee from that (**time**), and have declared it? ye are even my witnesses. Is there a God beside me? yea, there is no God; I know not any."

Nehemiah 12:**44** "And at that (**time**) were some appointed over the chambers for the treasures, for the offerings, for the firstfruits, and for the tithes, to gather into them out of the fields of the cities the portions of the law for the priests and Levites: for Judah rejoiced for the priests and for the Levites that waited."

Nehemiah 10:34 "And we cast the lots among the priests, the Levites, and the people, for the wood offering, to bring it into the house of our God, after the houses of our fathers, at (**times**) appointed year by year, to burn upon the altar of the LORD our God, as it is written in the law:" (10 + 34) = **44**.

1st Kings 18:**44** "And it came to pass at the seventh (**time**), that he said, Behold, there ariseth a little cloud out of the sea, like a man's hand. And he said, Go up, say unto Ahab, Prepare thy chariot, and get thee down that the rain stop thee not."

Jeremiah 50:**44** "Behold, he shall come up like a lion from the swelling of Jordan unto the habitation of the strong: but I will make them suddenly run away from her: and who is a chosen man, that I may appoint over her? for who is like me? and who will appoint me the (**time**)? and who is that shepherd that will stand before me?"

Judges **4:4** "And Deborah, a prophetess, the wife of Lapidoth, she judged Israel at that (**time**)."

Luke **19:44** "And shall lay thee even with the ground, and thy children within thee; and they shall not leave in thee one stone upon another; because thou knewest not the (**time**) of thy visitation."

Matthew 26:**44** says "And he left them, and went away again, and prayed the (**third time**), saying the same words."

Matthew **24:36** "But of that **day and hour** knoweth no man, no, not the angels of heaven, but my Father only." Here day and hour are mentioned and there are **24** hours in a day, and our verse numbers (24 + 36) = 60, as in **60** minutes in an hour. Our verse numbers multiplied (24 x 36) = **864**, just multiply by 100 to get (864 x 100) = **86,400**, the number of **seconds** in a day!

Matthew 24:**44** "Therefore be ye also ready: for in such an (**hour**) as ye think not the Son of man cometh." Here we have **24 as in 24** hours in a day with 'an hour as ye think not' and **44** is the Planck time.

Matthew **24:42** "Watch therefore: for ye know not what (**hour**) your Lord doth come." The number (**24**) is a mirror of the number **42** (the size of earth times the Planck length). Here we are warned about the hour (**24** hours in a day) that Jesus will return to the earth (size of earth is **42**) in verse 24:42 of the book of Matthew; a (**24 | 42**) mirror.

Matthew **24**:50 "The lord of that servant shall come in a **day** when he looketh not for him and in an (**hour**) that he is not aware of." Verse numbers (24 x 50) = 1200 or **12:00** o'clock.

John **2:4** "Jesus saith unto her, Woman, what have I to do with thee? mine (**hour**) is not yet come." **24 hours** in a day. Also (2 x 4) = (**8**) Jesus, who is about to turn (**2 + 4**) = **6** water-pots into wine!

Luke 12:12 "For the Holy Ghost shall teach you in the same (**hour**) what ye ought to say." (12 + 12) hours = **24** hours in a day.

Luke **24**:33 "And they rose up the same (**hour**), and returned to Jerusalem, and found the eleven gathered together, and them that were with them."

Matthew 25:19 "After a long (**time**) the lord of those servants cometh, and reckoneth with them." (25 + 19) = **44**.

Proverbs 25:19 "Confidence in an unfaithful man in (**time**) of trouble is like a broken tooth, and a foot out of joint." (25 + 19) = **44**.

2nd Kings 19:25 "Hast thou not heard long ago how I have done it, and of **ancient (times)** that I have formed it? now have I brought it to pass, that thou shouldest be to lay waste fenced cities into ruinous heaps." (19 + 25) = **44**.

Matthew 26:18 "And he said, Go into the city to such a man, and say unto him, The Master saith, My (**time**) is at hand; I will keep the passover at thy house with my disciples." (26 + 18) = **44**.

Leviticus 26:18 "And if ye will not yet for all this hearken unto me, then I will punish you seven (**times**) more for your sins." (26 + 18) = **44**.

1st Chronicles 12:32 "And of the children of Issachar, which were **men** that had **understanding** of the (**times**), to know what Israel ought to do; the heads of them were two hundred; and all their brethren were at their commandment." (12 + 32) = **44**.

Luke 15:29 "And he answering said to his father, Lo, these many years do I serve thee, neither transgressed I at any (**time**) thy commandment: and yet thou never gavest me a kid, that I might make merry with my friends." (15 + 29) = **44**.

Luke 4:11 "And in their hands they shall bear thee up, lest at any (**time**) thou dash thy foot against a stone." (4 x 11) = **44**.

Judges 11:4 "And it came to pass in process of (**time**), that the children of Ammon made war against Israel." (11 x 4) = **44**.

Ezra 4:11 "This is the copy of the letter that they sent unto him, even unto Artaxerxes the king; Thy servants the men on this side the river, and at such a (**time**)." (4 x 11) = **44**.

Jeremiah 4:11 "At that (**time**) shall it be said to this people and to Jerusalem, A dry wind of the high places in the wilderness toward the daughter of my people, not to fan, nor to cleanse." (4 x 11) = **44**.

Ezekiel 4:11 "Thou shalt drink also water by measure, the sixth part of an hin: from (**time**) to (**time**) shalt thou drink." (4 x 11) = **44**.

Also consider that (**44 x 3**) equals **132**; just add the unity factor of oneness (**132 + 1**) = **133**.

* Next is the number **31** dealing with **seeds**, (**offspring** and **increase**), and things that **rise** up.

Matthew **13:31** "Another parable put he forth unto them, saying, The kingdom of heaven is like to a grain of **mustard seed**, which a man took, and sowed in his field." The number **31** in the Bible means '*offspring*' and here we have a (13 | 31) mirror talking about **seeds** and things springing out of the ground. Speaking of offspring; on the cover of People weekly magazine dated February 25, 2002 exactly **31** women show up on the cover with their babies (**offspring**). These are the women whose husbands died in the World Trade Center attack. The mass of the electron is **10^-31** power as stated from Psalm 31, and we know that electrons are always springing off new photons of light. The verse numbers (13 + 31) = **44**, waiting the **time** (and **133 as time**) for the **seeds to grow**.

Job **31:8** "Then let me **sow**, and let another eat; yea, let my (**offspring**) be rooted out." Offspring on a **31** numbered verse.

Mark 4:27 "And should sleep, and rise night and day, and the (**seed**) should (**spring**) and **grow up**, he knoweth not how." The words 'seeds' and 'spring' and 'grow up' are here and (4 + 27) = **31**, the Bible number of '**offspring**'.

Mark 4:**31** "It is like a grain of (**mustard seed**), which, when it is sown in the earth, is less than all the **seeds** that be in the earth." Seeds springing up and growing in a **31** numbered verse.

Deuteronomy 22:9 say "Thou shalt not sow thy vineyard with divers **seeds**: lest the fruit of thy **seed** which thou hast **sown**, and the fruit of thy vineyard, be defiled." The word '**seeds**' appears in the Old Testament just **one** time and (22 + 9) = **31**.

Psalms 21:10 "Their **fruit** shalt thou destroy from the earth, and their (**seed**) from among the children of men." Seeds and (21 + 10) = **31**.

Jeremiah **31:27** "Behold, the days come, saith the LORD, that I will sow the house of Israel and the house of Judah with the (**seed**) of man, and with the (**seed**) of beast."

Jeremiah **31:36** "If those ordinances depart from before me, saith the LORD, then the (**seed**) of Israel also shall cease from being a nation before me for ever."

Jeremiah **31:37** "Thus saith the LORD; If heaven above can be measured, and the foundations of the earth searched out beneath, I will also cast off all the (**seed**) of Israel for all that they have done, saith the LORD."

Mark 8:**31** "And he began to teach them, that the Son of man must suffer many things, and be rejected of the elders, and of the chief priests, and scribes, and be killed, and after three days (**rise**) again."

Mark 9:**31** "For he taught his disciples, and said unto them, The Son of man is delivered into the hands of men, and they shall kill him; and after that he is killed, he shall (**rise**) the third day."

Luke 16:**31** "And he said unto him, If they hear not Moses and the prophets, neither will they be persuaded, though one **rose from the dead**."

John 11:**31** "The Jews then which were with her in the house, and comforted her, when they saw Mary, that **she rose up hastily** and went out, followed her, saying, She goeth unto the **grave to weep** there."

Luke 24:7 "Saying, The Son of man must be delivered into the hands of sinful men, and be crucified, and the third day (**rise**) again. Our **31** and rising again as $(24 + 7) = 31$.

Luke 9:22 "Saying, The Son of man must suffer many things, and be rejected of the elders and chief priests and scribes, and be slain, and be **raised** the third day." $(9 + 22) = 31$.

Acts 17:**31** "Because he hath appointed a day, in the which he will judge the world in righteousness by that man whom he hath ordained; whereof he hath given assurance unto all men, in that he hath **raised him** from the dead."

1st Corinthians 15:16 "For if the dead (**rise**) not, then is not Christ (**raised**)." Rising again and $(15 + 16) = 31$.

Exodus **12:31** "And he called for Moses and Aaron by night, and said, (**Rise up**), and get you forth from among my people, both ye and the children of Israel; and go, serve the LORD, as ye have said."

2nd Samuel 18:**31** "And, behold, Cushi came; and Cushi said, Tidings, my lord the king: for the LORD hath avenged thee this day of all them that **rose up against thee**."

Genesis 26:**31** proclaims "And **they rose up** betimes in the morning, and sware one to another: and Isaac sent them away, and they departed from him in peace."

Genesis **31**:17 says "Then **Jacob rose up**, and set his sons and his wives upon camels."

Genesis 32:**31** says "And as he passed over Penuel the **sun rose upon him,** and he halted upon his thigh."

Joshua **3:1** "And Joshua **rose early in the morning**; and they removed from Shittim, and came to Jordan, he and all the children of Israel, and lodged there before they passed over."

Nehemiah **3:1** "Then Eliashib the **high priest rose up** with his brethren the priests, and they builded the sheep gate; they sanctified it, and set up the doors of it; even unto the tower of Meah they sanctified it, unto the tower of Hananeel."

Psalms **3:1** "Lord, how are they increased that trouble me! many are they that **(rise)** up against me."

Colossians **3:1** "If ye then be **(risen)** with Christ, seek those things which are above, where Christ sitteth on the right hand of God."

Matthew 24:7 "For nation shall **(rise)** against nation, and kingdom against kingdom: and there shall be famines, and pestilences, and earthquakes, in divers places." Rising nations with (24 + 7) = **31**.

Luke **21:10** "Then said he unto them, Nation shall **(rise)** against nation, and kingdom against kingdom"; (21 + 10) = **31**.

Luke **11:31** "The queen of the south shall **(rise)** up in the judgment with the men of this generation, and condemn them: for she came from the utmost parts of the **(earth)** to hear the wisdom of Solomon; and, behold, a greater than Solomon is here." We have **31** and rise with the **earth** and $(11 + 31) = 42$, the Planck size of the earth at 10^{42} power.

The word '**risen**' appears exactly **31** times in the New Testament! It appears **20** times in the Old Testament for a total of **51** times in the whole Bible. You have just entered the real mystery of '**Area 51**' dealing with Jesus, generations, and resurrection life. 1st Corinthians **15:51** mystifies with: "Behold, I shew you a **mystery**; We shall not all sleep, but we shall all be changed"; this even reflects **51** with a (**15 | 51**) mirror. We know that the *generational* number (**14**) + Word of the Father (**37**) = **51**. The Torah numbers (304,805) added $(3 + 0 + 4 + 8 + 0 + 5) = 20$, the number of times *risen* shows up in the Old Testament. The Torah numbers, without the zeros $(85 - 34)$ also equal **51**, with the zeroes they are $(805 - 304) = 501$. The number **20** in the Bible means: *redemption*. The number 51 squared = (5 squared = **25** and 1 squared = **1**) which makes $(25 + 1) = $ **26**, the number of Jehovah. Acts **17:3** "Opening and alleging, that Christ must needs have suffered, and (**risen**) again from the dead; and that this Jesus, whom I preach unto you, is Christ"; verse numbers (**17 x 3**) = **51**, and (**17 + 3**) = **20** (the number of times **risen** appears in the **Old Testament**). 1st Corinthians 15:13 says "But if there be no resurrection of the dead, then is Christ not risen:" If there "be no resurrection" comes from verse numbers 15:13; but there really is a resurrection so let's look at the opposite, the mirror of (15:13 | **31:51**) ok then **31** and **51** that's more like it! If we multiply (**3 x 51**) we get **153** the 'great fishes' and 'Sons of God' number. The (**3 x 51**) if pasted together as **351** is the mirror to 153 a (**351 | 153**) mirror.

* Some more **light** scriptures at **34** like Psalm **34** with **lighten** and **brightness**.

Matthew 17:2 "And was transfigured before them: and his **face did shine** as the sun, and his raiment was white as the **light**." The verse numbers (17 x 2) = **34** and this says "…and his **face** did **shine** as the **sun**…" Now look at Psalm **34:5** "They looked unto him, and were **lightened**: and their **faces were not ashamed**." $10^{-34\text{th}}$ power is number for the minimum energy of a photon of light in joule seconds. Actually it is 6.626 x 10^-34 power. This is also called Planck's constant and in one of the most important constants in physics. This is the same value as Psalm **27** (which used erg seconds) to measure light. We are just using a different scale of measurement called joule seconds for our 10^-34 power number of light.

Habakkuk **3:4** "And his **brightness was as the light**; he had horns coming out of his hand: and there was the hiding of his power."

Luke **2:32** says "A light to **lighten the Gentiles**, and the glory of thy people Israel." Our verse numbers (2 + 32) = **34** again, as in $10^{\wedge}\text{-}34^{\text{th}}$ power, the number for the minimum energy of a photon of light in joule seconds.

Luke **11:34** "The **light** of the body is the eye: therefore when thine eye is single, thy whole body also is full of **light**; but when thine eye is evil, thy body also is full of darkness." We have **light** falling on a 34 numbered verse.

Job **3:4** "Let that day be darkness; let not God regard it from above, neither let the **light shine** upon it."

Psalm **34:5** "They looked unto him, and were **lightened**: and their faces were not ashamed."

Psalms 67:1 "God be merciful unto us, and bless us; and cause **his face to shine upon us**; Selah" (67 + 1) = 68, (**34** x 2) = 68.

Job 36:32 "With clouds he **covereth the light**; and commandeth it not to **shine by the cloud** that cometh betwixt." (36 + 32) = 68, (**34** x 2) = 68.

Isaiah 59:9 "Therefore is judgment far from us, neither doth justice overtake us: we wait for **light**, but behold obscurity; for **brightness**, but we walk in **darkness**." (59 + 9) = 68, (**34** x 2) = 68.

Luke 23:45 "And the **sun was darkened**, and the veil of the temple was rent in the midst." (23 + 45) = 68, (**34** x 2) = 68. Jesus died (**23**) to save (**45**) us. Thirty four is in the middle also 23:45.

James 1:**17** "Every good gift and every perfect gift is from above, and cometh down from the **Father of lights**, with whom is no variableness, **neither shadow of turning**." (17 x 2) = **34**.

1ˢᵗ John **1:7** "But if we walk in the **light**, as he is in the **light**, we have fellowship one with another, and the blood of Jesus Christ his Son cleanseth us from all sin." (17 x 2) = **34**.

* Here are scriptures referring to the numbers *666, 66,* and **18;** (6 + 6 + 6) = **18**.

John *6:66* "From that time many of his **disciples went back**, and walked no more with him." Many of His disciples turned away from Jesus on a '**666**' verse number. Revelation **13:18** "Here is wisdom. Let him that hath understanding count the number of the beast: for it is the number of a man; and his number is **Six hundred threescore and six**." (*666*). Keep in mind that (6 + 6 + 6) = **18**, the verse number in Revelation 13. The number 13 in the Bible means (**depravity** and **rebellion**) and 18 is bondage.

Luke **10:18** "And he said unto them, I beheld **Satan** as **lightning** fall from heaven." Here we have lightning (dealing with **electricity**) and the verse numbers of Revelation **13:18** (13 + 18) = **31** the mass of the electron; see how Psalm **31** is about computers and the net; maybe the beast is going to use (or even be) a computer! The Hartree energy (a scientific constant of 4.3597 x 10^{18} power joules) is what is used to measure the **energy** of the electron's orbit; it is 10^{18} power and Luke **10:18** is talking about Satan and lightning (*electricity*). The number 18 in the Bible means bondage! The ampere (a basic unit) defining the flow of electrons (*electricity*) is defined as 6.28 x $10^{18\text{th}}$ power **electrons** per second. Psalm **18:10** "And he rode upon a (**cherub**), and did **fly**: yea, he did **fly** upon the **wings of the wind**." It's interesting that these Psalm **18** verse numbers are (18 x 10) = **180**, because **electrons** have what is called spin ½, and 180 is ½ of 360 degrees, a full circle.

Job **1:8** "And the LORD said unto **Satan**, Hast thou considered my servant Job, that there is none like him in the earth, a perfect and an upright man, one that feareth God, and escheweth evil?"

Ezekiel **28:18** "Thou hast **defiled thy sanctuaries** by the multitude **of thine iniquities**, by the iniquity of thy traffick; therefore will I bring forth a fire from the midst of thee, it shall devour thee, and I will bring thee to ashes upon the earth in the sight of all them that behold thee." Just prior to this verse **Satan** is explained in: Ezekiel **28:14** "Thou art the anointed (**cherub**) that covereth; and I have set thee so: thou wast upon the holy mountain of God; thou hast walked up and down in the midst of the stones of fire." This scripture in Ezekiel is talking about **Satan** and his former state in heaven, here is the scripture afterwards: Ezekiel 28:15 "Thou wast perfect in thy ways from the day that thou wast created, till **iniquity** was found in thee."

Notice that Ezekiel 28:14 and Psalm **18:10** both mention (**cherub**).

Here is more 'lightning' and electricity in **18** numbered verses like Luke **10:18** "...I beheld **Satan** as lightning fall from heaven."

Psalm **18**:14 "Yea, he sent out his arrows, and scattered them; and he shot out **lightnings**, and discomfited them."

Psalms 77:**18** "The voice of thy thunder was in the heaven: **the lightnings lightened** the world: the earth trembled and shook."

Revelation 16:**18** says "And there were voices, and thunders, and **lightnings**; and there was a great earthquake, such as was not since men were upon the earth, so mighty an earthquake, and so great." The verse numbers (16 x 18) = **288**, the size of our **2 angels** on the Ark of the Covenant, and look who did this in the scripture before this one: Revelation 16:17 "And the seventh (**angel**) poured out his vial into the air; and there came a great voice out of the temple of heaven, from the throne, saying, It is done."

Revelation **18**:1 "And after these things I saw another **angel** come down from heaven, having great power; and the earth was **lightened** with his glory."

Exodus 20:**18** thunders: "And all the people saw the **thunderings**, and the **lightnings**, and the noise of the trumpet, and the mountain smoking: and when the people saw it, they removed, and stood afar off."

Revelation **18**:23 "And the **light** of a **candle shall shine** no more at all in thee; and the voice of the bridegroom and of the bride shall be heard no more at all in thee: for thy merchants were the great men of the earth; for by **thy sorceries were all nations deceived**." **18** is bondage and **23** is death and this is about **sorceries**.

Psalms **18**:28 "For thou wilt **light** my **candle**: the LORD my God will **enlighten** my **darkness**."

Luke 11:**18** "If **Satan** also be divided against himself, how shall his kingdom stand? because ye say that I cast out **devils** through **Beelzebub**."

Matthew 10:8 "Heal the sick, cleanse the lepers, raise the dead, **cast out devils**: freely ye have received, freely give." $(10 + 8) = $ **18**.

Mark 3:15 "And to have power to heal sicknesses, and to **cast out devils**." $(3 + 15) = $ **18**.

James 3:15 "This wisdom descendeth not from above, but is **earthly, sensual, devilish**." $(3 + 15) = $ **18**.

Matthew 11:**18** "For John came neither eating nor drinking, and they say, He hath a **devil**."

Matthew 17:**18** "And Jesus rebuked the **devil**; and he departed out of him: and the child was cured from that very hour."
Mark 5:**18** "And when he was come into the ship, he that had

been possessed with the **devil** prayed him that he might be with him."

Acts 26:**18** "To open their eyes, and to turn them from darkness to light, and from the **power of Satan** unto God, that they may receive forgiveness of sins, and inheritance among them which are sanctified by faith that is in me."

1st Thessalonians 2:**18** "Wherefore we would have come unto you, even I Paul, once and again; but **Satan hindered us**."

2nd Thessalonians 2:9 "Even him, whose coming is after the working of **Satan** with all power and signs and lying wonders", and verse numbers (2 x 9) = **18**.

Revelation 2:9 "I know thy works, and tribulation, and poverty, (but thou art rich) and I know the blasphemy of them which say they are Jews, and are not, but are the synagogue **of Satan**", (2 x 9) = **18**.

Matthew 12:24 "But when the Pharisees heard it, they said, This fellow doth not cast out **devils**, but by Beelzebub the prince of the devils." Verse numbers (12 + 24) = **36**, a multiple of **18** (**18 x 2**) = 36.

1st Timothy 3:6 "Not a novice, lest being lifted up with pride he fall into the **condemnation of the devil**." Another 36 (**18 x 2**) = 36 or (**3 x 6**) = **18**.

Mark 7:29 "And he said unto her, For this saying go thy way; the **devil is gone** out of thy daughter." (7 + 29) = **36** or (**18** x 2) and (**6 x 6**) = 36.

Romans 16:20 "And the God of peace shall **bruise Satan** under your feet shortly. The grace of our Lord Jesus Christ be with you. Amen." (16 + 20) = **36**, (**18 x 2**) = 36.

Luke 13:16 "And ought not this woman, being a daughter of

Abraham, whom **Satan** hath bound, lo, these (**eighteen years**), be loosed from this bond on the sabbath day?" Satan had her bound for eighteen years.

Luke 13:4 "Or those (**eighteen**), upon whom the tower in Siloam fell, and slew them, think ye that they were **sinners** above all men that dwelt in Jerusalem?" This is talking about sinners and the number eighteen and (**18**) is bondage.

Judges **10:8** "And that year they **vexed and oppressed** the children of Israel: (**eighteen years**), all the children of Israel that were on the other side Jordan in the land of the Amorites, which is in Gilead." The words **vexed, and oppressed** along with **eighteen years** are here, and of course (**10 + 8**) = **18**.

1st Chronicles **18:12** "Moreover Abishai the son of Zeruiah **slew** of the **Edomites** in the valley of salt (**eighteen thousand**)." He slew eighteen thousand Edomites on an **18** verse.

Ezra **8:18** "And by the **good hand of our God** upon us they brought us a man of understanding, of the sons of Mahli, the son of Levi, the son of Israel; and Sherebiah, with his sons and his brethren, (**eighteen**)." Here is a good scripture with the number **18** talking about "his brethren **eighteen**", (18 x 8 (*Jesus*)) = **144**, the size of the man or **angel** from Revelation 21:17. (**8 + 18**) = **26** Jehovah.

Revelation 9:20 "And the rest of the men which were not killed by these plagues yet repented not of the works of their hands, that they should not **worship devils**, and **idols of gold**, and silver, and brass, and stone, and of wood: which neither can **see, nor hear, nor walk**." (9 x 20) = **180** or (**18** x 10).

Revelation **18:2** "And he cried mightily with a strong voice, saying, Babylon the great is fallen, is fallen, and is become the **habitation of devils**, and the hold of **every foul spirit**, and a cage of every unclean and hateful bird."
* **God's** answer to *Harry Potter*: in **Deuteronomy 18**.

Deuteronomy 18:9-13 "When thou art come into the land which the LORD thy God giveth thee, thou shalt not learn to do after the **abominations** of those nations. There shall not be found among you any one that maketh his **son** or his **daughter** to pass through the fire, or that useth **divination**, or an observer of times, or an **enchanter**, or a **witch**. Or a charmer, or a consulter with **familiar spirits**, or a **wizard**, or a necromancer. For all that do these things are an abomination unto the LORD: and because of these **abominations** the LORD thy God doth **drive them out from before thee**. Thou shalt be **perfect** with the **LORD** thy **God**."

The word lightning is found in the Bible just 13 times. The word lightnings is in the Bible 14 times (13 + 14) = **27** like Psalm **27** "The Lord is my **light** and my salvation." Matthew **24:27** "For as the **lightning** cometh out of the east, and shineth even unto the west; so shall also the coming of the Son of man be." The number **18** is connected to *electricity* and (18 + 9 (Bible number of **manifestation**) = **27** light). The number 24 is Jesus' number of the Priesthood and **27** is light and He is coming back as **lightning**. The verse numbers of Revelation 13:18 are talking about the *666* number and (13 x 18) = **234**; but you do not have to be afraid, just look at the **234** of Psalm **23:4** "Yea, though I walk through the valley of the shadow of **death**, I will **fear no evil**: for thou art with me; thy rod and thy staff they comfort me." Now look at this in Revelation 21:17 "And he measured the wall thereof, an **hundred and forty and four cubits**, according to the measure of a man, that is, of the angel." Here we are talking about a man/angel again in Revelation 21:17 at a size of 144 cubits, knowing that Satan is a fallen angel. A cubit (which varied according to ancient peoples) is about **18** inches and 144 cubits x **18** inches = 216 feet; (*6 x 6 x 6*) also equals **216**!

* Now getting back to the *66* and *666* numbers in the scripture.

Matthew *26:66* "What think ye? They answered and said, He is guilty of **death**."
Genesis *6:6* says "And it **repented** the LORD that he had made

man on the earth, and it grieved him at his heart."

Matthew 2:16 "Then Herod, when he saw that he was mocked of the wise men, was exceeding wroth, and sent forth, and **slew all the children that were in Bethlehem,** and in all the coasts thereof, from two years old and under, according to the time which he had diligently enquired of the wise men." Herod slew all of the children in Bethlehem, a very **satanic** thing and our verse numbers 216 equal (*6 x 6 x 6*) = 216. Also (2 + 16) = **18.**

2nd Kings 21:6 "And he made his son pass through the fire, and observed times, and used **enchantments,** and dealt with **familiar spirits and wizards**: he wrought much wickedness in the sight of the LORD, to provoke him to anger." And as just stated (*6 x 6 x 6*) = 216.

1st Kings 11:6 "And Solomon **did evil** in the sight of the LORD, and went not fully after the LORD, as did David his father." Solomon did evil and verse numbers (6 x 11) = **66; 66** is the Bible number of *idol worship*.

Genesis 3:22 "And the LORD God said, Behold, the man is become as one of us, to know **good and evil**: and now, lest he put forth his hand, and take also of the tree of life, and eat, and live for ever." Verse numbers (3 x 22) = **66.** Man now had revelation light (**22**) of good and evil.

Mark 3:22 "And the scribes which came down from Jerusalem said, He hath **Beelzebub,** and by the prince of the **devils** casteth he out devils." Beelzebub, the prince of the devils and (3 x 22) = **66.**

Luke 22:3 "Then entered **Satan** into **Judas** surnamed Iscariot, being of the number of the twelve." **Satan** entered into **Judas** and (22 x 3) = **66.**

2nd Chronicles 33:2 "But did that which was **evil** in the sight of the LORD, like unto the abominations of the heathen, whom the LORD had cast out before the children of Israel." Evil in the sight of the Lord and (33 x 2) = **66**.

Isaiah *66*:4 "I also will choose their **delusions**, and will bring their **fears upon them**; because when I called, none did answer; when I spake, they did not hear: but they did **evil** before mine eyes, and chose that in which I delighted not." They did evil before my eyes with **66**:4.

Ezekiel 6:11 "Thus saith the Lord GOD; Smite with thine hand, and stamp with thy foot, and say, Alas for all the **evil abominations** of the house of Israel! for they shall fall by the sword, by the famine, and by the pestilence." Evil abominations and verse numbers (6 x 11) = **66**.

Micah 6:11 "Shall I count them pure with the **wicked balances**, and with the bag of **deceitful weights**?" (6 x 11) = **66**.

Genesis 6:11 "The earth also was **corrupt** before God, and the earth was filled with **violence**." (6 x 11) = **66**.

Ephesians 6:11 "Put on the whole **armour of God**, that ye may be able to stand against the wiles of the **devil**." Standing against the wiles of the devil and (6 x 11) = **66**. (6 + 11) = **17** (the *victory* number) because the '**armour**' is the **victory**!

Acts 7:59 says "And **they stoned** Stephen, calling upon God, and saying, Lord Jesus, receive my spirit." **Evil** men **stoning** Stephen (7 + 59) = **66**.

Revelation 22:3 "And there shall be **no more curse**: but the throne of God and of the Lamb shall be in it; and his servants shall serve him." No more **curse** (22 x 3) = **66**.

Matthew 25:41 "Then shall he say also unto them on the left hand, Depart from me, **ye cursed**, into everlasting fire, prepared for the **devil and his angels**." Our verse numbers (25 + 41) = **66**.

Hebrews **6:6** "If they shall **fall away**, to renew them again unto repentance; seeing they **crucify to themselves** the Son of God afresh, and put him to an **open shame**."

Luke 22:44 "And being in an **agony** he prayed more earnestly: and his **sweat** was as it were **great drops of blood** falling down to the ground." Jesus (the light **22**) is in agony for *sin* and (22 + 44) = **66**.

Isaiah *66*:3 "He that killeth an ox is as if he slew a man; he that sacrificeth a lamb, as if he cut off a dog's neck; he that offereth an oblation, as if he offered swine's blood; he that burneth incense, as if he blessed an **idol**. Yea, they have chosen their own ways, and their soul **delighteth in their abominations**." Talking about 'blessed an *idol*' and **66** in the Bible means *idol* worship.

* These are related to the numbers **38 and 39** as *gravity*, Jesus walking on the water, and the phrases: "**KING OF THE JEWS**" or "**JESUS OF NAZARETH**" relating to the *heavy cross*.

Matthew 14:24 "But the ship was now in the midst of the sea, **tossed with waves**: for the wind was contrary." Gravity is 10^{38} power controlling the elements and verse numbers (14 + 24) = **38**.

Matthew 14:25 "And in the fourth watch of the night Jesus went unto them, **walking on the sea**." Now Jesus is a little higher than *gravity* because He is walking on the water and verse numbers (14 + 25) = **39**.

Mark **4:38** "And he was in the hinder part of the ship, **asleep on a pillow**: and they awake him, and say unto him, Master, **carest thou not that we perish**?" Gravity again with the **forces of nature** and **waves of the sea saying** "…carest thou not that we perish", in a verse that has (**38**) gravity in it. Verse numbers (4 + 38) = **42** the Planck size of the **earth**! Matthew **28:18** "And Jesus came and spake unto them, saying, All **power** is given unto me in **heaven** and in **earth**." The earth's size **42** plus **4** seen dimensions (**heavens**) = 46; so does Matthew (**28 + 18**) = **46**. (**42 x 4**) = **168** and 168 is $10^{80} + 10^{88}$; (80 + 88) = **168**, which is the estimated number of all particles of **light** and **matter** in the Universe 10^**168**! Jesus (**8**) x (**21**) Holy Spirit equals **168** also, like the **821** (**Eightfold** Way) of particle physics.

Mark **4:39** "And he arose, and **rebuked the wind**, and said unto the sea, **Peace, be still**. And the wind ceased, and there was a great calm." Again we have a similar situation with Jesus and the sea in the book of Mark dealing with verse (**38**) gravity, and one number higher in the stilling of the sea with (**39**). Psalm 39 is about **speech** and He said "**Peace, be still**"; amazing! Psalm **39**:2 "I was dumb with silence, I held my **peace**..."

Matthew 11:28 "Come unto me, all ye that labour and are **heavy laden**, and I will give you **rest**."
Jesus is going beyond gravity (like Psalm 38 and **heavy laden**) and giving us rest as (11 + 28) = **39**.

Matthew 20:19 "And shall deliver him to the Gentiles to mock, and to scourge, and to **crucify him**: and the third day he shall **rise again**." This scripture says "...He shall **rise** again" and (20 + 19) = **39**. God's victory number (17) magnified ten times (17 x 10) = 170 and (170 + **39**) = **209**, landing in the 208-209 antigravity range!

Hebrews 12:27 "And this word, Yet once more, signifieth the removing of those things **that are shaken**, as of things that are made, that those things which **cannot be shaken** may remain." This is (12 + 27) = **39** talking about things that **cannot be shaken** above gravity (38 + 1) = **39**. Also our 39 number is (3 x 9) = 27 and (3 + 9) = 12, our verse numbers!

John 18:**39** "But ye have a custom, that I should **release** unto you one at the passover: will ye therefore that I release unto you the **King of the Jews**?" **Release** unto you **King of the Jews** on a **39** verse.

* This next set of **38's** is really amazing as they all point to the **KING OF KINGS** and **KING OF THE JEWS** and the cross.
Matthew **10:38** "And he that taketh not his **cross**, and followeth

after **me**, is not worthy of me." We know that **10^-38 power** is gravity, and Psalm 38 says "...an **heavy** burden they are too **heavy** for me"; and in Matthew 10:38 we are carrying something **heavy** – **a cross**. The word 'heavy' shows up in **38** different verses of the Bible and twice in Psalm 38 only, for a total of 39 different times.

Mark **10:38** "But Jesus said unto them, Ye know not what ye ask: can ye **drink of the cup that I drink of**? and be **baptized with the baptism** that I am baptized with? He is talking of the **cross** here.

John **19:19** "And Pilate wrote a title, and put it on the cross. And the writing was **JESUS OF NAZARETH THE KING OF THE JEWS**." Knowing that 10^-38 power is gravity: verse numbers (**19 + 19**) = **38**, the gravity and weight of our sins hanging on **His** cross.

Luke 23:**38** "And a superscription also was written over him in letters of Greek, and Latin, and Hebrew, **THIS IS THE KING OF THE JEWS**." The number 23 is the Bible number of death and again **38** is gravity. Verse numbers (23 + 38) = **61**, the size of the radius of the universe and the upside down **19** of John **19:19**.

Acts **10:38** says "How God anointed (**Jesus of Nazareth**) with the Holy Ghost and with power: who went about doing good, and healing all that were oppressed of the devil; for God was with him." We have the words '**JESUS OF NAZARETH**' in a 10^38th power numbered scripture healing all that were 'oppressed'. The number **38** in the Bible means '*slavery*' and in science it is '*gravity*' (10^38th power times weaker than the strong force); two of the same things that pull someone down.

Luke 4:34 "Saying, Let us alone; what have we to do with thee, thou **Jesus of Nazareth**? art thou come to destroy us? I know thee who thou art; the Holy One of God." We have (4 + 34) = **38** with **JESUS OF NAZARETH**.

Matthew 27:11 "And Jesus stood before the governor: and the

governor asked him, saying, Art thou the **King of the Jews**? And Jesus said unto him, Thou sayest." We have **KING OF THE JEWS** and (27 + 11) = **38**.

Mark 15:2 "And Pilate asked him, Art thou the **King of the Jews**? And he answering said unto them, Thou sayest it." Remember our **152** number and the English language and that "King of the Jews" = 152; so does (**38 x 4**) = **152** our verse numbers and **KING OF THE JEWS** is here again. Psalm **38:4** "For mine iniquities are gone over mine head: as an **heavy** burden they are too **heavy** for me."

Luke 19:**38** "Saying, Blessed be the **King** that cometh in the name of the Lord: peace in heaven, and glory in the highest." The **KING that cometh in the name of the LORD** is here again on a 38 verse. Our chapter number (19) x 2 = 38.

Revelation 19:16 "And he hath on his vesture and on his thigh a name written, **KING OF KINGS, AND LORD OF LORDS.**" Verse numbers multiplied out (19 x 16) = **304**; the first 3 Torah numbers and exactly divisible by **38** (*gravity*) as (304 / **38**) = **8** Jesus number of new beginnings. If you also remember, the first 4 Torah numbers 3048 are used to convert centimeters into inches/feet. Using 3048 / **38** (*gravity*) = 80.2 and we know that there are **10^80** power particles in the universe. In fact science says that there must be 'right at', but no more than about **10^80** power particles because of the *gravitational* constant! The mirror to the heaviness of the particles at 80.2 is 2.08 a (**80.2 | 2.08**) mirror of (208) our antigravity and rising number from Bismuth the 83rd element.

* These are scriptures that equal **45** and have to do with *preservation* and *salvation*.

Matthew 14:31 "And immediately Jesus stretched forth his hand, and caught him, and said unto him, O thou of little faith, wherefore didst thou doubt?" These verse numbers (14 + 31) = **45** and 45 is the number of preservation in the Bible and Jesus is *saving* Peter from drowning. Noah's Ark is (300 x 50 x 30) cubits which equals 450,000, also Elijah slayed 450 prophets of Baal.

Genesis **45**:5 "Now therefore be not grieved, nor angry with yourselves, that ye sold me hither: for God did send me before you to (**preserve**) life."

Genesis **45**:7 "And God sent me before you to (**preserve**) you a posterity in the earth, and to save your lives by a great deliverance."

Mark 15:30 "**Save** thyself, and come down from the cross." They were trying to get Jesus to **preserve (save)** his own life and (15 + 30) = **45** and (15 x 30) = **450**.

Revelation 21:24 "And the nations of them which are **saved** shall walk in the light of it: and the kings of the earth do bring their glory and honour into it." **Saved** and (21 + 24) = **45**.

1st Corinthians 3:15 "If any man's work shall be **burned**, he shall suffer loss: but he himself shall be **saved**; yet so as by **fire**." Saved by fire and (3 x 15) = **45**. (3 + 15) = **18** and the **fire** of *lightning*.

Romans 5:9 "Much more then, being now justified by his blood, we shall be **saved** from wrath through him." Saved from wrath and (5 x 9) = **45**.

1st Thessalonians 5:9 "For God hath not appointed us to wrath, but to obtain **salvation** by our Lord Jesus Christ." Salvation by Jesus and (5 x 9) = **45**.

Hebrews 5:9 "And being made perfect, he became the author of eternal **salvation** unto all them that obey him." Jesus the author of **salvation** and (5 x 9) = **45**.

2nd Peter 3:15 "And account that the longsuffering of our Lord is **salvation**; even as our beloved brother Paul also according to the wisdom given unto him hath written unto you." The longsuffering of our Lord is **salvation** and (3 x 15) = **45**.

2nd Timothy 3:15 "And that from a child thou hast known the **holy scriptures**, which are able to make thee **wise** unto **salvation** through faith which is in Christ Jesus." Becoming wise unto **salvation** and (3 x 15) = **45**.

* These next **22** scriptures are about '**words**', writing, and the number **22**. The number **22** being the number of characters in the Hebrew **alphabet** and the Bible number of **light**. Psalms 119:105 "Thy **word** is a **lamp** unto my **feet**, and a **light** unto my path." Verse numbers (**119 + 105**) = **224**; (**22** x 4) = **88**, the number of **photons of light** in the universe.

John 19:**22** "Pilate answered, What I have (**written**) I have (**written**)." The verse before: John 19:21 says "Then said the chief priests of the Jews to Pilate, **Write** not, The King of the Jews; but that he said, I am King of the Jews." Pilate wrote words (**22**) that can never be changed.

Luke **22**:37 "For I say unto you, that this that is (**written**) must yet be accomplished in me, And he was reckoned among the transgressors: for the things concerning me have an end." We have **written** again on a **22** numbered verse and **37** means "**Word** of the Father!"

Matthew 13:**22** "He also that received seed among the thorns is he that heareth the (**word**); and the care of this world, and the deceitfulness of riches, choke the (word), and he becometh unfruitful."

Matthew **22**:46 "And no man was able to answer him a (**word**), neither durst any man from that day forth ask him any more questions."

Mark **2:2** "And straightway many were gathered together, insomuch that there was no room to receive them, no, not so much as about the door: and he preached the (**word**) unto them."

Acts **2:22** "Ye men of Israel, hear these (**words**); Jesus of Nazareth, a man approved of God among you by miracles and wonders and signs, which God did by him in the midst of you, as ye yourselves also know."

Acts 7:**22** says "And Moses was learned in all the wisdom of the Egyptians, and was mighty in (**words**) and in deeds."

Acts 10:**22** "And they said, Cornelius the centurion, a just man, and one that feareth God, and of good report among all the **nation of the Jews**, was warned from God by an holy angel to send for thee into his house, and to hear (**words**) of thee."

Acts **22:2** "(And when they heard that he spake in the **Hebrew tongue** to them, they kept the more silence: and he saith)." There are **22** characters in the **Hebrew language**.

Acts **22:22** "And they gave him audience unto this (**word**), and then lifted up their **voices**, and said, Away with such a fellow from the earth: for it is not fit that he should live."

Matthew **22:22** "When they had heard these (**words**), they marvelled, and left him, and went their way."

Luke 4:**22** "And all bare him witness, and wondered at the gracious (**words**) which proceeded out of his mouth. And they said, Is not this Joseph's son?"

Luke **22**:61 says "And the Lord turned, and looked upon Peter. And Peter remembered the (**word**) of the Lord, how he had said unto him, Before the cock crow, thou shalt **deny me** thrice."

John 9:**22** "These (**words**) spake his parents, because they feared the Jews: for the Jews had agreed already, that if any man **did confess** that he was Christ, he should be put out of the synagogue."

John **2:22** "When therefore he was risen from the dead, his disciples remembered that he had said this unto them; and they believed the (**scripture**), and the (**word**) which Jesus had **said**."

2nd Thessalonians **2:2** "That ye be not soon shaken in mind, or be troubled, neither by spirit, nor by (**word**), nor by **letter** as from us, as that the day of Christ is at hand." The scripture is talking about 'by word and by letter' and equals **222**.

Hebrews **2:2** "For if the (**word**) spoken by angels was stedfast, and every transgression and disobedience received a just recompence of reward."

Hebrews 13:**22** "And I beseech you, brethren, suffer the word of exhortation: for I have written a **letter** unto you in few (**words**)."

James 1:**22** says "But be ye doers of the (**word**), and not hearers only, deceiving your own selves."

1st Peter **2:2** "As newborn babes, desire the sincere milk of the (**word**), that ye may grow thereby:"

Revelation **22**:18 "For I testify unto every man that heareth the (**words**) of the prophecy of this book, If any man shall add unto these things, God shall add unto him the plagues that are **written in this book**."

Revelation **22**:19 "And if any man **shall take away** from the (**words**) of the book of this prophecy, God shall take away his part out of the book of life, and out of the holy city, and from the things which are **written in this book**."

* The elements are melting and the **31** electron number.

2nd Peter **3:10** "But the day of the Lord will come as a thief in the night; in the which the heavens shall pass away with a great noise, and the (*elements*) shall melt with **fervent heat**, the earth also and the **works** that are therein shall be **burned up**." The verse numbers (3 x 10) = **30**; **Jesus** number of service and dedication, when He started His ministry; and this verse is talking about (the day of the **Lord**) referring to **Jesus**. All of the (**elements**) are burning up here and our verse numbers **310** contain (**31**), the mass of the electron or (31 x 10) = 310 and $10^{\wedge}-31^{st}$ power is the mass of the electron; see **Psalm 31**. Our verse numbers (3 + 10) = **13** the weak force. See Psalm 13 for an explanation of the weak force. These two are a (**13 | 31**) mirror of forces that actually do work together in the universe. Matthew **3:10** "And now also the axe is laid unto the **root of the trees**: therefore every tree which bringeth not forth good fruit is **hewn down, and cast into the fire**."

2nd Peter **3:11** "Seeing then that all these things **shall be dissolved**, what manner of persons ought ye to be in all **holy conversation and godliness**." All these things (**elements**) are going to be dissolved and we have (311) or 31 x 1 = **31** the mass of the electron again, or (**3 x 11**) = **33** the Planck length, the smallest measurement known where space and time merge together; see **Psalm 33** and *ten stringed* dimensions of the universe.

Only **5** scriptures in the Bible have the word 'earthly' in them and earthly refers to the senses of man; man has *5 earthly senses*. All of these scriptures have **31** (mass of the electron) in them except 2nd Corinthians **5:1**. We know that the electron refers to the **elements** of this earth.

John **3:12** "If I have told you **earthly things**, and ye believe not, how shall ye believe, if I tell you of heavenly things?"

John 3:**31** "He that cometh from above is above all: he that is of the earth **is earthly**, and speaketh of the earth: he that cometh from heaven is above all."

2nd Corinthians **5:1** "For we know that if our **earthly** house of this tabernacle were dissolved, we have a building of God, an house not made with hands, eternal in the heavens."

Philippians **3:19** "Whose end is destruction, whose God is their belly, and whose glory is in their shame, who mind **earthly** things."

James **3:15** "This wisdom descendeth not from above, but is **earthly**, sensual, devilish."

The **10^-31** power number here is the mass of the electron expressed in kilograms like Psalm 31. Another way to express the mass of the electron is in **GeV** or **G**iga **e**lectron **V**olts like this (**. 511**) and (**51**) is the beginning of our 2nd Corinthians **5:1** scripture. Here are **angels** spinning like **electrons** around the throne: Revelation **5:11** "And I beheld, and I heard the voice of **many angels round** about the **throne** and the beasts and the elders: and the number of them was **ten thousand times ten thousand**, and **thousands of thousands**."

* This last set deals with verse numbers dealing with **measurement** and numbers like **3.14, 33, 35, 40, 57, and 114**. We will also examine the last set dealing with the resurrection and numbers **38, 39, and 40**.

Matthew **6:27** "Which of you by taking **thought** can add one **cubit** unto his stature?" This is talking about adding one cubit (measurement) and verse numbers (6 + 27) = **33** the Planck length at 10^-33 centimeters, the smallest measurement in the universe; and what all measurement is gauged on. Also 10^-27 power is the smallest measurement of light energy and **6** is the number of man. (27 – 6) = **21**, recalling that the Jewish **cubit** was actually about **21** inches or 20.8 inches, and this is what we used for the *Ark of the Covenant.*

Isaiah **48:13** "Mine hand also hath laid the **foundation of the earth**, and my right hand hath **spanned the heavens**: when **I call unto them, they stand up together**." Verse numbers (48 + 13) = **61** and we know that the universe has a radius of 10^61 magnitudes above the Planck length. Added together (4 + 8 + 1 + 3) = **16**, the number of cancellations in string theory and mirror to our 61 number a (**16 | 61**) mirror.

Isaiah **44:13** "The carpenter **stretcheth** out his rule; he

marketh it out with a line; he fitteth it with planes, and he marketh it out with the **compass**, and maketh it after the **figure of a man**, according to the beauty of a man; that it may remain in the house." The scripture is talking about a compass, a rule, and the figure of a man. Verse numbers (44 x 13) = **572** and verse numbers added (44 + 13) = **57**, about one tenth of our **572** number actually (**10.035**). We also know that man is about **10^35** powers (in centimeters) in size above the Planck length as in our (**572 / 57**) number = (10.035). In relation to a **compass** using our **572** number (**5 x 72**) = 360, the number of degrees in circle. In relation to the figure of a man the **572** again (57 x 2) = **114** as in John 1:14 "And the **Word** was made flesh..." In relation again to the **572** number and the word compass; **RADIANS** are what is used to measure a **circle** and there are **57.2957** degrees in a **RADIAN**, very close to the **572** number if divided by ten: (**572 / 10**) = **57.2**. There are **6.28** RADIANS in a circle (**2 x pi**). All of this in a scripture talking about a **carpenter and his rule**, and marking with a **compass** the figure of a **man**. This scripture is really loaded with real **math measurements**.

Gen **2:2** "And on the **seventh** day God ended his work which he had made; and he rested on the **seventh** day from all his **work** which he had **made**." We know there are **22** characters in the Hebrew language and that the Jews believe that the universe is constructed out of them. We live in a circular universe (see Psalm 90:4) and that this is the *'seventh'* day after God has finished creation and verse numbers **2:2** divided by **seven** (**22 / 7**) = pi **3.1428**, the number we use to compute the circumference of a circle. Hebrews **7:22** says "By so much was Jesus made a surety of a **better testament**." Here is **22** again in the only scripture with the word **circle** in it: Isaiah 40:**22** "It is he that sitteth upon the **circle** of the earth, and the inhabitants thereof are as grasshoppers; that **stretcheth out the heavens as a curtain**, and spreadeth them out as a tent to dwell in." As just stated, we know the radius size of the universe is **10^61** powers above the Planck length, and our verse numbers (40 + 22) = **62**, representing Him "...that sitteth upon the **circle**." We have 62, which is one Planck size larger than the universe at 10^61 power. Also 62 is a mirror to 26, the numerical name of JEHOVAH a (**62 | 26**) mirror. Oddly enough when both sides of the mirror are added (62 + 26) = **88**; they equal the number of photons of light in the universe. See Psalm 88 talking about God's waves. Take the photons of light and split them in half (88 / 2) = **44**, the Planck time (see Psalm 44). Split time in half (44 / 2) = **22**, the Hebrew alphabet. Split the Hebrew alphabet in half (22 / 2) = **11**, the number of dimensions of the universe. Split eleven in half (11 / 2) = **5. 5**, or how about two tablets of stone (**5 + 5**) = *The 10 Commandments*. Split 5.5 in half (5.5 / 2) = **2.75** the mirror to our carpenters rule of Isaiah 44:13, a (**2.75 | 57.2 RADIANS**) mirror, even the decimals are in the right place! One more time split **2.75** in half (2.75 / 2) = **1.375** and we know that **137** is the mystery constant. If you take the angle that primordia grow, using the center of the seed head as a reference from plants in regards to the Fibonacci sequence, then one gets an angle of **137. 5** degrees. After doing all of this splitting in half consider the number **57** as the (**half life – radioactive decay**) of carbon **14**, which is a little bit over **5700** years. A small number of particles stay around quite a bit longer than the half life *called the mean life*; and the decay process obeys unchanging rules. The mean life of these particles that stick around are equal to **1. 44** times the half life, and we know that 144 or (1.44 x 100) = **144** the size of the man or angel from Revelation 21:17. The half life of carbon **14** is **5730** years, so lets compute the mean life of one of these particles by multiplying (1.44 x 5730) = **8251. 2**. This number is really interesting. We have (8)251.2 because Jesus' number is **8**, and then 8(**251. 2**); knowing that **251. 2** is embedded in our numbers from Exodus **25:12** where the 'Ark of the Covenant' is being built. These are close to our numbers from Psalm 80 where (80 x **pi**) = **251. 3**. We know that the '*Ark of the Covenant*' was in the '*Tabernacle* of Moses'; now read **2ⁿᵈ** Corinthians **5:1** "For we know that if our earthly house of this (**tabernacle**) were dissolved, we have a (**building of God**), an house not made with hands, **eternal in the heavens**." The numbers of this Corinthian scripture are **251** because this is **2ⁿᵈ** Corinthians **5:1** talking about a (**tabernacle**), quite amazing! Deuteronomy **25:13** says "Thou shalt not have in thy bag divers **weights**, a great and a small"; (25 + 13) = 38 *gravity!* I am still looking into this, but I wonder about the **25** number here in relation to the Ark of the Covenant. The Ark is where the presence of God dwelt and this would be like a singularity in our world; a singularity is a term used with black holes. The closed off region of space (information) inside a black hole, can't be any greater than one quarter (**25%**) of the horizon of the black holes surface area.

Proverbs **8:27** "When he prepared the **heavens**, I was there: when he set a **compass** upon the face of the depth." **Light** from the sun takes **8** minutes and **27** seconds to reach the earth." The words 'earth' and 'sun' appear together in the Bible in just **8** scriptures. One of these is 2nd Samuel **23:4** "And he shall be as the (**light**) of the morning, when the (**sun**) riseth, even a morning without clouds; as the tender grass springing out of the (**earth**) by clear shining after rain." Scripture numbers (23 x 4) = **92** and 92 x 10^6 power is the distance from the earth to the sun at the sun's closest point. Verse numbers (23 + 4) = **27** as in Psalm **27** and '**light**'; the core of the sun is 27,000,000 (**27** million) degrees Fahrenheit. All verse numbers multiplied (2 x 3 x 4) = **24** and the earth is **10^24** power weight in kilograms. Even verse numbers subtracted (**23 - 4**) = **19** and Psalm **19** says "...In them hath he set a tabernacle for the **sun**..."

Genesis **8:22** promises: "While the earth remaineth, **seedtime** and harvest, and cold and heat, and **summer** and **winter**, and **day** and **night** shall not cease." The word 'seedtime' is in the Bible just one time. Our verse numbers (8 + 22) = 30, like **30** days in a month. All numbers added (8 + 2 + 2) = 12, like **12** months in a year. Multiplied (8 x 2 x 2) = **32** the Bible number of Covenant (God's promises).

Mark **10:6** "But from the **beginning of the creation** God made them **male and female**." This is talking about the **beginning** of creation and verse numbers 10 x 6 = **60**, knowing that 10^60 magnitudes is about the size of the broken universe above the Planck length, and **6** is the number of man; see Psalm **60**.

Matthew **4:10** "Then saith Jesus unto him, Get thee hence, Satan: for it is written, Thou shalt worship the Lord thy God, and him only shalt thou serve." This is the last temptation after **40** days in the wilderness and verse numbers **(4 x 10) = 40**.

* **40** and the **Resurrection, rising**, and **ascending**.

Acts **1:3** "To whom also he shewed himself alive after his passion by many infallible proofs, being seen of them **(forty days)**, and speaking of the things pertaining to the kingdom of God." Jesus showed Himself for **(40)** forty days after His Resurrection. The word *'resurrection'* appears in exactly **40** different scriptures of the Bible. The word 'rise' appears **140** times in the Bible.

Acts **10:40** "Him God **(raised)** up the third day, and shewed him openly."

Acts **4:10** "Be it known unto you all, and to all the people of Israel, that by the name of Jesus Christ of Nazareth, whom ye crucified, whom God **(raised)** from the dead, even by him doth this man stand here before you whole."

Matthew 17:23 "And they shall **kill him**, and the third day he shall be **(raised)** again. And they were exceeding sorry." Twenty-three **(23)** is the Bible number of **death** (see Psalm **23**:4) and (17) is God's victory number (17 + 23) = **40**; *resurrection powe*r!

Isaiah 26:14 "They are dead, they shall not live; they are deceased, they shall not **(rise)**: therefore hast thou visited and destroyed them, and made all their memory to perish." (26 + 14) = **40**.

Ecclesiastes **10:4** "If the spirit of the ruler **(rise)** up against thee, leave not thy place; for yielding pacifieth great offences." (10 x 4) = **40**.

Ephesians **4:10** "He that descended is the same also that **ascended up far above all heavens**, that he might fill all things." (4 x 10) = **40**.

John 20:17 "Jesus saith unto her, Touch me not; **(for I am not**

yet ascended to my Father): but go to my brethren, and say unto them, **I ascend unto my Father**, and your **Father**; and to my God, and your God." Jesus has **not ascended yet** (20 + 17) = **37** (3 short of **40**); **37** means **"Word of the Father"** in the Bible. All of the full-ness of the Godhead (**3 in 1**) is in Jesus (**3 + 37**) = **40** (**when he ascends**). It looks like when **Jesus** ascends we will have **40** now because of John 10:30 "**I and my Father** are **one**." (10 + 30) = **40**; and **30** is **Jesus** number of blood and divine service.

Acts 2:34 "For (**David is not ascended into the heavens**): but he saith himself, The Lord said unto my Lord, Sit thou on my right hand." **David has not ascended** and is lower than Jesus (2 + 34) = **36**.

John 3:13 "And **no man hath ascended up to heaven**, but he that came **down from heaven**, even the **Son of man** which is in heaven." **No man has ascended** into heaven because (**3 x 13**) = **39**, **1** under 40. The "…he that came down from heaven…" was Jesus that died for our (**39**) diseases before ascending (**39 + 1**) = **40**.

Proverbs 30:4 asks: "Who hath **ascended up into heaven**, or descended? who hath gathered the wind in his fists? who hath bound the waters in a garment? who hath established all the ends of the earth? what is **his name**, and **what is his son's name**, if thou canst tell?" The number (30 + 4) = '**34**'; and **34** in the Bible means: **the naming of a son**! (30 x 4) = **120**; which is evenly divisible by **40** (120 / **40**) = 3.

Judges 20:**40** "But when the flame began to arise up out of the city with a pillar of smoke, the Benjamites looked behind them, and, behold, the **flame of the city ascended up to heaven**."

Proverbs 28:12 "When righteous men do rejoice, there is great glory: but when the wicked (**rise**), a man is hidden." (28 + 12) = **40**. And 28 is **man** as in "…a man is hidden."

Exodus 21:19 "If he (**rise**) again, and walk abroad upon his staff, then shall he that smote him be quit: only he shall pay for the loss of his time, and shall cause him to be thoroughly healed." (21 + 19) = **40**.

Psalms **140**:10 "Let burning coals fall upon them: let them be cast into the fire; into deep pits, that they (**rise**) not up again."

Matthew 27:53 "And came out of the **graves** (**after his resurrection**), and went into the holy city, and appeared unto many." We have other people **resurrected** (27 + 53) = 80 and (**40 x 2**) = 80.

If the number **31** has to do with **rising** and offspring where does the number **40** come in with resurrection? Didn't Jesus promise us that He would send the Holy Spirit (**9**) because there are 9 gifts and 9 fruits of the Spirit?" Take **31** and just add **9** you get **40**! If you add all 18 gifts and fruits (9 + 9) = 18 to 31 you get **49**; remember the feasts of Pentecost and (7 x 7) = **49** days, and that the feast was on the next (50th day). Take the unity (**1**) oneness of the body of Christ and add it to **49** (49 + 1) = **50** Pentecost.

* Here is what I am talking about with the **9** and **31**.

Mark **9:31** "For he taught his disciples, and said unto them, The Son of man is delivered into the hands of men, and they **shall kill him**; and after that he is killed, he shall (**rise**) the third day." Nine (**9**) + thirty-one (**31**) = forty (**40**).

* The resurrection of Jesus and the progression of the numbers: **38, 39, and 40**.

At (**38**) He carries the heavy cross (*gravity*) for our sins. Matthew 10:38 "And he that taketh not his cross, and followeth after me, is not worthy of me." Hanging on the cross: Luke 23:**38** "And a superscription also was written over him in letters of Greek, and Latin, and Hebrew, **THIS IS THE KING OF THE JEWS**." John 19:19 "And Pilate wrote a title, and put it on the cross. And the writing was **JESUS OF NAZARETH THE KING OF THE JEWS**"; (19 + 19) = **38**.

At (**39**) He faces his mockers and is still silent (**39** has to do with words and **39** = disease). Proverbs 18:21 "**Death** and **life** are in the **power** of the **tongue**: and they that love it shall eat the fruit thereof"; and (18 + 21) = **39**. Psalm **39:1** "I said, I will take heed to my ways, that I sin not with my **tongue**: I will keep my **mouth with a bridle**, while the wicked is before me." He was mocked and beaten for our **39** diseases. Matthew **20:19** "And shall deliver him to the **Gentiles to mock**, and to **scourge**, and to **crucify him**: and the **third day** he shall **rise** again." Our verse numbers (20 + 19) = **39**.

At **(40)** He 'shall rise' from the dead on the third day and we are repeating the Mark 9:31 scripture to show the progression of the 38, 39, and 40 numbers relating to the resurrection.

Mark 9:31 "For he taught his disciples, and said unto them, The Son of man is delivered into the hands of men, and they **shall kill him**; and after that he is killed, he (**shall rise**) the third day"; and (9 + 31) = **40**.

Acts **4:10** "Be it known unto you all, and to all the people of Israel, that by the name of **Jesus Christ** of Nazareth, whom ye **crucified**, whom God (**raised**) from the dead, even by him doth this man stand here before you whole"; (4 x 10) = **40**.

Acts **10:40** "Him God (**raised**) up the **third day**, and **shewed** him **openly**."

* With all of this '**numerical evidence**' seen by these groups of **related data**, we see that the **scripture numbers** are **magnetic** to the scripture **meanings**. We have witnessed a mind-boggling array of a vast number of the '**most key**' scriptures of the Bible; where the **meaning** of the scriptures gravitate towards appearing in scriptures of the **equivalent numerical** value.

CHAPTER 10

Secrets, Numbers, and the life of Don Christie

H ere are some unusual numbers that have occurred in Don Christie's life on these dates. I was born on August 2nd, 1948 and in 1948 Israel became a nation. I discovered the **821** and **882** ELS Bible codes in the center of the Torah next to the name of Jesus. Here is my birthday lined up by month, day, and year 821948 or (**821**)948. Here are my birthday numbers in a circle, as if the numbers touched the six-pointed star of David; remembering I found the 8821 in the creation numbers squared, and in the Torah, and 8821 is the name of Jesus squared in English with the (**1288 | 8821**) mirror. You can see that 8821 and 1288 are both included here by reading clockwise or counter-clockwise using my birthday numbers.

8

8   **2**

4   **1**

9

My father was **21** when I was born and look at my birthday again: 8(**21**)948; my mother was **19** when I was born: 82(**19**)48. My grandfather Reuben Christie was born in 1900 making him **48** in the year that I was born: 8219(**48**); he passed away in 1986. My mother's birthday is December the 8th and December is the 12th month and her birthday is **128** numerically, the mirror to **821**: (128 | 821). My mother passed away in 1996. September is the **9th** month and my father's birthday is September the **29th** or **929** numerically; there are **929** chapters in the Old Testament, and this is where I found these **821** codes. My grandmother Beulah Christie is 101 years old this year in 2002. Psalm **48:2** "Beautiful for situation, the joy of the whole earth, is (**mount** Zion), on the sides of the north, the city of the great King." I was born in **Mount** Pleasant, Michigan (located in the center of the **palm** of the state of Michigan) at **9:14** pm August 2, 1948 (look at the circle again for 914).

I was in the U. S. Navy from 1966 to 1969 and received my orders near the end of boot camp to go to my first ship, having no say on what ship I would end up on. My first ship was a Destroyer called the U. S. S. Stickell DD **888**; yes the hull number was '**888**' and we know that Jesus' name in the (**Greek**) numerically adds up to '888'. I received Christ (got saved) on the deck of this ship in January of 1969 while the ship was at sea. The international call sign of this ship was: **RED CROSS**. This ship was sold to (**Greece**) in 1972 and was given the name Kanaris. I went back into the Navy in the 1970's. My second ship was the guided missile cruiser U. S. S. Biddle CG **34**; that's hull number **34** and Planck's constant is 10^-34 power like Psalm 34; the first three Torah numbers are 304. My third ship was another guided missile cruiser called the U. S. S. Harry E. Yarnell CG **17**; knowing that **17** is God's victory number and that (17 x 2) = **34**. I was married on November 18, 1972 in Detroit Michigan; here is the date lined up numerically because November is the 11th month (1118) and (111 x 8) = '**888**' again. These numbers 1118 multiplied this way (11 x 18) = **198**; my full name is: DONALD GEORGE CHRISTIE and my name added together using the **English** code = **198**. I don't believe that these numbers are magical in any way, but rather that these are God's numbers and the way that He would have them. He is a mathematical God of precise measurement as we see from the scriptures, and He always leaves a pattern of order in what He does. I didn't have any prior knowledge about these numbers, because I only started to come to know and write about them in relation to the Bible and science about three years ago from the year 2002.

The Secret of the Higgs Boson and the number **114**

We have talked about a secret to be revealed throughout the book about the particle or field that gives 'mass' to everything in the universe. Here is a recap and some basic facts about science and the Higgs Boson related to the number 114. What I have also seen related to super-symmetry is that a light Higgs boson is guaranteed under 130 GeV.

* Ununquadium is a newly discovered element and its Atomic number is **114**. This new element is said to be an island of stability surrounded by a group of more unstable elements. The atomic weight of this element is 289 and (2 x 8 x 9) = **144**, the size of the man or angel from Revelation 21:17.

* The measurements of Ark of the Covenant (using **cubits**) are 114 inches when multiplied by **20. 8** (the atomic weight of anti-gravity the 83rd element Bismuth); (**2. 5** x 20.8) = 52, (**1. 5** x 20.8) = 31.2 (for two sides) yielding (52 + 31.2 + 31.2) = **114.4**. Remembering also, that the Torah numbers **30.48** convert from centimeters into inches. We know that the Jewish cubit at this time in history was about **21** inches, which is very close to our **20. 8** anti-gravity number: (**208 / 10**) =20.8. Psalm **20:8** "They are brought down and fallen: but we are **risen**, and **stand upright**."

* If you take our **114** number of inches measurement from the Ark of the Covenant and convert it to centimeters as in (114 x **2. 54**) it equals **289. 5**. This is about the atomic weight of Ununquadium the 114th element. God's perfect victory number is 17 and (17 x 17) also equals 289, the atomic weight of the 114th element! We also know that 114 + 30 (Jesus number of blood and divine service) = **144** the size of the man.

* The quantum vacuum (so-called empty space) has a measurement of **10^114 power** and Psalm **114**:4-7 proclaims: "The mountains

skipped like rams, and the little hills like lambs. What ailed thee, O thou sea, that thou fleddest? thou Jordan, that thou wast driven back? Ye mountains, that ye skipped like rams; and ye little hills, like lambs? **Tremble, thou earth**, at the presence of the Lord, at the **presence of the God of Jacob**." We know that all of the Psalms contain the mathematical and scientific power numbers, and that we can rely on them to give us the right information about the universe.

* Psalm 110:4 says "The LORD hath sworn, and will not repent, Thou art a **priest for ever** after the order of **Melchizedek**"; and (110 + 4) our verse numbers = **114**.

* The number **619** represents our Psalm 10^19 electricity constant, and 10^61 power size of the universe number (joined together as 6(1)9) equals (6 x 19) = **114**; and that 619 actually is the **114**[th] prime number! There are also many power scriptures that contain these 619 numbers; especially Hebrews **6:19** "Which hope we have as an **anchor of the soul**, both sure and stedfast, and which entereth into that **within the veil**." The ancient peoples of the Old Testament tried to enter this heavenly veil in a (114 scripture): Genesis **11:4** "And they said, Go to, let us build us a city and a tower, whose top may **reach unto heaven**; and let us make us a **name**, lest we be scattered abroad upon the face of the whole earth."

* We know that Jesus is the **light** of the world and that He created the world because of this (114 scripture) in Genesis **1:14** "And God said, Let there be **lights** in the firmament of the heaven to divide the day from the night; and let them be for signs, and for seasons, and for days, and years."

* The generational number is **14** confirmed in Psalm 14:5 "There were they in great fear: for God is in the (**generation**) of the righteous." The body has 10^14 power cells. The word 'generations' is found **114** times in the Bible! A key fourteen numbered verse: Numbers **14:18** "The LORD is longsuffering, and of great mercy, forgiving iniquity and transgression, and by no means clearing the guilty, visiting the iniquity of the fathers upon the children unto the third and fourth (**generation**)."

* Our **gravity** $10\wedge38$ power Psalm **38:3** says "There is no sound-ness in my flesh because of thine anger; neither is there any rest in my bones because of my sin. For mine iniquities are gone over mine head: as an **heavy** burden they are too **heavy** for me."; verse numbers (**38 x 3** dimensions) = **114**.

* If we take our mysterious **251** number from Exodus where the Ark is being built; which is the **54**[th] prime number (**54** is the 4 forces of the universe combined); and divide by **61** (radius size of the universe), we have (251 / 61) = **4.114**.

* When you square all of the numbers of the total number of char-acters in the Torah (first 5 books of the Bible) which is (304,805) characters: (9 + 0 + 16 + 64 + 0 + 25) they equal **114**.

* If we do the operation of (61 divided into 19 = .3114), the number **114** repeats every **61**[st] character in the decimals. Here we have the quantum vacuum energy of the universe (114) power number; repeating itself (circling) exactly every 61st number; knowing that 61 is the radius size number of the universe and 19 is the electricity number.

Even in the English language (which seems to be scientifically coded), expressed as numbers we have:

P	E	T	E	R		H	I	G	G	S	
16	5	20	5	18		8	9	7	7	19	= (**114**)

Peter Higgs is who the Higgs boson is named after = (**114**)

H	I	G	G	S		B	O	S	O	N	
8	9	7	7	19		2	15	19	15	14	= (**115**)

If the words were HIGGS BOSOM they would equal 114.

Referring to Jesus Christ in English:

O	N	L	Y		S	O	N	
15	14	12	25		19	15	14	= (**114**)

G O D **(26)** + B E G O T T E N **(88)** = **(114)**

From John **1:14** "And the Word was made flesh…"
"AND THE WORD WAS MADE FLESH…" = **(228)**, an exact multiple of 114 **(114 x 2)** = 228.

John **1:14** "…and **dwelt among** us, (and we beheld his glory, the glory as of the **only begotten** of the **Father**,) full of grace and truth."

DWELT AMONG = **(114)**

Genesis 1:1 "In the beginning God created the heaven and the earth."
"In the beginning God created the heaven and the earth" = **(411)** in English the information number; and the mirror to 114: a **(114 | 411)** mirror.

The full scripture in **John 1:14** "And the **Word** was made **flesh**, and dwelt among us, (and we beheld his glory, the glory as of the only begotten of the Father,) full of grace and truth." He is also coming back again in: Jude **1:14** "And Enoch also, the seventh from Adam, prophesied of these, saying, Behold, the **Lord cometh** with **ten thousands** of his saints."

Standby for the SECRET!

A further definition of the Higgs boson is that the Higgs field condenses (disappears into the vacuum), spontaneously breaking the symmetry of the electro-**weak** interaction and gives masses to the fermions (particles of matter) and weak bosons (light particles). The HIGGS is the most sought after thing today in physics and would complete the standard model of particle physics. We know from Psalm 13 that the **weak force** is 10^{13} power times weaker than the strong force, and that Jesus is the one who holds everything in the universe together, and look what we have in Hebrews **1:3** "Who being the brightness of his glory, and the express image of his person, and (**upholding all things** by the **word** of his power),

212

when he had by himself purged our sins, sat down on the right hand of the Majesty on high." The ultimate example of the weak force at **10^13 power**: 2nd Corinthians **13:4** "For though he was crucified through (**weakness**), yet he liveth by the power of God. For we also are (**weak**) in him, but we shall live with him by the (**power**) of God toward you." Our verse numbers (13 x 4) also equal 52, near the weight (10^52) of the whole universe in kilograms! Let's look at one more **10^13** power number in the scriptures and Jesus number of eight (**8**) together in Hebrews **13:8** "Jesus Christ the same yesterday, and to day, and for ever." What do our Hebrew verse numbers (13 x 8) equal? They equal 104, as in Psalm 104:2 "Who coverest thyself with **light** as with a **garment**: who **stretchest out the heavens** like a **curtain**." SECRET HERE: Could the name '**HIGGS BOSON**' merely be an acronym for "**HIS ONLY BEGOTTEN SON**"; and will the HIGGS BOSON (the field that gives all particles their mass) be discovered at **114 GeV**? With all of this information (**411**) from the Bible; would we have the (**114**) power to say so? **John 1:14** "And the **Word** was made **flesh**, and **dwelt among us**, (and we beheld his glory, the glory as of the **only begotten** of the Father,) full of grace and truth."

HIS ONLY BEGOTTEN SON
HIS ONLY **BEGOTTEN SON**

CHAPTER 11

The Final Chapter and Summary of Major Verses

What will the final chapter of your life look like? Do you know the One who put all of these scientific power numbers in the Bible in such a consistent pattern? Do you know the One who prophesied all of these events in the Palms 2,900 years before they happened? He must be really powerful to have left this much 'proof' as He inspired His holy prophets to write the books of the Bible. The Bible is an amazing compilation of 66 books, written over a period of about 1,400 years by 40 different authors. The 'evidence' of God and His son Jesus Christ is seen on the surface of the text of the Bible in its verse numbers that match many related science words, forces of nature, and years of events. These patterns are in plain site that anyone can see and understand. The mathematical odds of the '38 matching Psalms'; the 'Tabernacle of Moses' equaling the latest facts of the universe; the 'Ark of the Covenant' equaling the basic particles and their spins; and much more as we have seen, would all have astronomical odds to be here by random accident or chance. Recall also that many of the Psalms' constants 'key words' are actually found in the Bible that many times such as: Psalm 27 and LIGHT with lightning(s) found (27) times; Psalm 31 about the ELECTRON and the words (speed, speedily, speedy) found 31 times; Psalm 38 GRAVITY and the word 'heavy' found in (38) scriptures; Psalm 42 and 'wave(s)' found (42) times and so on.

If the Bible is not true, then how could not only all of the right 'key words' land on the right Psalms, but also be coded in the Bible exactly that many times; and by many different men who did not possess this information, over hundreds of years? Most of the 'key words' for scientific numbers show up in the first 5 verses of the Psalms, showing an incredible pattern, and many of the 'years of the Psalms expressions' occur on the correct month of the verse number. Even common sense and simple logic show that the obvious numbers and their patterns point to the creator Himself. The "Actual Proof of My Existence" book shows this because the signature of God is His word. The 'science numbers' and 'years for events' in the Psalms that we have just learned about in the last 200 years were all encoded and signed by God thousands of years ago. This creator has a name. His name is Jesus Christ and He made all things. This is the same Jesus in John 1:1 "In the beginning was the **Word**, and the **Word** was with God, and the **Word** was God"; and in John 1:3 "All **things** were **made by him**; and without **him** was not any **thing made** that was **made**." This God is a kind and merciful God who wishes that none would perish. In fact, God the Father isn't just sitting in the heavens waiting to zap you with lightning if you do something wrong. The father doesn't judge anyone, as he has left all judgment up to the Son. John 5:22 "For the Father judgeth no man, but hath committed all judgment unto the Son." Jesus is very gentle and kind as seen in Matthew 12:20 "A bruised reed shall he not break, and smoking flax shall he not quench, till he send forth judgment unto victory." All of us were born in sin, we were all born wrong, and that is why we must be born again. Romans 3:23 says "For all have sinned, and come short of the glory of God." Now the remedy is in John 3:7 "Marvel not that I said unto thee, Ye must be born again." How do we do that? In 1st John 1:9 "If we confess our sins, he is faithful and just to forgive us our sins, and to cleanse us from all unrighteousness." Do this simple thing and actually turn from sin and have a change of mind as stated in Romans 10:10 "For with the heart man believeth unto righteousness; and with the mouth confession is made unto salvation." Here is what will happen if you confess: Romans 10:9 "That if thou shalt confess with thy mouth the Lord Jesus, and shalt believe in thine heart that God hath raised him from the dead, thou shalt be saved."

Why Jesus and not somebody else: 1st Timothy 2:5 "For there is one God, and one mediator between God and men, the man Christ Jesus." And the great miracle that He did for you at the cross: 2nd Corinthians 5:21 "For he hath made him to be sin for us, who knew no sin; that we might be made the righteousness of God in him." He has already made the provision of eternal life for you, just reach out and take the gift as stated in Romans 6:23 "For the wages of sin is death; but the gift of God is eternal life through Jesus Christ our Lord." Here is the simple and incredible fact of who God really is: 1st John 4:16 "And we have known and believed the love that God hath to us. God is love; and he that dwelleth in love dwelleth in God, and God in him." Jesus didn't just come to start a religion, Jesus primarily came to bring life: John **10:10** "The thief cometh not, but for to steal, and to kill, and to destroy: I am come that they might have **life**, and that they might have it more **abundantly**." He wants to give you a (**10 x 10**) = **100** % full **abundant** life.

Condensed reference lists of **Historical** and **Scientific data**

Here is a list of all the scientific Psalms in a more condensed format for your ready reference and easier study.

Psalm **8:3**   "When I consider thy heavens, the work of thy fingers, the moon and the stars, which thou hast ordained." Eight (**8**) is Jesus' number in the Bible and (**150 x 10^8th power**) is the radius size of the universe in billions of light years (15,000,000,000). There are **150** Psalms.

Psalm **13:1**   "... O LORD my God: **lighten mine eyes**, lest I sleep the **sleep of death**." **10^-13th power** is the relative power of the weak force (*compared to the strong force set to* **1**) and beta decay. This is the *death* of particles involved with bosons of *light*. In this process the particle such as a neutron decays (*dies*) and is transformed into another particle. Particles of (*light*) like **photons** with mass called vector bosons are also involved in this process. The weak force is carried out by three particles called bosons, the W+, W-, and Z bosons. These particles of the weak force are extremely short lived and can only travel a very short distance on the subatomic scale, and then they disappear.

Psalm 14:5

"There were they in great fear: for God is in the generation of the righteous." 10^{14} power is the number of cells in your body and **Psalm 14** talks about "**God** is in the **generation** of the righteous"; having to do with our **genes** (*cells*). The word 'generations' is found in the Bible **114 times**; John **1:14** "And the Word was made **flesh**..." Matthew 1:17 "So all the **generations** from Abraham to David are **fourteen** generations; and from David until the carrying away into Babylon are **fourteen** generations; and from the carrying away into Babylon unto Christ are **fourteen** generations."

Psalm 18:10

"And he rode upon a (**cherub**), and did **fly**: yea, he did **fly** upon the **wings of the wind**." The Hartree energy (a scientific constant of 4.3597 x 10^{18} power joules) is what is used to measure the **energy** of the **electron's** orbit; it's 10^{18} power and Luke **10:18** is talking about Satan and lightning (*electricity*): Luke **10:18** "And he said unto them, I beheld **Satan** as **lightning** fall from heaven." The ampere (a basic unit) defining the flow of electrons and (*electricity*) is defined as 6.28 x 10^{18} power electrons per second. This all seems to be related to the **electron** and **electricity**, and also Psalm 31 the mass of the electron coming ahead. The weak force (13) + the Hartree energy (18) = **31**. It's interesting that these Psalm **18** verse numbers are (18 x 10) = **180**, because **electrons** have what is called spin ½, and 180 is ½ of 360 degrees, a full circle. Although, as stated before, the electron must make 2 full revolutions (720 degrees) before returning to its original state.

Psalm **19:1**   "The heavens declare the glory of God; and the firmament sheweth his handywork. Day unto day uttereth speech, and night unto night sheweth knowledge. There is no speech nor language, where their voice is not heard. Their line is gone out through all the earth, and their words to the end of the world. In them hath he set a tabernacle for the **sun**, Which is as a bridegroom coming out of his chamber, and rejoiceth as a strong man to run a race. His going forth is from the **end of the heaven**, and his **circuit** unto the ends of it: and there is nothing hid from the **heat** thereof." The number for electrical energy (*heat*) is 10 to the -**19th power** and this is also referred to as the Planck mass. This number 10 to the -19th power joules is associated with one **electron** volt. A joule is a unit of energy required to lift something weighing one pound about nine inches. Another use is 10 to the **+19th power** (GeV); this is the Planck energy. The words 'sun' and 'light' appear together in **19** scriptures of the Bible. The charge of the **electron** is 10^-**19** power.

Psalm **23:4**   "Yea, though I walk through the valley of the shadow of **death**, I will fear no evil: for thou art with me; thy rod and thy staff they comfort me." Psalm 23:3 says "He **restoreth** my **soul**." Remember that man was created by God '*breathing*' into him and then man became a *living soul.* Ten to the **23rd power** (6.022 x **10^23**) is the Avogadro Constant that matches the **Psalm 23** number because this constant is all about the air (**gases**) we breathe that keep us alive. The Boltzmann constant is 1.3806 x **10^-23 power** and is defined as: the ratio of the 'universal gas constant' to the Avogadro number. **Psalm 23:4 (23 x 4) = 92** the number of natural **elements** on the earth, and this 10^{23} power number is all about gases and molecules and their measurement, simply awesome.

Psalm **24:1**

"The **earth** is the LORD's, and the fulness thereof; the world, and they that dwell therein." **6 x 10^{24th}** power is the mass (*weight*) of the **Earth** as measured in kilograms (1 kilogram = 2.2 pounds); and this is Psalm 24 talking about the **Earth** in the first verse! The earth's weight can also be expressed as **6 x 10^{21st}** power metric tons: Psalm **21:10** "Their fruit shalt thou destroy from the **earth**, and their seed from among the children of men." A metric ton is 2204.6 pounds.

Psalm **27:1**

"The LORD is my **light** and my salvation; whom shall I fear?" **10^{-27th}** power is the number for the minimum energy of a **photon** of *light* in erg seconds. This is also called Planck's constant and is one of the most important constants in physics. The words **'light**ning' and **'light**nings' together are found **27 times in the Bible.** Matthew **10:27** "What I tell you in darkness, that speak ye in (**light**): and what ye hear in the ear, that preach ye upon the housetops." See also Psalm **34.** The words **'God and light'** appear together in **27** different scriptures of the Bible.

Psalm **29:7**

"The voice of the LORD **divideth** the *flames of fire*." **10^{29th} power** is the temperature of the heat of the creation event when the universe was 10^{-37th} power of a second old. This Psalm **29** shows the Lord **dividing the flames** of fire in creation, and matches the scientific number of 10^{29} power. If you subtract (**29 – 7**) you get **22,** the number of letters in the Hebrew alphabet, and science says that there are **7** curled up dimensions. Hebrews 12:**29** "For our God is a consuming **fire**."

Psalm **31:2**   "Bow down thine ear to me; deliver me **speedily**: be thou my strong rock, for an house of defence to save me." Psalm 31:4 "Pull me out of the **net** that they have laid privily for me: for thou art my strength." **10^-31 power** is the rest **mass** of the electron; actually 9.10938 x   10^-31power expressed as kilograms. The key to the electron is its incredible *speed* as it orbits the atom and Psalm 31:2 says "...deliver me **speedily**." The tiny electron orbits the atom at 2.2 million meters per second or **220** million centimeters per second! The two verse numbers where the key words *'speedily'* and *'net'* are found is **31:2** (31 x 2) = **62** and **31:4** (31 x 4) = **124**. Just add the results as (62 + 124) = **186**, the base number for **light speed**. The word *'speedily'* is found **19** times in the Bible, the word *'speed'* is found **11** times, and *'speedy'* is found **1** time. In the Bible there are (**19 + 11 + 1**) = **31** instances of the words speed, speedily, and speedy. In **1911** Ernest Rutherford discovered that the atom has a nucleus and **electrons** surrounding it! Psalm 18:10 says "And he rode upon a (**cherub**), and did **fly**: yea, he did **fly** upon the **wings of the wind**." The Hartree energy (a scientific constant of 4.3597 x **10^18** power joules) is what is used to measure the **energy** of the **electron's** orbit. The words *'fly'* and *'speedily'* seem to go together as both are about the electron whirling around the atom. The weak force (**13**) + the Hartree energy (**18**) = **31**. The Electron 31 is a mirror to the weak force 13 a (**13 | 31**) mirror.

Psalm **33:1-2**   "Rejoice in the LORD, O ye righteous: for praise is comely for the upright. Praise the LORD with harp: sing unto him with the psaltery and an instrument of **ten strings**." The number of the Planck length, the smallest length measurement in the universe is 10 to the -**33rd** power expressed as centimeters in length. This **10 to the -33 power** is the basic length (or a multiple of this length) of the length of vibrating loops of energy called strings. The theory of the universe where these strings vibrate in the **ten dimensions** of space is called **super-string** theory. This Psalm 33 is about vibrating **ten strings** in the universe. God said that He would write His (10) laws (strings) upon our hearts.

Psalm **34:5**   "They looked unto **him**, and were **lightened**: and their faces were not ashamed." **10^-34th** power is the number for the minimum energy of a photon of **light** in joule seconds. Actually it's 6.626 x 10^-34 power. This is also called Planck's constant and is one of the most important constants in physics. This is the same value as Psalm 27 which used erg seconds. We are just using a different scale of measurement called joule seconds for our **10^-34 power** number. This Planck's constant relates the *quantum* of energy of a *photon of light* to its frequency and is used in many equations in quantum theory. The words 'Lord' and 'light' appear together in **34 verses** in the Bible and this verse starts out "They looked unto **him**!"

Psalm **38:3**   "There is no soundness in my flesh because of thine anger; neither is there any rest in my bones because of my sin. For mine iniquities are gone over mine head: as an **heavy** burden they are too **heavy** for me." Gravity is **10^-38th** **power**

222

compared to the *strong force*, and Psalm 38 talks of "*an heavy burden*" and something "*too heavy*" called sin. The word '*heavy*' is found in exactly **38 different verses** of the Bible! The word *heavy* is in this verse **twice**, and this is the only verse that it's in twice in the whole Bible, for a total of 39 times.

Psalm **39:1** "I said, I will take heed to my ways, that I sin not with my **tongue**: I will keep my **mouth** with a bridle, while the wicked is before me." This is a prophecy of Jesus Christ who said nothing to Pilate just before He was crucified; and was also beaten with **39 stripes**. The tension strength of a string in super-string theory is $10^{\wedge}+39^{th}$ **power** (*a number with 39 zeroes in it*) tons. This $10^{\wedge}+39^{th}$ **power** number seems to have to do with the power of **speech** and **words** as a **"string vibration."** Proverbs **18:21**says "Death and life are in the power of the **tongue**: and they that love it shall eat the fruit thereof"; $(18 + 21) = 39$. Isaiah 28:11 "For with stammering **lips** and **another tongue** will he speak to this people", and $(28 + 11) = 39$. Psalms **139**:4 "For there is not a **word** in my **tongue**, but, lo, O LORD, thou knowest it altogether."

Psalm **42:7** "Deep calleth unto deep at the noise of thy waterspouts: all thy **waves** and thy **billows** are gone over me." This **Psalm 42** talks about '*waves*' which relates to the Planck frequency. This frequency is a kilogram (2.2 pounds) of mass whose energy equals the energy of a group of photons (*of light*) whose frequencies sum to $10^{\wedge}42^{nd}$ power. This Planck frequency means *cycles per second* or frequency of **waves at $10^{\wedge}42$** power matching Psalm 42 talking about **waves**. The word '**waves**' shows up in 26 verses and the word '**wave**' appears in 16 different verses of the Bible for a total of (26 + 16) = **42 verses**.

Psalm **44:1**

"We have heard with our ears, O God, our fathers have told us, what work thou didst in their days, in the **times** of old." This is 10 to the **-44th power** of a second. This is the smallest *time* that can be measured! This is the time that it takes light to cross the Planck length. This Psalm 44 has to do with the major physics constant of the smallest measurement of time; 10^-44 power of a second. From the New Testament: Galatians **4:4** "But when the fulness of the (**time**) was come, God sent forth his Son, made of a woman, made under the law, To redeem them that were under the law, that we might receive the adoption of sons."

Psalm **60:1**

"O God, thou hast cast us off, thou hast scattered us, thou hast been displeased; O turn thyself to us again. Thou hast made the **earth to tremble**; thou hast **broken it**: heal the breaches thereof; for it shaketh." The key phrase to Psalm **60** is "**thou hast broken it**" and this is exactly what science says; that the universe exists as a **broken symmetry**. You can say that the whole universe spans a range of about (**60-61**) magnitudes of the power of 10 using the Planck length. This is from 10 to the -33rd power, the smallest size in centimeters; to the largest (radius size of the whole universe) which is about 10 to the 27th power expressed in length as centimeters. Adding the two powers we get (33 + 27 = **60**). The universe that we live in is said by scientists to have a *broken symmetry* and not a perfect symmetry.

Psalm **61:2**

"From the **end of the earth** will I **cry unto thee**, when my heart is overwhelmed: lead me to the **rock** that is higher than I." This is the Psalm of the stretched universe at **10^61** magnitudes above the Planck length. If we **cry unto God** with the 'power' of faith (which is **19** from **Psalm 19**), from the **end of the earth** (**42**) we have (19 + 42) = **61**, the radius size of the stretched universe and this Psalms number! This makes Jesus (**61**) the rock that is higher than I. If 61 is Planck size of the radius of the universe then (61 + 61) = **122** must be the diameter in Planck lengths. If we look at 122 this way as (1 x 22) = **22**; this is the number of characters in the Hebrew alphabet and the Bible number of light. Wow, this is even verse number (**61 x 2**) = **122**. If we measured the circumference of the universe in **Planck units** it would be (61 x 6.28) = **383**. This looks like gravity (**38**) and anti-gravity (**83**) held together by the eight 3(**8**)3. The circumference of the universe in billions of **light years** is (15 billion x 6.28) = **94.2** billion.

Psalm **72:5**   "They shall fear thee as long as the sun and **moon** endure, throughout all generations." This is **Psalm 72:5** talking about the sun and **moon** and of course the moon orbits the earth, and the earth orbits the sun, and the verse numbers of (72:5) multiplied (72 x 5) = **360**; like a 360 degree orbit. We landed on the **moon** on (**7/20**/1969) and this **Psalm 72** talks about the moon. We landed on the **moon** at 4:18 pm EDT and (4 x 18) = **72**, this Psalm's number again! In regards to Psalm **104:19** mentioning 'appointed the **moon** for seasons' the verse numbers (**104 x 19**) = **1976**, the year of our nation's bicentennial and when most of the **moon** trees (tree seeds that were taken to the moon) were planted around the world! Psalms **72:7** "In his days shall the righteous flourish; and abundance of peace so long as the **moon** endureth." This is a reflection of Psalms **27** 'sunlight' off of Psalms **72** 'moonlight'; a (**27 | 72**) mirror. Revelation **6**:12 "And I beheld when he had opened the **sixth** seal, and, lo, there was a great earthquake; and the sun became black as sackcloth of hair, and the **moon** became as blood"; (6 x 12) = **72**.

Psalm **80:1** "Give ear, O Shepherd of Israel, thou that leadest Joseph like a flock; thou that **dwellest between** the cherubims, **shine forth**." There are **10^80** power particles in the universe and Psalm 80 is talking about "thou that **dwellest** between the **cherubims, shine** forth." This is the place where God's **spirit** and **matter** met in the **Ark of the Covenant**. The *"thou that dwellest between the cherubims"* is referring here to the **Lord God** who dwelt between the **cherubims** (angels) that are on top of the Ark of the Covenant. The Greek symbol for pi (π) has a numerical value of **80**. Multiply the eighty (**80**) by pi (3.14159) and as we see it yields (**80** x 3.14159) = **251. 3**. The **Psalm 80** verse number (**80** times pi) refers to the same area of **Exodus** 25:10-13 or (**25:13**) and both are talking about the **Ark of the Covenant**. There are two cherubim here or two angels on the mercy seat of the Ark. Multiply the size of two angels (**144 x 2**) and you have **288**. Now we are talking about Psalm **80** (and there are **10^80** **power** particles in the universe). Add (**80** to the **208** atomic weight of Bismuth) and you have **288** (the size of the **2** angels). The **288** is the mirror to the E8 x E8 (**882**) string theory of living between **2** worlds: (heaven and earth). The 'Ark of the Covenant' and the 'Tabernacle of Moses' are models of the universe and both contain all of the basic numbers, particles, spins, dimensions, etc. of the universe, all written about 3,400 years ago.

Psalm **83:18**   "That men may know that thou, whose name alone is **JEHOVAH**, art the **most high** over all the earth." This is the anti-gravity Psalm with the expression: "**JEHOVAH**, art the **most high** over all the earth" and mirror to Psalm 38 (gravity); a (-**38 | +83**) mirror. If you want to escape the gravity and **weight** of sin in Psalm **38**, then you must **rise** and experience the anti-gravity of JEHOVAH the *"most high"* in **Psalm 83**. To go along with the Psalm 83:18 meaning of anti-gravity, the **83rd** element is called Bismuth. This element has an atomic number of 83. This Bismuth element has the *highest electrical resistance* when placed in a magnetic field (*qualities of anti-gravity*), than any other element. Hebrews **8:3** "For every **high priest** is ordained to offer gifts and sacrifices: wherefore it is of necessity that this man have somewhat also to offer." Daniel **8:3** "Then I **lifted up** mine eyes, and saw, and, behold, there stood before the river a ram which had two horns: and the two horns were **high**; but one was **higher** than the other, and the **higher** came up last." Bismuth has an atomic weight of **208**. Psalm **20:8** "They are brought down and **fallen**: but we are **risen**, and stand **upright**." John **20:8**-9 "Then went in also that other disciple, which came first to the **sepulchre**, and he saw, and believed. For as yet they knew not the scripture, that he must **rise again** from the dead." Act **20:8** "And there were many lights in the **upper chamber**, where they were gathered together." 2nd Kings **20:8** "And Hezekiah said unto Isaiah, What shall be the sign that the LORD will heal me, and that I shall go **up into the house** of the LORD the (**third day**)?"

Psalm **88:7**   "Thy wrath lieth hard upon me, and thou hast afflicted me with all thy **waves**. Selah." This one goes along with **Psalm 42** that says "...**all thy**

waves and thy billows are gone over me." 10^42 is a power number that measures the frequency of photons of (light wave) cycles per second in one kilogram of mass. We are talking about (waves of photons) in **Psalm 88** and 10 to the **88th power** is the number of photons in the universe with "all thy **waves**." Also remember that God says that He is light!

Psalm **90:4**

"For a **thousand years** in thy sight are but as **yesterday** when it is past, and as a watch in the night." Here we have Einstein's relativity in a circular universe where even time is curved and has its own shape. Psalm number 90 times verse number 4 (**90 x 4**) = **360**, the number of degrees in a circle. 2nd Peter **3:8** says, "But, beloved, be not ignorant of this one thing, that one day is with the Lord as a **thousand years**, and a **thousand years** as one day." This is verse **3:8** in 2nd Peter and gravity is **10^-38** power; knowing also that the curvature (360 degrees) of the universe is gravity. These are the only two verses (Psalm **90:4** and 2nd Peter **3:8**) where these relativity scriptures (*thousand years* as a **day**) can be found; and they both contain numbers defining the *curvature* and *gravity* of the universe, utterly amazing! Peter was the one who walked on the water with Jesus and thus defied **gravity**.

Psalm **92:3**

"Upon an instrument of **ten strings**, and upon the psaltery; upon the harp with a solemn sound." There are **92** natural elements that are known to exist on earth and the **vibration frequency** of a string is what gives the **92 natural elements** their masses and force charges. This Psalm 92 represents strings defining atoms at atomic size. Only Psalms 33, **92**, and 144 say *"an instrument of ten strings"*, and this shows a natural three level progression of size from the tiniest strings at size (10^{-33} centimeters), to atomic size with 92 (natural elements), and size 144 (size of the man or angel) in Psalm 144.

Psalm **104:2**   "Who coverest thyself with **light** as with a garment: who **stretchest out the heavens** like a curtain:" The name Jehovah which is **JHVH** in the Hebrew language has a numerical value of (J=10, H=5, V=6, H=5). When these are added they are (10 + 5 + 6 + 5) = **26**. Another fact of the number 26 is that the limit of the observable universe (***cosmic horizon***) is 10 to the 26th power meters. There are four (**4**) seen dimensions to the universe: length, width, height, and time and (**4 x 26 = 104**). It is **Jehovah (26)** who "stretchest out the heavens (**4**) like a curtain" in **Psalm 104**! All verse numbers **1042** represents the earth at 10^{42nd} Planck size!

Psalm **104:19**   "He appointed the **moon** for seasons: the sun knoweth his going down." In regards to Psalm **104:19** mentioning 'appointed the moon for seasons' the verse numbers (**104 x 19) = 1976**, the year of our nation's bicentennial and when most of the **moon trees** were planted! See also Psalm **72:5** for the full story.

Psalm **114:4-7**   "The mountains **skipped like rams**, and the little hills like lambs. What ailed thee, O thou sea, that thou fleddest? thou Jordan, that thou wast driven back? Ye mountains, that ye skipped like rams; and ye little hills, like lambs? **Tremble, thou earth**, at the presence of the Lord, at the **presence of the God of Jacob**." 10^{114} power is the energy of the quantum vacuum. This 114 power number is actually the measurement of the energy of a cubic meter of empty space using the joules measurement system, a power number with 114 zeros in it. The power of the God of Jacob in **Psalm 114** can certainly make the whole earth to **shake and tremble**, remembering that the **fear of the Lord** is the beginning of wisdom.

Psalm **144:9**   "I will sing a new song unto thee, O God: upon a psaltery and an instrument of **ten strings** will I sing praises unto thee." Only Psalms 33, 92, and **144** say "an instrument of **ten strings**." This shows a natural three level progression of size from the tiniest strings at size (10^{-33} centimeters), to atomic size with 92 (natural elements), and size 144 (size of the man or angel) defined in: Revelation 21:17 "And he measured the wall thereof, an **hundred and forty and four cubits**, according to the measure of a man, that is, of the angel." The (half life – radioactive decay) of carbon **14** is a little bit over 5700 years. A small number of particles stay around quite a bit longer than the half life called the *mean life*; and the decay process obeys strict rules. The *mean life* of these particles that stick around are equal to **1.44** times the **half life**, and (1.44 x 100) = **144**. Everything about the numbers **14, 114**, and **144** have to do with the *generations* of Jesus and the size of the man, especially in light of science and carbon **14**. The word 'generations' appears **114** times in the Bible.

Here is a condensed list of the years of matching Psalm numbers with significant historical events for your reference.

Psalm **12:**   Year **1912.** Psalm 12 is the year **1912** and the sinking of the Titanic, if you remember: "Not even God can sink this ship!" This era in 1912 was called the *'Gilded age'* where many rich people flourished and had forgotten about God. We've all seen the movie and know the facts. Psalm **12:3** at the end says "...the tongue that speaketh proud things." Psalm **12:4** "...who is the lord over us?" This is Psalm **12:4** in relation to 1912 and the Titanic sank in the **4th** month (April). The Titanic was written up in many papers and magazines as unsinkable because of her **16** watertight compartments and our Psalm numbers 12:4 (12 + 4) =**16**. Our other Psalm numbers 12:3 (12 + 3) = **15** the morning she sank April **15th** 1912 at 2:20 am! The word *Titanic* is encoded in Psalm **124** at **12140 skip codes**. **Psalm 124:4** "Then the waters had overwhelmed us, the stream had gone over our soul."

Psalm **18**:   Year **1918.** The ending of the first World War; WWI in 1918. Psalm 18:14 "Yea, he sent out his **arrows**, and scattered them; and he shot out **light-nings**, and discomfited them." Psalm 18:29 "For by thee I have run through a **troop**; and by my God have I **leaped over a wall**." Psalm 18:34 "He teacheth my hands to **war**, so that a **bow of steel** is broken by mine arms."

Psalm **33**:   Year **1933.** This is the end of the great depression in 1933 when many were without jobs and hungry. Psalm 33:19 "To deliver their soul from **death**, and to keep them alive in **famine**." This one even lands on verse 19 as in **1933**.

Psalm **41**:   Year **1941.** The attack on Pearl Harbor was December 7th, **1941**. The Japanese ambassadors were falsely negotiating peace right up to the time of the attack; Psalm **41**:9 "...familiar friend, in whom I trusted, which did eat of my bread, hath *lifted up his heel against me*." Notice that verse 41:11 says "...because mine **enemy** doth not *triumph* over me." Take the end of the 11th month of November in **1941** as in verse numbers 41:11 and add our verse numbers (4 + 1 + 1 + 1) and you get 7, the day of the attack in the next month, December 7th! Psalm 41:11 "By this I know that thou favourest me, because mine **enemy doth not triumph over me**." Psalm 41:12 "And as for me, thou **upholdest me in mine integrity**, and settest me before thy face for ever." War was declared on Japan on December 8, 1941 and our verse numbers for Psalm **41**:12 are year **1941**, verse 12 as in the **12th** month December; and all verse numbers (4 + 1 + 1 + 2) = **8**, the day we declared war; but we know that God will *'upholdest me in mine integrity'* referring to the United States of America and her allies.

Psalm **43**:   Year **1943**. Psalm 43:1 "Judge me, O God, and plead my cause against an **ungodly nation**: O deliver me from the *deceitful and unjust man*." Psalm **43**:2 "For thou art the God of my strength: why dost thou **cast me off**? why go I mourning because of the *oppression of the enemy*?" Jesus is talking to the Jews about missing their day of visitation: Luke **19**:**43** "For the days shall come upon thee, that **thine enemies** shall cast a **trench about thee**, and **compass thee round**, and keep thee in on every side." The year is **1943** and Psalm 43:1 says: "...plead my case against an **ungodly nation**"; and 43:2 says "...oppression of the **enemy**." This of course relates to the Nazi's and the oppression of the Jews during World War II in **1943**.

Psalm **44**:   Year **1944**. Psalm 44:5 "Through thee will we **push down** our **enemies**: through thy name will we tread them under that rise up against us." We were getting ready for D-day in May the (5th

month), **1944**. Psalm 44:6 "For I will not *trust in my bow*, neither shall my sword save me." In June (the sixth month) the 6th day 1944 you really needed to trust in God, and not just in your **bow or sword** on this beach-head. Psalm 44:7 "But thou hast *saved us from our enemies*, and hast put them to shame that *hated us*." We landed our troops and pushed the enemy back in July the (7th month), **1944**.

Psalm **45**:   Year **1945**. Psalm 45:5 "Thine *arrows are sharp* in the heart of the *king's enemies*; whereby the people fall under thee." The Germans attacked the '**King and Queen**' (*king's enemies*) of England. This is the falling of our **enemies** in Germany because of the sharp **arrows** of our **armed forces and allies**! This is verse **45:5** and the **5**th month is May and **May** 8th is when Germany surrendered in **1945**.

Psalm **46**:   Year **1946**. Psalm 46:8 "Come, behold the works of the LORD, what **desolations** he hath made in the **earth**." Psalm **46**:9 "He maketh **wars to cease** unto the end of the earth; he **breaketh the bow**, and cutteth the **spear** in sunder; he **burneth** the **chariot in the fire**." The year is **1946** and Psalm 46:9 says "He maketh **wars** to cease", the first full year after 1945 and **WWII**. Notice that this is verse 46:**9** and the **9**th month is September, exactly one year after the surrender.

Psalm **48**:   Year **1948**. Psalm 48:2 says "Beautiful for situation, the joy of the whole earth, is **mount Zion**, on the sides of the north, the **city** of the **great King**." The city of the great king *(mount Zion)* is of course **Jerusalem** and in **1948** Israel became a nation. The 2 middle Torah numbers are '**48**': 30(**48**)05. The other Torah numbers are **30** 48 **05**

= **(30 x 5)** = the **150** Psalms we are presently talking about. **(150 – 48)** = **102** which is Psalm **102**, which in Psalm talk is this year **2002** as I am writing this.

Psalm **87**:   Year **1987**. Psalm 87:4 "I will make mention of Rahab and *(Babylon)* to them that know me: behold *Philistia*, and Tyre, with Ethiopia; this man was born there." There was the restoring of the ancient Babylonian **(Babylon)** empire in **1987** by Saddam Hussein with a **big feast** that lasted thirty days from October to November. This was a really large celebration with **singers** and **bands** from all over the world and Psalm **87**:7 declares "As well the **singers as the players on instruments** shall be there: all my springs are in thee."

Psalm **89**:   Year **1989**. Psalm 89:40 "Thou hast broken down all his **hedges**; thou hast brought his **strong holds to ruin**." Thou hast **broken down** all his 'hedges' referring to the Berlin **wall** falling; which came down on November 9, **1989**. The word 'hedges' is only in the whole Bible 6 times and this one happens to land here. We know that the Berlin wall led to the breakup of the Soviet Union, which fell in 1991. Psalm 89:10 "Thou hast **broken** *(Rahab)* in pieces, as one that is slain; thou hast *scattered thine enemies* with thy strong arm." The beginning of the coming down of the Soviet empire and the *"scattering of thine enemies"*; the breaking up of the USSR into other countries which occurred in 1991.

Psalm **91**:   Year **1991**. Psalm 91:5 "Thou shalt not be afraid for the terror by night; nor for the **arrow that flieth** by day." This is the terror *(terror by night)* from Saddam Hussein and the scud missiles (**arrow** that *flieth* by day) during the Gulf War in

1991. Israel has now built its own new anti-missile defense system to combat scud missiles in 2002 and it's called the '**Arrow**' system.

Psalm **93**:   Year **1993**. Psalm 93:3 "The **floods** have lifted up, O LORD, the floods have lifted up their voice; the **floods** lift up their **waves**." Psalm 93:4 "The LORD on high is mightier than the noise of many **waters**, yea, than the **mighty waves of the sea**." This is the **1993** Midwest **floods** that were the among the worst in U.S. history.

Psalm **98**:   Year **1998**. Psalm 98:7 "Let the **sea roar**, and the fulness thereof; the world, and they that dwell therein." This was the year of El Niño, and of course the **seas** really did roar and affected parts of the whole earth with flooding.

Psalm **99**:   Year **1999**. Psalm 99:**8** "Thou answeredst them, O LORD our God: thou wast a God that forgavest them, though thou tookest **vengeance of their inventions**." God took vengeance on our inventions, the **computers** and the **Y2K** problem and all of the expense and time involved to fix them. This is verse 8 and we know that all computers are based on the number 8, especially seen in memory chips: 64k 128k, 256k, 1024k etc..; numbers all evenly divisible by eight (8).

Psalm **100**:   Year **2000**. Psalm 100:**1** "Make a **joyful noise** unto the LORD, all ye lands." The **millennium celebration** in the Year **2000**. This is also on the first verse and the first month is **January.**

Psalm **101**:   Year **2001**. Psalm 101:8 "I will early destroy all **the wicked** of the land; that I may cut off all **wicked doers** from the (**city**) of the LORD." Looks like something is about to happen (**WTC** attack of September 11, 2001) in the (**city**) and God is going to judge the **wicked terrorists**. Notice also this is the last verse of Psalm 101 verse 8 (August is the 8th month). **If** there was a next verse (**9** for September) it would have been verse 101:9 or **9:101** backwards. The verse numbers (101 + 9) would have equaled a **110** story building! The expression "**THE BIG APPLE**" using the English language code equals **101**, this Psalms number!

Psalm **102**: Year **2002.** Psalm **102**:3 "For my days are **consumed like smoke**, and my **bones are burned** as an hearth." Psalm 102:9 "For I have eaten **ashes** like bread, and mingled my drink with **weeping**." The mood and grieving of the people after the smoke and ashes of the World Trade Center attack. Psalm 102:8 "Mine *enemies reproach me all the day*; and they that are **mad against** me are **sworn** against me." The constant threats of the **terrorists** in America and in Israel. Here is some **hope**: Psalm 102:13 "Thou shalt arise, and have mercy upon **Zion**: for the **time** to favour her, yea, the **set time**, is come."

The approximate odds of **38** matching Psalms would be about **10^38** power or written out like this: **100,000,000,000,000,000,000,000,000,000,000,000,000** to **1**; that all of these science constants and historical events would all appear by random accident or chance and land on these Psalm numbers with the correct phrases. These odds don't count three factors: (**1**) the number of 'times appearing' such as 38 scriptures for the word 'heavy' in Psalm 38 for scientific constants; (**2**) the fact that almost all scientific constants appear in the first seven verses; (**3**) many 'years' of significant events appear on the correct month of the verse number. I suppose that if we figured those odds in, then the zeroes would be just too ridiculous to write down.

Major verses with significant matching data

Exodus **25:10** "And they shall make an ark of shittim wood: **two cubits** and a **half** shall be the length thereof, and a **cubit** and a **half** the breadth thereof, and a **cubit** and a **half** the height thereof." The verse numbers of Exodus (**25 / 10**) = **2. 5** or 5/2 the first length measurement of the Ark! Go back two verses to Exodus **25:8** "And let them make me a sanctuary; that I may **dwell** among them"; these verse numbers divided with (**25 / 8**) = **3.12** or **3/2** or 31.2 inches, the width of the Ark. Bismuth the anti-gravity element no. (83) has an atomic weight of **208**. The Jewish cubit was 21 inches. If you multiply (**20.8** inches x **2.5**), the Arks length, you get exactly **52** inches, which amazingly looks like the **5/2** fraction (52) or (2.5 cubits). If you multiply (**20.8 x 1.5**) you get **31.2** inches and there are two of these 1.5 cubit sides; and 31.2 inches (312) looks amazingly like the **3/2** fraction (1.5 cubits)! All dimensions added together (52 + 31.2 + 31.2) = **114**.4 inches, and Jesus is our modern day Ark in John **1:14**. The measurements of 52, 31.2, and 31.2 inches for the Ark contain the actual super-symmetry numbers of **spin** that science is looking for. These are talked about in Psalm 83 in relation to the length of the Ark with **5/2** (**5** regular matter particles with ½ spin) or (**5** super-symmetry particles with ½ spin (5 x ½ = 2.5)). The two widths of **3/2** are the 3/2 (**2** super-symmetry **gravitons** with a spin of **3/2**). In the Greek language pi = **80**; (pi x 80) = **251.3** and the Ark is being built in Exodus **25:13**. Psalm **80** talks about "...thou that dwellest between the cherubims, shine forth", referring to the Ark of the Covenant.

The Ark's measurements of **3/2**, **5/2**, and **3/2** look just like the attack on Pearl Harbor and the bomb that was dropped on Hiroshima Japan August 6, 1945. The surrender was signed on **9/2/45** and Uranium (what the bomb was made of) is the **92**[nd] element. All dimensions (3 x 5 x 3 x 2 x 2 x 2) = **360** (like a circular fireball). This 360 number is the mirror for the ship where the surrender was signed, the U. S. S. Missouri BB **63**, a (360 | 063) mirror of fireball and surrender.

3   5   3   There were **353** planes in the attack on Pearl
Harbor.

— — —

2   2   2   There were **6** Japanese aircraft carriers 2 + 2 + 2
= **6**.
The attack was launched from about **222** miles
away.

3 x   5 x   3 = **45** (as in **1945**)

— — —

2 x   2 x   2 = **8** (the 8th month, **August**)
2 +   2 +   2 = **6** (the 6th day of the month of **August**)

The bomb was a uranium **235** device and 235 can be read up
both sides of the measurements of the Ark. The aircraft that
dropped the bomb was a B-**29** Super-fortress a (**29 | 92**) mirror of
the date of surrender; and of matter and energy. The aircraft was **29**
feet **7** inches high see Psalm **29:7** and fire. The serial number of the
aircraft was 44-86**292**. The 44-**86**292 (**86**) numbers are August (8th
month) the 6th.

2nd Chronicles 35:3 "And said unto the Levites that taught all
Israel, which were holy unto the LORD, Put the holy (**ark**) in the
house which Solomon the son of David king of Israel did build; it
shall not be a **burden** upon your shoulders: serve now the LORD
your God, and his people Israel." (35 + 3) = **38**.

The **Tabernacle of Moses** looks just like what modern day
science says about the 5 string-theories and M-theory with the duality of its 5 and 5 curtain sets. The 5 and 6 curtain sets being
'coupled together' looks like what science describes as the (10 and
11) dimensional universe, including the fold in the **eleventh** dimension. The first curtain set is (4 x 10 x 28) cubits and 4 x10^28th
power is the number of particles in the average human being. All of
this is described in Exodus **26** and **26** is the total number of dimensions before math cancellations are done; Jehovah = **26** in the
Hebrew language. There are **8** boards with **16** silver sockets; **silver**
in the Bible always speaks of redemption and the **cancellation** of

our sin debt. There are **16 cancellations** in string theory (26 – 16) = **10** getting back to the '**ten string**' or 'ten dimensional' universe. The number **16** in the Bible means *love*. Exodus **26:7** says "And thou shalt make curtains of goats' hair to be a covering upon the tabernacle: **eleven curtains** shalt thou make." Verse numbers (**26 + 7**) = **33**; Psalm **33:2** "…sing unto him with the psaltery and an instrument of *ten strings*"; **ten** space dimensions + **one** time dimension equals *eleven dimensions*.

The **Torah numbers** are the number of characters in the first 5 books of the Bible (**304,805**). To convert centimeters to feet use **30.48**, because 30.48 centimeters is exactly one foot. This is the same as saying that there are **2.54** centimeters to one inch. (2.54 x 12 *inches*) = **30.48** *centimeters*, and the first four Torah numbers are **3048**! If you multiply 186 (base number for light speed in mps) by **pi** (186 x 3.14159) = **584.3**36. The Torah numbers (without zero's) are now mirrored in this number in the first 4 digits, a (**5843 | 3485**) mirror. The Torah numbers **3,485** are about how many years ago that the Torah was written.

The **Fibonacci number series** mirrors the most important scriptures backwards, especially 2nd Corinthians 3:18 and the mirror parity violation of the weak force (**13**) with the expression: "the same image." The **8**th book of the New Testament (**2**nd Corinthians) in chapter **3** verse **18** (a **2:318** mirror of the Fibonacci numbers **8132**) contains the answer to the mirror parity violation ("changed into the *same image*"); and the **8**th Fibonacci number is **13**, the weak force of Psalm **13** where this violation occurs!

Fibonacci numbers forwards:
(0, 1, 1, (**2, 3, 5**), (**8, 13, 2**)1, (**34**, (**5**)5, **8**)9, (**144**), (**233**))

Fibonacci numbers Backwards:
(**33:2, 44:1**, 9(**8, 55, 43**), 1(**2, 31, 8**), (**5, 3, 2**), 1, 1, 0)

Backwards: Psalm **33:2** Ten strings and **Space**; Psalm **44:1** **Time**; Torah numbers **85, 43** or **34, 58**; 2nd Corinthians **3:18**; Ephesians **5:32** "This is a great **mystery**: but I speak concerning

Christ and the **church**."

The **882** numbers representing the E8 x E8 and SO(32) string theories, along with the **Eightfold way (821)** of particle physics are encoded by **(ELS)** in the very center of the **Torah** in Leviticus 13:10; all of the words starting positions span just 4 characters!

English	Verse	Position	Skip	Hebrew word
offering	Leviticus 13:10	158592	882	מתנה
priest	Leviticus 13:10	158593	-882	גלח
Jesus	Leviticus 13:10	**158594**	**8**	ישוע
Levitical	Leviticus 13:10	**158594**	**-821**	לויי
symmetry	Leviticus 13:10	158595	821	תואם

882 – 821 = **61** the radius size of the universe in Planck units and the year (19**61**) that the **821** 'Eightfold Way' of particle physics was discovered.

JESUS = 74 in English. To science the number **.74** is the difference between matter and anti-matter. All of the name of Jesus in English squared and added (J=100 + E=25 + S=361 + U=441 + S=361) = **1288**; and the mirror to 1288 is a (**1288 | 8821**) mirror. These numbers are from the center of the Torah and the progression of elevens of the creation event, matching the 821 and 882 numbers of particle physics (**8821**). With the **74** number also consider that (7 + 4) = **11** and that (**7 x 4**) = 28 just add the ones (**11**): (**128 | 821**).

A cross sampling of over **400** scriptures (and many are key scriptures), appear in *groups* related to science and Bible numbers that refer to the *meaning* contained in the scriptures using the numbers: 18 lightning and satanic kingdom, 22 light and Hebrew alphabet and blind men, 27 light, 31 offspring and rising, 34 light, 35 size of man a (35 | 53) mirror, 38 and 39 gravity, 40 resurrection, 42 earth, 44 time, 45 preservation, 53 and 54 heavens and universe, 66 idol worship and 666 satanic kingdom, 133 Cessium atom and time, and the 153 great fish number.

The following **20** 'key words' actually appear in the **Bible** the same amount of **times** that match their scientific or biblical **numerical** meanings.

1. "**Heavy**" meaning the Gravity of Psalm **38** appears in (**38**) scriptures. Psalm 38 "…as an **heavy** burden they are too **heavy** for me."

2. "**Speed(ily)**"meaning the Electron (**31**) of Psalm 31, also flame, lamps, and risen (N. T.), all appear 31 times. Thirty one (**31**) is also the Bible number of offspring and increase. **Psalm 31:2** "Bow down thine ear to me; deliver me **speedily**…"

3. "**Generations**" means the (**114**) of John **1:14** "And the Word was made flesh…" Fourteen (**14**) is the generational number of Psalm **14** and '*generations*' appears **114** times in the Bible. The word '**times**' appears **114** times in the Old Testament. The word '**times**' appears **27** times in the New Testament and the New Testament has **27** books. The word '**times**' appears **141** times in the whole Bible, a generational (**14 | 41**) mirror to itself.

4. "**Sun** and **Light**" appear in (**19**) scriptures together meaning the Suns' energy (**19**) of Psalm **19** and electrical energy 10^19 power. Psalm 19 "…In them hath he set a tabernacle for the **sun**…"

5. "**Earth** and **Sun**" appear together in (**8**) scriptures and it takes **8** minutes for the light of the sun to reach the earth. Proverbs **8:27** "When he prepared the **heavens**, I was there: when he set a **compass** upon the face of the depth." **Light** from the sun takes **8** minutes and **27** seconds to reach the earth.

6. "**Lord** and **light**" appear together (**34**) times like the **light** of Psalm **34** "They looked unto **him**, and were **lightened**."

7. The words "**lightning(s)**" together are found (**27**) times in the Bible; Psalm 27 is about light! Psalm 27 "The LORD is my **light** and my salvation…"

8. The words **"God** and **light"** appear together in **27** different scriptures of the Bible; Psalm **27** is about light and **10^-27** power is a photon of **light** in science.

9. **"Wave(s)"** shows up in **(42)** verses of the Bible and $10^{42^{nd}}$ power is how science measures waves; Psalm **42** "...all thy **waves** and thy **billows** are gone over me."

10. The word **'earth'** is found **906** times in the Bible. Take 905.6 (almost 906) and divide by the earth's weight power number **24** (in kilograms); (905.6 / 24) = **37.73**. The Genesis creation verse of the Bible: **Genesis 1:1** "In the beginning God created the heaven and the **earth"** = 2701 in Hebrew or multiples **(37 x 73)** = **2701**.

11. To figure the approximate **circumference of the whole universe**: take a 15 billion light year radius and use the formula 2 x (pi 6.28) x RADIUS (15) = **94.2** billion light years. The Word **Jesus** appears **942** times in the King James Version of the Bible, all in the New Testament.

12. There are **2** cherubims on the Ark. The word **'cherubims'** appears in the Bible **57** times and **(57 x 2** cherubims) = **114**, and our measurement of the Ark (52 + 31.2 + 31.2) inches = **114.4**. **2nd** Chronicles **5:7** "And the priests brought in the **ark of the covenant** of the LORD unto his place, to the oracle of the house, into the most holy place, even under the wings of the **cherubims"**; and again **(2nd x 57)** = **114**.

13. The word 'angel' or 'angels' shows up **(286)** times in the Bible, and the word seraphim(s) shows up only **twice** in Isaiah Chapter 6; (286 angels + **2** seraphims) = **288**! The size of the man or angel is 144 from Rev. 21:17 and **(144 x 2)** = **288**, and there are **2** angels on the Ark of the Covenant. The number 288 is a mirror of the 'two worlds' of the **882** or E8 x E8 string theory, a **(288 | 882)** mirror.

14. The **128** mystery **constant** is a critical measurement in science for higher energies; the word **'measure'** as the root word in: measure, measures, or measured, shows up **128** times in the Bible.

The only place in the whole Bible where the word '*constant*' shows up is in: **1**st Chronicles **28**:7 "Moreover I will establish his kingdom for ever, if he be (*constant*) to do my commandments and my judgments, as at this day." This number seems to have to do with *generations* also as one generation **(14)** + **(114)** = **128**. Genesis **1:28** "And God blessed them, and God said unto them, Be **fruitful, and multiply**, and **replenish the earth**, and subdue it: and have dominion over the fish of the sea, and over the fowl of the air, and over every living thing that moveth upon the earth." The result of being fruitful is: Psalm **128**:6 "Yea, thou shalt see thy **children's children**, and peace upon Israel." The word '**flesh**' appears **128** times in the New Testament. We also know that the **28** number is about the body and soul, and that (4×10^{28th}) power is the number of particles (neutrons and protons) in the human body. Genesis **1:27** "So God created **man** in his **own image**, in the **image of God** created he him; **male and female** created he **them**"; $(1 + 27) = 28$. The full verse numbers: **(1. 27** x 2 people) = **2. 54**; which is our 2.54 number to convert centimeters into inches. Isn't this stuff mindboggling?

15. The word "**seed**" shows up **254** times in the Bible, and **2. 54** is how we convert centimeters into inches. This would be God's 'measure' as there is a lot said about **seeds** in the Bible. Planck lengths are measured in centimeters or meters. The Torah numbers are also based this on this conversion because $(2.54 \times 12) = 30.48$, the first 4 Torah numbers.

16. The words '**Ark**' and '**covenant**' appear together in **45** scriptures of the Old Testament and just once in the New Testament in Hebrews 9:4. The top of Ark of the Covenant measured is $(3 \times 5 \times 3) = 45$, and Noah's Ark is 300 x 50 x 30 cubits = 450,000. In the Bible **45** means preservation; and this is what it was also for America in 19**45**.

17. Jesus showed Himself for **(40)** forty days after His **Resurrection**. The word '*resurrection*' appears in exactly **40** different scriptures of the Bible. The word '**rise**' appears **140** times in the Bible.

18. If you recall, Psalm **83** is the anti-gravity Psalm: Psalm 83:**18** "That men may know that thou, whose name alone is **JEHOVAH**, art the **most high** over all the earth." This was the only Psalm meaning past the 7th verse landing on the **18th** and last verse of Psalm 83; except for the **Hartree energy** which also is an **eighteen** number: **10^-18** power, landing right on Psalm **18:10**! We are also aware that **Satan** tried to take **God's** place but was seen falling out of heaven on an **18** numbered verse: Luke **10:18** "And he said unto them, I beheld **Satan** as **lightning** fall from **heaven**." 1st Thessalonians **2:18** "Wherefore we would have come unto you, even I Paul, once and again; but **Satan** hindered us." Acts **26:18** "To open their eyes, and to turn them from darkness to light, and from the power of **Satan** unto God, that they may receive forgiveness of sins, and inheritance among them which are sanctified by faith that is in me." Luke **11:18** "If **Satan** also be divided against himself, how shall his kingdom stand? because ye say that I cast out **devils** through **Beelzebub**." Satan couldn't rise above God because God is the **highest** in Psalm 83:**18** "...**most high** over all the earth"; the word '**HIGHEST**' appears (**18**) times in the Bible. Psalms **18**:13 "The **LORD** also **thundered** in the **heavens**, and the **Highest** gave his voice; hail stones and coals of **fire**."

19. A **string** is a 'one-brane' object because it exists in just one dimension. There are however, higher dimensional **branes** possible. For example, a 'three-brane' is an object existing in 3 spatial dimensions. These strings are called membranes if they have more space dimensions than one. These **strings** can have extra space dimensions up to **nine** spatial dimensions, **nine** is the limit! The word '**string**' shows up exactly **nine** (**9**) times in the Bible in all of its forms. The word '**string**' appears (**2** times), '**strings**' (**4** times), and '**stringed**' (**3** times), (2 + 4 + 3) = **9**. There are **5** string theories which are joined by the coupling constant **137**; the word '**couple**' appears **5** times when referring to '**joining together**' in the Bible. The word '**coupled**' appears **11** times like the 11 dimensional-universe. The word '**coupling**' appears in **8** different scriptures, for a total of **10** times within those **8** scriptures; like the '**Eightfold Way**' of particle physics and (8 x 10) = **80** or 10^**80** power particles in the universe. The 2 key scriptures where the (50 + 50) loops are

joined together is: Exodus 26:10 "And thou shalt make **fifty loops** on the edge of the **one curtain** that is outmost in the **coupling**, and **fifty loops** in the edge of the curtain which **coupleth the second**." Exodus **26:11** "And thou shalt make **fifty taches** of brass, and put the taches into the **loops**, and **couple** the tent together, that it may **be one**." (50 + 50 = **100**) loops + verse numbers (26 + 11 = **37**) = **137**, the mystery constant. Exodus **6:20** "And Amram took him Jochebed his father's sister to wife; and she bare him **Aaron and Moses**: and the years of the life of **Amram** were an (**hundred** and **thirty** and **seven years**)." Verse numbers (**6 x 20**) = **120** and Deuteronomy 34:7 says "And **Moses** was an (**hundred** and **twenty** years old) when he died: his eye was not dim, nor his natural force abated."

20. The word '**WORLD**' appears **249** times in the Bible. The earth has a circumference around the equator of (**249** x 100) = **24,900** miles. Our size of the universe number and the 'times **JESUS** appears' in the Bible is **942**. These numbers are mirrors; a (**249 | 942**) mirror of the circumference of the **WORLD** and the circumference of the **UNIVERSE**! If we multiply (**249 x 942**) we get **234558**. The mysterious **Fibonacci** number sequence holds these numbers: (2 **34558**) starting at the **tenth** number: (0, 1, 1, 2, 3, 5, 8, 13, 21, **34, 55, 8**9, 144, 233). These are also **Torah** numbers!

Now just imagine the intelligence and power of a supreme being, who could encode all of these things in the Bible down through history; and do it exactly a certain number of times; matching the numbers of the scientific data. God did this using 40 different people, spread out over hundreds of years (1400 years), in 66 different books, who didn't know what these things were to begin with! This being is of course, the **God** of the Bible, and His name is **Jesus Christ**. We have seen from all of these incredible things that the **Bible** agrees with science and nature. Actually it's the other way around, science and nature must agree with **God** and the **Bible**. The Bible has revealed itself to us to be the infallible "**Word of God**." We now have, beyond a shadow of a doubt, our actual '**proof**' of God's existence.

Printed in the United States
1380300003B/97-99